SECURITY CLEARANCE MANUAL

HOW TO REDUCE THE TIME IT TAKES TO GET YOUR GOVERNMENT CLEARANCE

William H. Henderson

Last Post Publishing
Pacific Grove, California

ii

Every effort was made to insure that the information in this book is current, accurate, and complete as possible. However, government policies change often and are not always consistent across all governmental agencies. This book was written to provide information on security clearance processing (application, investigation and adjudication). It is sold with the understanding that the writer and publisher are not engaged in rendering legal advice. If legal assistance is required, the services of a competent attorney specializing in security clearance law should be sought.

Published by
Last Post Publishing
1120 Forest Avenue, PMB 274
Pacific Grove, CA 93950
editor@LastPostPublishing.com
http://LastPostPublishing.com

Printed in the United States of America

Publisher's Cataloging-in-Publication
(Provided by Quality Books, Inc.)

Henderson, William H., 1949-
    Security clearance manual : how to reduce the time it
takes to get your government clearance / by William H.
Henderson.
    p. cm.
    Includes bibliographical references and index.
    LCCN 2007924526
    ISBN-13: 978-0-9793466-0-6
    ISBN-10: 0-9793466-0-6

    1. Security clearances--United States--Handbooks,
manuals, etc.   I. Title.

JK734.H46 2007   352.3'79
                        QBI07-600095

LACK OF TRANSPARENCY

"All applicants for government employment, as well as those seeking contractor positions that require government review, must be provided with clear information in writing about the security vetting process. Currently, applicants, employees, and contractors typically are provided little information on the process. Promoting a greater understanding of the process should help to improve overall accountability, both for employees and for those responsible for administering security programs . . . .

"Most agencies make little effort to disseminate any information regarding the personnel security process to applicants, contractors, and employees subject to investigation or reinvestigation. These individuals thus remain largely uninformed with respect to basic, unclassified information concerning the overall process, the length of time it takes, the standards applied, and their own status . . . . In addition, those subjected to the clearance process often do not understand it. Some assume, for example, that they will be denied a clearance for reasons that are not actually grounds for rejection."

REPORT OF THE COMMISSION ON PROTECTING AND REDUCING GOVERNMENT SECRECY (WASHINGTON, DC: GOVERNMENT PRINTING OFFICE, 1997)

ABOUT THE AUTHOR

William Henderson is a retired federal investigator who worked as a field agent and supervisor for the Defense Investigative Service (DIS) and its successor organizations (Defense Security Service— DSS and Federal Investigative Services Division of the Office of Personnel Management—OPM) for over 20 years. He was previously an Army Counterintelligence Agent and a security manager at the Satellite Control Facilities Operation of Ford Aerospace & Communications Corporation.

He wrote his first personnel security investigation report in 1970 for the U.S. Army. His assignments included CI Special Operations in Japan and Korea, Source Administration in Vietnam, CI field office duty in Chicago, tactical CI operations in Colorado Springs, and a position on the J2 staff at CINCLANT.

While with DIS, DSS and OPM, he held assignments as a Special Agent, Senior Resident Agent, and Assistant Special Agent-in-Charge. His duty station was in Monterey, California where he conducted numerous security investigations of former Soviet Bloc Émigrés And Refugees teaching at the Defense Language Institute; however, he frequently conducted investigations in major metropolitan areas throughout the United States.

CONTENTS

Introduction   vii

Part I — SECURITY CLEARANCE PROCESS   1

Chapter 1   Investigations, Access, & Clearances   3
Chapter 2   Applying for a Security Clearance   19
Chapter 3   The Investigative Process   31
Chapter 4   Adjudication & Post-Adjudicative Action   41

Part II — SECURITY CLEARANCE APPLICATION   55
FORM

Chapter 5   Personal Identifying Information & U.S.   57
            Citizenship
Chapter 6   Residence, Education & Employment   67
Chapter 7   Character References, Relatives & Associates   83
Chapter 8   Military Service, Foreign Connections/Travel &   95
            Selective Service
Chapter 9   Mental Health, Police Records & Drug Use   109
Chapter 10 Alcohol, Prior Investigations & Finances   123
Chapter 11 Court Actions, Organizations, Technology &   139
            Sexual Behavior

Conclusion   149

Appendix A — REFERENCES   A-1

Appendix B — ADJUDICATIVE GUIDELINES   B-1

Appendix C — STANDARD FORM 86   C-1

Index

INTRODUCTION

The purpose of this book is to help people, who have been nominated for a government security clearance, obtain it as quickly as possible. Even if you have never experienced any problems, such as those enumerated in the "Adjudicative Guidelines for Determining Eligibility For Access to Classified Information,"[1] your clearance could take longer unless you understand the security clearance process and do everything you can to speed it along. By filling out your security form in a way that will facilitate the investigation, you greatly increase your chances of having your case completed ahead of others and in the shortest amount of time possible. If there are security or suitability issues in your case, the way you present information during a personal interview with an investigator can affect the level at which your case is adjudicated and the length of time required to process your case.

In its February 2007 report to Congress, the Security Clearance Oversight Group (SCOG) stated that all investigations completed by the Office of Personnel Management (OPM) after October 1, 2006 averaged 166 days, plus 39 days for adjudication (205 days total).[2] In its testimony before Congress on May 17, 2007, the General Accountability Office (GAO)[3] took issue with the SCOG report and cited the findings in its September 28, 2006 report (GAO-06-1070).[4] GAO claimed that statistics the Office of Management and Budget (OMB) and the Office of Personnel Management (OPM) provided to the SCOG for their report to Congress on the timeliness of the clearance process did not portray the full length of time it takes many applicants to receive a clearance. Specifically, they fail to include the processing time before an investigation is opened at OPM

---

[1] National Security Advisor memorandum, Subject: Adjudicative Guidelines, with attachments, 29 December 2005 (The White House, Washington, DC).

[2] Report of The Security Clearance Oversight Group Consistent with Title III of the Intelligence Reform and Terrorism Prevention Act of 2004, February 2007.

[3] United States Government Accountability Office, Testimony Before the Subcommittee on Oversight of Government Management, the Federal Workforce, and the District of Columbia, Committee on Homeland Security and Governmental Affairs, U.S. Senate, "DoD Personnel Clearances—Delays and Inadequate Document Found for Industry Personnel, May 17, 2007 (GAO-07-842T).

[4] United States Government Accountability Office (GAO), Report to Congressional Requesters, entitled: DoD Personnel Clearances: Additional OMB Actions Needed to Improve the Security Clearance Process, GAO-06-1070, September 28, 2006.

and the additional time spent on cases returned from requestors because the cases did not meet national investigative standards.

The independent analysis conducted and reported by GAO in September 2006 reviewed 2,259 Department of Defense (DoD) contractor personnel Top Secret clearances granted in January and February 2006 and determined that it took an average of 446 days for an initial clearance and 545 days for a clearance update. The report provided a breakdown of the processing time for initial Top Secret clearances for DoD contractor personnel as 111 days for application submission, 286 days for investigation, and 39 days for adjudication. For updating Top Secret clearances on DoD contractor personnel it took 81 days for application submission, 419 days for investigation, and 36 days for adjudication. The average days for the phases do not sum to the average days for the total clearance process, because the number of applicable cases varies for each calculation.

Bear in mind that these are only averages, and averages are merely mathematical calculations. There are Top Secret clearances that are granted in less than one-fourth of the average time and some that take much longer than the average. You can significantly influence how long your clearance takes.

The figures cited above from GAO-06-1070 represent only cases adjudicated by the Defense Industrial Security Clearance Office (DISCO). DISCO is authorized to grant or continue security clearances on completely clean cases and cases where only minor unfavorable information exists. If DISCO is unable to grant or continue a security clearance, the case is forwarded to the Defense Office of Hearings and Appeals (DOHA). In 2004 the Office of the Secretary of Defense mandated that all DoD Central Adjudication Facilities (CAFs), including DISCO, achieve an overall response time of 30 days. However, response time does not mean the time taken to reach a final adjudicative decision. It means the time to reach a favorable decision and grant the clearance or the time to reach a preliminary unfavorable decision and issue a "Letter of Intent" (LOI) to deny a security clearance (or in the case of DISCO, forward the case to DOHA). There are no reliable figures available regarding the length of time it takes from the issuance of an LOI to a final clearance decision, but anecdotal information suggests a period of three to six months. If a clearance is denied or revoked, the appeal process can take an additional two to seven months.[5]

In most instances having a current Secret or "L" Clearance will not reduce the time necessary to obtain a final higher level clearance. Likewise, having had a Top Secret or "Q" Clearance[6] more than five years ago will not reduce the

---

[5] Department of Defense, Office of the Inspector General, Audit Report: Personnel Security in the Department of Defense, Report No. 97-197, July 25, 1997.

[6] The Department of Energy uses the term "Access Authorization" instead of the term "Clearance." Within the Department of Defense the term "Access Authorization" has a different meaning from the term "Clear-

time necessary to obtain a new final clearance at the same level. If your spouse and parents hold security clearances, it will not reduce the time necessary for your clearance.

The greatest impediment to getting a security clearance as quickly as possible is failing to provide complete, accurate and detailed information on your Questionnaire for National Security Positions (Standard Form 86—SF86). Almost everyone who completes an SF86 (or its electronic equivalent) is so focused on himself that he does not stop to consider how the information is going to be used. The people who will spend the most time reading and analyzing your SF86 are investigators and investigative support personnel. Investigators use this form as a road map in conducting your investigation. If they can follow the map easily, they can complete your investigation in a week or two, once they begin working on it. Choosing the right people to list as character references and those who can verify your residence, education, and employment can reduce processing time by weeks. To choose correctly you need to understand the investigator's goals and methodology.

Merely following the instructions on the SF86 and providing the requested information is not enough. Often the questions on the form are not clear. Some questions require specialized knowledge to answer correctly. If you are applying for a Top Secret clearance, the instructions on the SF86 are incomplete. There are supplement instructions that many applicants never receive. There are situations where it is to your advantage to provide more information than the form requests. There are also situations where it is to your advantage to disclose only the information requested.

Currently there are three different methods of submitting an application for a security clearance—a paper SF86, an Electronic Personnel Security Questionnaire (EPSQ) and a new web-based application called eQIP (electronic Questionnaires for Investigations Processing). According to OPM about 11 percent of the February 2005 clearance investigation requests submitted outside of eQIP were returned to the requesting offices, because missing or discrepant information could not be obtained telephonically before the investigation was opened. Having your application rejected in this manner can easily add an extra month to the process. Also according to OPM about 9 percent of the May 2006 clearance investigations requests submitted through eQIP were rejected.

The second greatest impediment to getting a security clearance as quickly as possible is the presence of unfavorable information in your SF86 and in your case reports. If you present such information properly in your SF86 and during your Personal Subject Interview (PRSI) or Special Interview (SPIN), it will allow the investigators and the adjudicator (who reviews your case and makes

---

ance." Within this book the terms "Access Authorization" and "Clearance" are used according to the Department of Defense definitions.

the initial decision to grant or not grant your clearance) to process your investigation ahead of other problematic cases. You can do more to influence the outcome of your clearance request than anyone else simply by completing your security clearance application form properly and being proactive during your personal interview.

An analysis of 12,212 Defense Investigative Service (DIS) security clearance investigations was conducted in 1995. Of the 3,777 initial investigations for Top Secret clearances, only 12 percent were considered clean, 69 percent contained minor derogatory information, and 19 percent contained major derogatory information.[7] Historically rates of derogatory information in investigations for Confidential and Secret clearances have been higher. The implementation of the NACLC (National Agency Check with Local Agency Checks and Credit Check) in 1998 for Confidential and Secret clearances resulted in even higher rates of derogatory information in these investigations. This was because of the credit bureau report and local police records checks that were added to the standard National Agency Check (NAC), which had previously been the basis for granting Confidential and Secret clearances. There are no current reliable figures available for the rate of major derogatory information in initial investigations for Confidential and Secret clearance. An estimate of over 25 percent would not be unreasonable.

Investigators and adjudicators are constantly faced with conflicting priorities and incredible pressure to process as many cases as possible, as quickly as possible. They are human beings who respond to overwhelming workload in the same way as others. They naturally focus on those cases they can do quickly and easily and set other cases aside to be worked later, perhaps much later.

This book was written primarily for the person who is applying for a security clearance from DoD, because DoD grants about 80 percent of all security clearances in the federal government and uses standardized investigations as the basis for those clearances. Other federal agencies rely on a variety of different investigations for employment and security clearance purposes too numerous to cover adequately in one book. OPM conducts 90 percent of all federal background investigations[8] and services more than 100 federal agencies and de-

---

[7] Defense Personnel Security Research Center (PERSEREC), Screening of Personnel Security Investigations, Kent S. Crawford and James A Riedel, undated (Monterey, California).

[8] The following departments/agencies have statutory or delegated authority to conduct background investigations: Central Intelligence Agency; Department of State; Department of the Treasury; Internal Revenue Service; Bureau of Engraving and Printing; Federal Bureau of Investigation; National Security Agency; Defense Intelligence Agency; U.S. Agency for International Development; Department of Homeland Security; Bureau of Customs and Border Protection; U.S. Secret Service; Small Business Administration; Broadcasting Board of Governors; Department of Justice—Bureau of Alcohol, Tobacco, Firearms, and Explosives; U.S. Postal Service; Tennessee Valley Authority; National Reconnaissance Office; and Peace Corps. Even though these agencies have authority to conduct their own investigations, some of them request OPM to conduct all or part of their investigations.

partments, including DoD.[9]

In this book you will find information that will help you distinguish between serious and minor unfavorable information, and how that information is applicable to the security clearance process. You will learn what information (about you) the investigator and adjudicator need to do their jobs as quickly as possible. It may seem that this book advises the applicant to do a lot of the investigator's work for him. It does. Every security investigator handles literally hundreds of investigations each year. Most applicants will only have one initial security investigation in their entire lives. You should be willing to spend a few extra hours of your time to do some of the investigator's work for him, if it will result in reducing the processing time by weeks or even months.

ORGANIZATION OF THE BOOK

Chapters 1 through 4 of this book provide information regarding types of security clearances, investigative standards, processes involved in applying for the clearance, the investigation, adjudication, and post-adjudicative actions. Chapters 5 through 11 are divided into sections addressing each of the sections of the SF86. These chapters provide information on how to fill out each section of the form and how each section of the form relates to the investigative process and the adjudicative standards, including applicable excerpts from the Adjudicative Guidelines. However, parts of *Guideline E: Personal Conduct* that relate to intentional omission/falsification of information and vulnerability to blackmail, apply to all sections of the SF86 (as well as the PRSI and SPIN) and are therefore not repeated in each section, unless there is special applicability to that section.

Instructions for the SF86 (including supplemental instructions for Single Scope Background Investigations) require inclusion of information covering different periods of time for different sections of the questionnaire. Often the National Investigative Standards (see Chapter 1, pages 6–15) specify time periods that are not the same as the instructions in the SF86. Additionally, OPM implementation of the National Investigative Standards sometimes specify slightly different time periods, particularly as they pertain to young people. Instructions in this book are based on a combination of the SF86 instructions and the National Investigative Standards (see Appendix C).

The December 2005 *Adjudicative Guidelines for Determining Eligibility*

---

[9] The National Security Agency, Defense Intelligence Agency, and National Reconnaissance Office each have a 1-year waiver that allows them to contract for their own personnel security clearance investigations. DoD officials say they do not anticipate that the waivers will be granted after the current waivers expire.

For Access to Classified Information is reprinted in its entirety at Appendix B. Examples of cases adjudicated by the Defense Office of Hearings and Appeals are presented, so the reader can see under what circumstances clearances were granted and denied. To the extent possible information in these chapters follows the same sequence as the questions on the SF86. Much of the information presented in this book is extracted directly from public documents.

Within investigative and adjudicative documents dealing with security clearances, the applicant is often referred to as the "subject" of the investigation. Throughout this book the terms **Applicant** and **Subject** are used interchangeably.

NOTES

Headings entitled: SECURITY FORM, APPLICABLE ADJUDICATIVE GUIDELINES, NACLC, SSBI/SSBI-PR, and EXAMPLES OF CLEARANCE ADJUDICATION repeatedly appear throughout Chapters 5 through 11 of this book. Information under those headings relies heavily on five sources. Rather than repeatedly citing these sources as footnotes for the information under those headings, the sources are cited below.

- SECURITY FORM refers to the U.S. Office of Personnel Management Standard Form 86 (EG), revised September 1995.

- Information under the heading APPLICABLE ADJUDICATIVE GUIDELINES was extracted from an attachment to the Memorandum for the Director, Information Security Oversight Office from the Assistant to the President for National Security Affairs, Subject: Adjudicative Guidelines, 29 December 2005 (The White House, Washington, DC), entitled: Adjudicative Guidelines for Determining Eligibility For Access to Classified Information.

- Information under the headings NACLC and SSBI/SSBI-PR relied upon the contents of Director of Central Intelligence Directive No. 6/4, Annex A—Investigative Standards for Background Investigations for Access to Classified Information, 2 July 1998 and Department of Defense Regulation 5200.2-R, "DoD Personnel Security Program," Appendix 1— Investigative Scope, January 1987 (Administrative Reissuance Incorporating Through Change 3, February 23, 1996).

- Information under the heading EXAMPLES OF CLEARANCE ADJUDICA-TION was obtained from the Defense Office of Hearings and Appeals website, http://www.dod.mil/dodgc/doha/industrial/.

NUMBER OF SECURITY CLEARANCES

There are about 3.2 million people who hold security clearances granted by the Federal government. Almost 2.5 million of these individuals are affiliated with the Department of Defense (DoD civilian, military and contractor personnel). For fiscal year 2006 (October 2005 through September 2006), OPM received about 713,000 requests for security clearance investigations and about 1,000,000 requests for other government background investigations. OPM anticipates a larger number of requests in fiscal year 2007.

COST OF INVESTIGATIONS

For over 40 years there has been a persistent myth that the cost of a full field security investigation such as a Single Scope Background Investigation was about $10,000. It is doubtful that it was ever that expensive. Before the Defense Investigative Service (DIS) was established in 1972, there was decentralized case control and considerable duplication of effort, because each of the military services operated independently. Military investigators were typing their own reports on manual typewriters with four carbon copies, writing separate reports for each interview and record check, and repeating the same lengthy verbiage in most of their reports. DIS changed all of that. They consolidated all the military investigators into one agency, immediately gaining economy of scale. They introduced abbreviated report writing, hired clerical staff, established centralized case control, and implemented the electronic transmission of reports and modern techniques for file management and retrieval.[10]

Today there are six investigative organizations working for OPM (the Office of Personnel Management)—one federal workforce and five contractor workforces.[11] The economy of scale once enjoyed by DIS has been lost, and the costs of investigations have increased due to partial privatization. Nevertheless,

---

[10] In 1996 the Defense Investigative Service changed its name to the Defense Security Service. In February 2005 all DSS investigative personnel transferred to the Federal Investigative Services Division of the U.S. Office of Personnel Management. DSS continued its Industrial Security function, including the operation of the Defense Industrial Security Clearance Office.

[11] OPM Federal Investigative Services, U.S. Investigative Services, Inc., CACI-PTI, Kroll, Inc., Omniplex World Services Corp., and Systems Application and Technologies, Inc.

as of October 1, 2006 OPM charged their customers (including DoD) the following amounts:[12]

INVESTIGATION TYPE	Priority Handling	Standard Service
NACLC (National Agency Check with Law and Credit)	$240	$192
ANACI (Access National Agency Check and Inquiries)	$260	$220
SSBI-PR (Periodic Reinvestigation for SSBI)	$2,625	$2,400
SSBI (Single Scope Background Investigation)	$3,900	$3,550

FEE FOR SERVICE

Each of the military services pays OPM for its security clearance investigations. Their cost represents a fraction of a percent of their overall budget. The Defense Security Service (DSS) is appropriated money to cover the cost of clearance investigations on Defense Contractor personnel (also known as industrial cases) processed by its Defense Industrial Security Clearance Office (DISCO). In May 2006 DSS announced that it could no longer submit requests to OPM for Priority Investigations on industrial cases due to lack of funds. Later that same month it announced that it had to stop submitting all requests for investigations on industrial cases. They claimed that within the first eight months of the fiscal year, requests for industrial cases had exceeded their projections (and funding) for the entire year. They subsequently obtained supplemental funding and on July 10, 2006 DISCO resumed accepting applications from industry for all types of personnel security investigations.

Recently there has been discussion about Defense contractors paying for their own investigations. This raises many questions regarding how DoD contractors will pay for investigations. It's possible that some may choose to have the applicant pay for the investigation. Others may have the applicant pay for the investigation, then reimburse the applicant over a period of time. Some will add the cost of investigations to their contracts.

BEFORE YOU CAN APPLY
FOR A SECURITY CLEARANCE

Before you can apply for a security clearance, you must be hired for a position that requires a clearance. Most of these jobs exist in the Armed Forces (including reserves and National Guard), DoD civilian positions, and DoD contractor positions. Some exist in the Department of Homeland Security, in the Department of Energy (DoE), at DoE contractors, and to a more limited extent

---

[12] OPM Federal Investigative Notice No. 06-08, Subject: Investigations Reimbursable Billing Rates for FY 2007, dated September 11, 2006.

with other federal agencies and their contractors.

If you foresee the lack of a security clearance as limiting your ability to get the job that you want, there are ways to get the security clearance first by accepting part-time employment while preparing yourself for your eventual career. If you are a student and you eventually want to work for a defense contractor, apply for a part-time position at a security guard company that provides services to a DoD cleared contractor facility or at a DoD cleared contractor facility that has an in-house security guard force. If you don't mind a long-term commitment, you can join a reserve component of the Armed Forces or a National Guard unit. Be sure that your enlistment contract guarantees a specialty that requires a security clearance (preferably a Top Secret clearance).

U.S. military operations in Iraq and the war on terrorism have created thousands of position in the defense industry, many of which require security clearances. Defense contractors are actively recruiting personnel with security clearances for a variety of technical and professional positions. The number of positions available far exceeds the number of cleared applicants. So much so that defense contractors are offering bonuses and other inducements to recruit cleared personnel from their competitors and from the federal government.

PART I

SECURITY CLEARANCE

PROCESS

CHAPTER 1

INVESTIGATIONS, ACCESS, & CLEARANCES

INVESTIGATIONS

In the past there were many different security investigations within DoD. They were known as Background Investigations (BI), Special Background Investigations (SBI), Expanded Background Investigations (EBI), Interview-Oriented Background Investigations (IBI), National Agency Checks (NAC), Expanded National Agency Checks (ENAC), Entrance National Agency Checks (ENTNAC), etc.

Today within DoD and DoE for initial security clearance purposes, there are three investigations—the Single Scope Background Investigation (SSBI), the National Agency Check with Local Agency Checks and Credit Check (NACLC), and the Access National Agency Check and Inquiries (ANACI). There are many other types of investigations conducted by OPM and the few federal agencies authorized to conduct their own investigations. Many of these investigations are primarily for employment purposes, but they may be acceptable for security clearances, if they meet the requirements of an SSBI or NACLC.

NATIONAL AGENCY CHECK

The National Agency Check (NAC) is part of all investigations and reinvestigations and is described below:[13]

The scope[14] for a NAC is five years or to age 18, whichever is the shorter period. At a minimum, the first three of the described Agencies (DCII, FBI/HQ, and FBI/ID),

---

[13] DoD 5200.2-R, "DoD Personnel Security Program," January 1987 (Administrative Reissuance Incorporating Through Change 3, February 23, 1996).

[14] The "Period Of Investigation or POI" is sometimes referred to as the "scope." More properly the term "scope" is used to refer to the breadth of an investigation—the aggregate of its components. The term POI is

below, shall be included in each complete NAC; however, a NAC may also include a check of any or all of the other described Agencies, if appropriate.

1. The DCII database consists of an alphabetical index of personal names and impersonal titles that appear as subjects, co-subjects, victims, or cross-referenced incidental subjects, in investigative documents maintained by DoD criminal, counterintelligence, fraud, and personnel security investigative activities. Additionally, personnel security adjudicative determinations are maintained, by subject, in the DCII. DCII records will be checked on all subjects of DoD investigations.[15]

2. FBI/HQ has on file copies of investigations conducted by the FBI. The FBI/HQ check, included in every NAC, consists of a review of files for information of a security nature and that developed during applicant-type investigations.

3. An FBI/ID check, included in every NAC (but not ENTNAC), is based upon a technical fingerprint search that consists of a classification the subject's fingerprints and comparison with fingerprint cards submitted by law enforcement activities. If the fingerprint card is not classifiable, a "name check only" of these files is automatically conducted.

4. OPM. The files of OPM contain the results of investigations conducted by OPM under E.O. 9835 and 10450, those requested by the Nuclear Regulatory Commission (NRC), the Department of Energy (DOE), and those requested since August 1952 to serve as a basis for "Q" clearances. OPM records are checked on all persons who are, or who have been, civilian employees of the U.S. Government; or U.S. citizens who are, or who have been, employed by a United Nations organization or other public international organization; and on those who have been granted security clearances by the NRC or the DOE.[16]

5. Immigration and Naturalization Service (I&NS).[17] The files of I&NS contain (or show where filed) naturalization certificates, certificates of derivative citizenship, all military certificates of naturalization, repatriation files, petitions for naturalization and declaration of intention, visitors' visas, and records of aliens (including government officials and representatives of international organizations) admitted temporarily into the U.S. I&NS records are checked when the subject is:

    5.1. An alien in the United States, or

    5.2. A naturalized citizen whose naturalization has not been verified, or

    5.3. An immigrant alien, or

---

used to refer to the overall number of years coverage for an investigation or the number of months of coverage for an individual component of an investigation.

[15] The DCII is being maintained but not updated with new clearance data. Since July 2005 new data are being entered into the Joints Personnel Adjudication System (JPAS).

[16] A check of OPM's Security and Investigations Index (SII) and employment files is now a standard part of all NACs.

[17] Immigration and Naturalization Service is now know as Citizenship and Immigration Services.

5.4. A U.S. citizen who receives derivative citizenship through the naturalization of one or both parents, provided that such citizenship has not been verified in a prior investigation.

6. State Department. The State Department maintains the following records:

6.1. Security Division (S/D) files contain information pertinent to matters of security, violations of security, personnel investigations pertinent to that agency, and correspondence files from 1950 to date. These files are checked on all former State Department employees.

6.2. Passport Division (P/D) shall be checked if subject indicates U.S. citizenship due to birth in a foreign country of American parents. This is a check of State Department Embassy files to determine if subject's birth was registered at the U.S. Embassy in the country where he was born. Verification of this registration is verification of citizenship.

7. Central Intelligence Agency (CIA). The CIA maintains the following records:

7.1. Directorate of Operations (CIA-DO/IMS) maintains the Foreign Intelligence/Counterintelligence database. This database shall be checked for all aliens residing outside the United States requiring access to classified information (i.e., LAA[18]). If the requester provides complete personal identifying information (Complete Name, Date of Birth, Place of Birth, and Citizenship), all alien co-subjects (on SSBIs) residing outside the United States are also checked. In addition, this database shall be queried on the Subject any time there is a counterintelligence concern raised during the conduct of the personnel security investigation.

7.2. Office of Security (CIA-SEC) maintains information on present and former employees, including members of the Office of Strategic Services (OSS), and applicants for employment. These files shall be checked if subject has been an employee of the CIA or when other sources indicate that CIA may have pertinent information.

8. Military Personnel Record Center files are maintained by separate Departments of the Armed Forces, General Services Administration and the Reserve Records Centers. They consist of the Master Personnel Records of retired, separated, Reserve, and active duty members of the Armed Forces. These records shall be checked when the requester provides required identifying data indicating service during the last 5 years.

9. Treasury Department. The files of Treasury Department Agencies (Secret Service, Internal Revenue Service, and Bureau of Customs) will be checked only when available information indicates that an Agency of the Treasury Department may be reasonably expected to have pertinent information.

---

[18] An LAA (Limited Access Authorization) is the equivalent of a security clearance for non-U.S. citizens.

10. The files of other Agencies, such as the National Guard Bureau, the Defense Industrial Security Clearance Office (DISCO), etc., will be checked when pertinent to the purpose for which the investigation is being conducted.

As of 1 March 2005 (as part of a NAC) OPM requests an Interpol (International Criminal Police Organization) records check through the U.S. National Central Bureau (USNCB) when, for six months or more, the Subject of an investigation: (1) had a non-military foreign residence; (2) had non-military employment overseas; (3) was engaged in academic activities abroad; or (4) when the Subject admits to, or there is developed, criminal activity overseas within the investigative coverage period.[19]

"The following investigative standards are established for all U.S. Government civilian and military personnel, consultants, contractors, employees of contractors, licensees, certificate holder or grantees and their employees and other individuals who require access to classified information, to include Sensitive Compartmented Information (SCI) and Special Access Programs (SAPs), and are to be used by government departments and agencies as the investigative basis for final clearance determinations. However, nothing in these standards prohibits an agency from using any lawful investigative procedures in addition to these requirements in order to resolve any issue identified in the course of a background investigation or reinvestigation."[20]

NATIONAL AGENCY CHECK WITH LOCAL AGENCY CHECKS AND CREDIT CHECK

COMPONENTS OF A NACLC:[21]

Completion of Forms

Completion of Standard Form 86, including applicable releases and supporting documentation.

National Agency Check

Completion of a National Agency Check (on the applicant).

---

[19] OPM Federal Investigative Notice No. 05-01, March 1, 2005.

[20] Memorandum from the Assistant to the President for National Security Affairs, Subject: Implementation of Executive Order 12968, March 24, 1997, Attachment: Final Investigative Standards.

[21] Ibid

Financial Review

Verification of the subject's financial status, including credit bureau checks covering all locations where the subject has resided, been employed, or attended school for six months or more for the past seven years.

Birth

Corroboration of date and place of birth through a check of appropriate documentation, if *not* completed in any previous investigation; a check of Bureau of Vital Statistics records when any discrepancy is found to exist.

Local Agency Checks

As a minimum, all investigations will include checks of law enforcement agencies having jurisdiction where the subject has lived, worked, and/or attended school within the last five years, and, if applicable, of the appropriate agency for any identified arrests.

Expanding for Issues

The investigation may be expanded if necessary to determine if access is clearly consistent with the national security.

ACCESS NATIONAL AGENCY CHECK WITH INQUIRIES

The ANACI includes the same components as the NACLC. Additionally, OPM sends inquiry letters to employers, schools, and personal references to confirm the subject's background and to obtain information about their basic suitability for employment. This investigation is not used for military or contractor personnel. This investigation is used only for new civilian federal employees whose position will require a Secret or "L" clearance. It is a combination of the National Agency Check with Inquiries (NACI) used for federal employment purposes and the NACLC used for security clearance purposes. Civilian federal employees who require a Secret or "L" clearance after they are hired are submitted for a NACLC, since a NACI was previously conducted on them. Because the ANACI is used for a combination of employment and security clearance purposes, and because the security clearance aspects of the ANACI are the same as the NACLC, the ANACI is not addressed separately in this book, except that footnotes are included in the applicable sections to explain any differences between the two investigations. ANACIs are expanded in the same manner and using the same criteria as NACLCs.

SINGLE SCOPE BACKGROUND INVESTIGATION

COMPONENTS OF AN SSBI:[22]

Completion of Forms

Completion of Standard Form 86, including applicable releases and supporting documentation.

Scope

Past ten (10) years. If the applicant is under 28 years of age, back to the 18th birthday or two years, whichever is longer.

National Agency Check

Completion of a National Agency Check (on the applicant).

National Agency Check for the Spouse or Cohabitant (if applicable)

Completion of a National Agency Check, without fingerprint cards, for the spouse or cohabitant.[23]

Birth

Corroboration of date and place of birth through a check of appropriate documentation and a check of Bureau of Vital Statistics records when any discrepancy is found to exist.

Citizenship

For individuals born outside the United States, verification of US citizenship directly from the appropriate registration authority; verification of US citizenship or legal status of foreign-born immediate family members (spouse, cohabitant, father, mother, sons, daughters, brothers, sisters).

Education

Corroboration of most recent or most significant claimed attendance, degree, or diploma. Interviews of appropriate educational sources[24] if education is a primary activity of the Subject during the most recent three years.

---

[22] Ibid..

[23] Cohabitant is defined as a person living in a spouse-like relationship with the Subject of an investigation.

[24] Although the SSBI investigative standards for education, employment, and neighborhoods do not specify the number of sources to be interviewed; since the words "sources" and "neighbors" are plural, it is generally accepted that a minimum of two sources must be interviewed at each venue, if possible.

Employment

Verification of all employments for the past seven years; personal interviews of sources (supervisors, coworkers, or both)[25] for each employment of six months or more; corroboration through records or sources of all periods of unemployment exceeding sixty days; verification of all prior federal and military service, including discharge type. For military members, all service within one branch of the armed forces will be considered as one employment, regardless of assignments.

References

References: four references, of whom at least two are developed; to the extent practicable, all should have social knowledge of the Subject and collectively span at least the last seven years.

Former Spouse

An interview of any former spouse divorced within the last ten years.

Neighborhoods

Confirmation of all residences for the last three years through appropriate interviews with neighbors[26] and through records reviews.

Financial Review

Verification of the Subject's financial status, including credit bureau checks covering all locations where Subject has resided, been employed, and/or attended school for six months or more for the last seven years.

Local Agency Checks

A check of appropriate criminal history records covering all locations where, for the last ten years, the Subject has resided, been employed, and/or attended school for six months or more, including current residence regardless of duration. (NOTE: If no residence, employment or education exceeds six months, local agency checks should be performed as deemed appropriate.)

Public Records

Verification of divorces, bankruptcies, and other court actions, whether civil or criminal, involving the Subject.

---

[25] Ibid.

[26] Ibid.

Subject Interview

A Subject Interview, conducted by trained security, investigative, or counterintelligence personnel. During the investigation, additional Subject Interviews may be conducted to collect relevant information, to resolve significant inconsistencies, or both. Sworn statements and unsworn declarations may be taken whenever appropriate.

Polygraph (only agencies with approved personnel security polygraph programs):

In departments or agencies with policies sanctioning the use of the polygraph for personnel security purposes, the investigation may include a polygraph examination, conducted by a qualified polygraph examiner.

Expanding the Investigation.

The investigation may be expanded as necessary. As appropriate, interviews with anyone able to provide information or to resolve issues, including but not limited to cohabitants, relatives, psychiatrists, psychologists, other medical professional, and law enforcement professionals may be conducted.

PERIODIC REINVESTIGATIONS

INTERVALS AND STANDARDS
Individuals holding security clearances must be reinvestigated periodically to maintain their clearances. Intervals for Periodic Reinvestigations (PR) are:[27]

Confidential Clearance—15 years
Secret & "L" Clearance—10 years
Top Secret & "Q" Clearance—5 years

The investigative standard for PRs for Confidential and Secret clearances is the same as the standard for an initial Confidential or Secret clearance—the NACLC. There are two investigative standards for PRs for Top Secret clearances and for others whose initial investigation was an SSBI. The standards are an SSBI-PR and a Phased Periodic Reinvestigation (PPR).

COMPONENTS OF AN SSBI-PR:[28]

---

[27] Memorandum from the Assistant to the President for National Security Affairs, Subject: Implementation of Executive Order 12968, March 24, 1997, Attachment: Final Investigative Standards.

[28] Ibid.

Completion of Forms

Completion of Standard Form 86, including applicable releases and supporting documents.

National Agency Check

Completion of a National Agency Check (fingerprint cards are required only if there has not been a previous valid technical check of the FBI).

National Agency Check for the Spouse or Cohabitant (if applicable)

Completion of a National Agency Check, without fingerprint cards, for the spouse or cohabitant. The National Agency Check for the spouse or cohabitant is *not* required if already completed in conjunction with a previous investigation or reinvestigation.

Employment

Verification of all employments since the last investigation. Attempts to interview a sufficient number of sources (supervisors, coworkers, or both)[29] at all employments of six months or more. For military members, all service within one branch of the armed forces will be considered as one employment, regardless of assignments.

References

Interviews with two character references who are knowledgeable of the subject; at least one will be a developed reference. To the extent practical, both should have social knowledge of the Subject and collectively span the entire period of the reinvestigation. As appropriate, additional interviews may be conducted, including cohabitants and relatives.

Neighborhoods

Interviews of two neighbors in the vicinity of the subject's most recent residence of six months or more. Confirmation of current residence regardless of length.

Financial Review

(1) **Financial Status:** Verification of the subject's financial status, including credit bureau checks covering all locations where subject has resided, been employed, and/or attended school for six months or more for the period covered by the rein-

---

[29] Although the SSBI-PR investigative standard for employment does not specify the number of employment sources to be interviewed; since the word "sources" is plural, it is generally accepted that a minimum of two sources must be interviewed, if possible.

vestigation;

(2) **Check of Treasury's Financial Data Base:** Agencies may request the Department of the Treasury, under terms and conditions prescribed by the Secretary of the Treasury, to search automated data bases consisting of reports of currency transactions by financial institutions, international transportation of currency or monetary instruments, foreign bank and financial accounts, and transactions under $10,000 that are reported as possible money laundering violations.

Local Agency Checks

Check of appropriate criminal history records covering locations where, during the period covered by the reinvestigation, the subject has resided, been employed, and/or attended school for six months or more, including current residence regardless of duration. (NOTE: If no residence, employment or education exceeds six months, local agency checks should be performed as deemed appropriate.)

Former Spouse

An interview with any former spouse unless the divorce took place before the date of the last investigation or reinvestigation.

Public Records

Verification of divorces, bankruptcies and other court actions, whether civil or criminal, involving the Subject since the date of the last investigation.

Subject Interview

A Subject Interview, conducted by trained security, investigative, or counterintelligence personnel. During the reinvestigation, additional Subject Interviews may be conducted to collect relevant information, to resolve significant inconsistencies, or both. Sworn statements and unsworn declarations may be taken whenever appropriate.

Expanding the Reinvestigation

The reinvestigation may be expanded as necessary. As appropriate, interviews with anyone able to provide information or to resolve issues, including but not limited to cohabitants, relatives, psychiatrists, psychologists, other medical professionals, and law enforcement professionals may be conducted.

PHASED PERIODIC REINVESTIGATION (PPR) FOR SSBIS:

"The phased approach to periodic reinvestigations involves conducting a

*reinvestigation in two phases; a more extensive reinvestigation would be con-
ducted only if potential security issues were identified in the initial phase. Specifically, investigative staff would verify residency records and conduct interviews of listed references, references developed during the investigation, and
individuals residing in the neighborhood only if potential security issues were
identified in other parts of the standard reinvestigation process. . . . In December 2004, the President approved the use of the phased PR for personnel need-
ing to renew their top secret clearances.*[30]

Essentially Government departments and agencies may, in their discretion,
exclude SSBI-PR requirements noted under **References** and **Neighborhoods**
when no information of security concern is listed on the applicant's SF86 or is
developed during the other aspects of the investigation. If there is information
of security concern, the SSBI-PR requirements under **References** and **Neighborhoods** must be met as well as the requirement under **Expanding the Reinvestigation**.

CONDITIONS THAT WOULD REQUIRE A FULL SCOPE SSBI-PR ARE DESCRIBED AS:[31]

Self-Disclosed Security Concerns Requiring Processing of a Full Scope SSBI-PR
A positive response by the subject, or subject-provided information related to the following questions on the Standard Form 86, Questionnaire for National Security Positions, may indicate a security concern. A positive response to any of the following
questions will result in investigations submitted as a PPR (case type 19) to be scheduled
as a full scope SSBI-PR (case type 18) and billed accordingly.

SF 86 Question Response

8a	Citizenship	"I am not a U.S. Citizen" checked
8d	Dual Citizenship	Checked
17	Your Foreign Activities	A positive response to questions b, c, or d.
21	Your Medical Record	A positive response
23	Your Police Record	A positive response to questions a, b, c, d, e, or f
24	Your Use Of Illegal Drugs And Drug Activity	A positive response to questions a, b, or c
25	Your Use Of Alcohol	A positive response
26	Your Investigations Record	A positive response to question b
30	Your Association Record	A positive response to questions a or b

---

[30] United States Government Accountability Office (GAO), Testimony Before the Subcommittee on Oversight of Government Management, the Federal Workforce, and the District of Columbia, Committee on
Homeland Security and Governmental Affairs, U.S. Senate, GAO-05-842T, June 28, 2005.

[31] OPM Federal Investigations Notice No. 05-04 Subject: Reinvestigation Products for Positions Requiring
Q, Top Secret or SCI Access, September 16, 2005.

Developed Security Concerns Requiring Processing of an Expanded PPR

If certain issues are developed during the conduct of the field-work portion of any PPR, OPM will automatically expand the investigation to include reference, residence and education coverage. The cost to expand a PPR once the investigation has begun is in addition to the basic PPR cost, and the additional charge will be billed at the time the investigation is expanded. The following issues, when developed during the course of the investigation, will result in expansion and applied surcharge:

- Evidence that the Subject is not a U.S. citizen, or has renounced or otherwise lost his U.S. citizenship since the time of the last investigation;
- Evidence that the Subject is a dual citizen or has obtained dual citizenship since the time of the last investigation;
- Evidence that the Subject has been employed by or acted as a consultant for any foreign government, firm or agency; that the Subject has engaged in any contact with a foreign government or its establishments or representatives on other than official U.S. government business; that the Subject holds or has been issued a foreign passport;
- Evidence that the Subject has undergone mental health treatment (except marital, family or grief counseling, not related to violence by the Subject) since the last investigation, whether this treatment began before or after the last investigation;
- Evidence that the Subject has been charged with or convicted of any criminal offenses (excluding traffic violations resulting in fines less than $150) since the last investigation;
- Evidence that the Subject used any drugs (illegally) since the last investigation;
- Evidence that the Subject has abused alcohol or has received any alcohol-related treatment or counseling since the last investigation;
- Evidence that the Subject has had a clearance or access authorization denied, suspended or revoked, or has been debarred from Federal employment since the last investigation; and
- Evidence that the Subject has associated with any individuals or groups dedicated to the violent overthrow of the United States government or that the Subject has acted to do so.

For the most part all federal background investigations contain some or all of the components (sources) listed under the three investigative standards (four if you count the PPR separately) described above. For security clearance investigations the information collected from these sources should be directly related to the Adjudicative Guidelines. Investigations conducted for employment purposes and for a combination of employment and security clearance purposes use basically some or all of the same investigative sources. However, differences exist in the nature of the information collected, because the criteria for employment is often different than the criteria for granting security clearances.

Table 1 (below) was extracted from GAO Report 06-1070, September 2006[32] and presents a comparison of the NACLC, SSBI and SSBI-PR.

---

[32] United States Government Accountability Office (GAO), Report to Congressional Requesters, entitled: DoD Personnel Clearances: Additional OMB Actions Needed to Improve the Security Clearance Process, GAO-06-1070, September 28, 2006.

Table 1: Information Gathered in an Investigation to Determine Eligibility for a Security Clearance

Type of information gathered	Type of security clearance and investigation		
	Confidential/Secret	Top Secret	
	Initial investigation & reinvestigation	Initial investigation	Reinves-tigation
1. Personnel security questionnaire: The subject's self-reported answers on a paper SF-86 form or electronic form	X	X	X
2. National agency check: Data from Federal Bureau of Investigation, military records, and other agencies as required	X	X	X
3. Credit check: Data from credit bureaus where the subject lived/worked/attended school for at least 6 months	X	X	X
4. Local agency checks: Data from law enforcement agencies where the subject lived/worked/attended school during the past 10 year or—in the case of reinvestigations—since the last security clearance investigation	X	X	X
5. Date and place of birth: Corroboration of information supplied on the personnel security questionnaire	X	X	
6. Citizenship: For individuals born outside of the United States verification of U.S. citizenship directly from the appropriate registration authority		X	
7. Education: Verification of most recent or significant claimed attendance, degree, or diploma[33]		X	X
8. Employment: Review of employment records and interviews with workplace references, such as supervisors and coworkers		X	X
9. References: Data from interviews with subject identified and investigator-developed leads		X	X
10. National agency check for spouse or cohabitant: National agency check without fingerprints		X	X
11. Former spouse: Data from interview(s) conducted with spouse(s) divorced within the last 10 years or since the last investigation or reinvestigation		X	X
12. Neighborhoods: Interviews with neighbors and verification of residence through records check		X	X
13. Public Records: Verification of issues, such as bankruptcy, divorce, and criminal and civil court cases		X	X
14. Subject interview: Collection of relevant data, resolution of significant inconsistencies, or both		X	X

Source DOD and OPM

---

[33] Under the National Investigative Standards verification of education as listed in Table 1, item 7 is not a required component of an SSBI-PR and educational sources are required for an SSBI, if the education was a primary activity within the most recent three years.

FINAL AND INTERIM SECURITY CLEARANCES

The SSBI is required for final Top Secret clearances and "Q" clearances and for access to SCI and designated SAPs at any classification level. The NACLC is required for final "L" clearances, Confidential clearances, and Secret clearances, not involving access to SCI or designated SAPs.

An Interim Security clearance is based on the completion of minimum investigative requirements. It is granted on a temporary basis, pending the completion of the full investigative requirements.

An Interim Top Secret clearance may be granted on the basis of a favorable NAC, a favorable review of the applicant's SF-86, a favorable review of local personnel, base/military police, medical, and other security records as appropriate, and the submission of a request for an SSBI.

An Interim Secret clearance may be granted on the basis of a favorable review of the applicant's SF86, a favorable review of local personnel, base military police, medical, and security records as appropriate, and the submission of a request for a NACLC.[34]

CLEARANCE TERMINATION, DOWNGRADE & REINSTATMENT

A security clearance remains in force until the individual granted the clearance leaves the position for which the clearance was needed. If they remain with the same employer in a position that doesn't require a clearance, their clearance is administratively downgraded or withdrawn. In this case, the clearance can be administratively upgraded or reinstated provided the underlying investigation is not out of date. If they terminate their employment, their clearance is terminated. If they are again hired into a position that requires the same or lower level clearance, the clearance can be reinstated provided two years have not elapsed since the clearance was terminated and the underlying investigation is not out of date.

When an individual has had a break in service (i.e., terminated employment where they held a security clearance and subsequently hired for a job that requires a security clearance), there are time limits during which a clearance can be reinstated without an investigation. Any break in service of 24 months or more requires a new initial investigation regardless of the date of the last investigation. If there is a break in service of less than 24 months and the time since the last investigation is not greater than the interval specified for the periodic

---

[34] DCID 6/4, Annex A - Investigative Standards for Background Investigations for Access to Classified Information, 2 July 1998.

reinvestigation, the clearance can be reinstated without an investigation. When hired for a position requiring a security clearance of a lower level than previously held, the interval for the lower level clearance applies. Under certain circumstances a person with a break in service of less than 24 months whose prior investigation for a Top Secret or Q clearance occurred more than five years ago, may only have to have an SSBI-PR. In any event the applicant may be required to submit a new SF86, even if a new investigation is not required.[35]

CLEARANCES VERSUS ACCESS

Within DoD there are only three levels of classified material and three clearances—Confidential, Secret, and Top Secret. The Department of Energy (DoE) basically has two levels of security clearances—"Q" clearances and "L" clearances.[36] "L" clearances are comparable to DoD Confidential and Secret clearances, and "Q" clearances are comparable to DoD Top Secret clearances.[37]

Access to classified information is based on having the appropriate security clearance (Confidential, Secret or Top Secret) and a "need to know." This need-to-know can be either a formal or informal determination. Generally all classified information exists within one of these two "need-to-know" realms. Information that falls into the realm of informal need-to-know determinations is often referred to as "Collateral Classified" information or "GENSER" for general service message traffic. Information that falls into the realm requiring formal access authorizations (just another term for need-to-know) is controlled within Special Access Programs (SAP) and Sensitive Compartmented Information (SCI). Access to SCI is regulated by the Central Intelligence Agency (CIA) under Director of Central Intelligence Directive (DCID) 6/4.

Acronyms such as SAP, SCI, CNWDI (Critical Nuclear Weapons Design Information), SIOP-ESI (Single Integrated Operations Plan—Exceptionally Sensitive Information), RD (Restricted Data), FRD (Formerly Restricted Data), ATOMAL (NATO Atomic Material), COSMIC Top Secret, SPECAT, CRYPTO, COMSEC, etc., are not clearances. They refer to categories of classified information, some of which involve extra need-to-know restrictions or spe-

---

[35] Memorandum from the Assistant to the President for National Security Affairs, Subject: Implementation of Executive Order 12968, March 24, 1997, Attachment: Final Investigative Standards.

[36] The Department of Energy uses the term "Access Authorization" instead of the term "Clearance." Within the Department of Defense the term "Access Authorization" has a different meaning from the term "Clearance." Within this book the terms "Access Authorization" and "Clearance" are used according to the Department of Defense definitions. Central Adjudication Facilities often use the term, "eligibility for access," in place of the terms, clearance and access authorization.

[37] The Department of Energy also has QX and LX clearances that are granted to individuals employed by a DOE access permittee. QX is for access to Secret and/or Confidential Restricted Data, and LX is for Confidential Restricted Data. Information regarding the DoE access permit program is found in 10 CFR 725.

cial access authorizations. For instance, the term COSMIC stands for "Control of Secret Material in an International Command." COSMIC Top Secret is merely the term used for NATO Top Secret Information. There are many caveats stamped or printed on classified documents with exotic sounding words, but most are only acronyms or short titles for special administrative handling procedures.

CHAPTER 2

APPLYING FOR A SECURITY CLEARANCE

Applications for security clearances must be preceded by a Request for Investigation. The Request for Investigation can only be initiated by an agency of the federal government or a private company that has a contract with a federal agency to perform classified work under the National Industrial Security Program. Since July 2005 these requests have been electronically initiated through the Joint Personnel Adjudication System.

In spring 2005 OPM launched eQIP (electronic Questionnaires for Investigations Processing). After the Request for Investigation has been submitted, the employee is given instructions on how to access the eQIP program at the OPM website and completes an electronic version of the Questionnaire for National Security Positions—Standard Form 86 (SF86) online.

OPM continues to accept requests and applications based on the EPSQ (Electronic Personnel Security Questionnaire) developed by the Defense Security Service (DSS) almost a decade ago as an electronic replacement of the SF86. However, OPM's computer system is not compatible with the EPSQ. OPM prints out the EPSQ into paper forms, then retypes them into their system. OPM anticipates that 100 percent of clearance applications from major requestors will be made using eQIP by the end of 2007.

Both systems have their own shortcomings. eQIP users who previously used the EPSQ will find that it takes considerably longer to input all the necessary data. Whichever system you use, it is important to print and keep a copy of the form the program creates.

COMPLETING THE SF86

Completing the SF86 is the only step in the security clearance process that you have complete control over and is therefore extremely important. There are a few other steps in the process where you can influence the outcome of your investigation. They are:

- the screening interview conducted before the request for an SSBIs is submitted;
- the Personal Subject Interview (PRSI) conducted as part of all SSBIs and SSBI-PRs;
- the Special Interview (SPIN) conducted to address significant unfavorable or discrepant information in any investigation;
- the written rebuttal or administrative hearing following a tentative denial or revocation of a security clearance; and
- the formal appeal to have an adverse decision reversed.

Get a paper copy of the SF86 (including the instructions) and fill it out before you begin completing one of the electronic versions. The form is available at *www.gsa.gov.* Just click on the Forms Library link. There are minor differences in the information requested in some data fields of the paper and electronic versions, but the time and frustration involved in completing an electronic version will be significantly less if you complete a paper version first. There are good instructions at the U.S. Coast Guard's website (*www.cgaux.info/g_ocx/administration/security/sf86_guide.pdf*) for filling out an SF86. DSS also has a website with an SF86 worksheet that might be helpful (*www.dss.mil/epsq/sf86work.doc*).

The paper version of the form is divided into two parts. Part 1 covers **background information**, including where you lived, worked, and attended school, as well as information about your family, associates, and foreign activities. Part 2 asks about **potential issue information** such as prior investigations, military service, mental health issues, problems at work, arrests, substance abuse, and financial problems. The SF86 instructions indicate that for background information and some potential issue information, data covering the past seven years is required. However, if submitting an application for an SSBI, you should be given supplemental instructions that direct you to provide information covering the past 10 years for residences, education, employment, police record, and civil court actions. This is because the SF86 is also used for positions that are not covered under the SSBI requirements of National Security Directive 63.[38]

It is helpful to think of the questions on the SF86 as being related to either background information or potential issue information, even though the electronic versions of the security forms are not divided into Part 1 and Part 2, like the paper version. That's not to say that background information never becomes a security or suitability issue.

The paper instructions for the SF86 state that, *"Some investigations will include an interview with you as a normal part of the investigative process. This provides you the opportunity to update, clarify, and explain information on*

---

[38] If you are over 20 but under 25 years of age, you are only required to include information back to your 18th birthday. If you are under 20 years of age you should include information back to your 16th birthday.

your form more completely, which often helps to complete your investigation faster. It is important that the interview be conducted as soon as possible, after you are contacted. Postponements will delay the processing of your investigation, and declining to be interviewed may result in your investigation being delayed or canceled."

Declining to be interviewed will definitely result in having your investigation canceled and your clearance denied. Don't count on using the Personal Subject Interview (PRSI) as an opportunity to clarify or explain information on your form so that your investigation will be completed faster. When an investigation is opened, all known investigative actions are tasked simultaneously to the different field offices involved in your case and to the headquarters element of OPM that conducts the National Agency Checks and Credit Check. If your investigation is a NACLC, a PRSI will not be tasked. With SSBIs and SSBI-PRs the field office that is tasked to conduct your PRSI may have a greater backlog of cases than other field offices involved in your case. If so, your PRSI may be the last initially tasked action completed on the case. Depending on the results of the PRSI, additional investigative actions may need to be tasked and accomplished before the investigation is completed.

Accuracy of names, dates, addresses (including postal ZIP codes), and telephone numbers is important in filling out the SF86. Take the time to dig through your old personal records, use telephone and other directories, and find the addresses of your former employers and educational institutions by searching the internet. Postal ZIP codes are particularly important because the computer program that processes your SF86 will use these ZIP codes to assign investigative work to various field offices. If you list the wrong ZIP code, it could result in your investigation being delayed. All post offices and most libraries have ZIP code directories. You can also search the online ZIP Code Directory at *http://zip4.usps.com/zip4/welcome.jsp*.

If there is unfavorable information about you in a record (i.e., police, court, medical, rental, credit bureau report, other credit file, IRS, bankruptcy court, divorce, county tax, etc.) that is less than ten years old, try to get a copy of the record to see exactly what it says.

You should go online and get a free copy of your credit reports at *www.annualcreditreport.com/cra/index.jsp*. You are entitled to receive one free credit file disclosure every 12 months from each of the three nationwide consumer credit reporting companies – Equifax, Experian and TransUnion. This free credit file can be requested through this website, by phone, or by mail.

Do not assume the attitude that if you don't know about a claim against you, you don't have to list it on your SF86. A credit bureau report will be obtained by OPM as part of your investigation. If unfavorable credit information exists and you fail to provide it in your SF86 or during your PRSI, you may be questioned about it later during a Special Interview (SPIN). This will add more time to your investigation, and your honesty may also become an issue.

The hours you invest completing your application properly could result in obtaining your clearance weeks, even months earlier than if you fail to provide complete and accurate data. Provide all the information requested as honestly and accurately as possible. Every section of the electronic forms has a data field for comments. There is a large comment section at the end of the paper version of the SF86, and you can append as many extra pages of information as needed to the paper SF86. If you are unable to provide the information required on the SF86, use the comment section to explain an inaccuracy or lack of data.

You will only undergo an investigation once every 5 to 15 years. A field investigator will handle a few dozen investigations every month. Security investigators do not work on one case at a time. They always have 20 to 40 cases that they work on concurrently—some are completed in a week or two, and some take four or more months to complete. Most investigators fail to complete some of their cases by their suspense dates. They are often faced with the choice of setting aside a case with a problematic SF86, so they can complete several other cases by their suspense dates, or working the case with a problematic SF86 and missing the suspense dates on several other cases. So, it's not surprising that many cases with problematic SF86s languish for months before the investigator chooses to finish them.

Bear in mind that an improperly completed form could be rejected by OPM before an investigation is even opened. It could take weeks before the form is rejected and you are eventually required to submit a new one. As previously stated, according to OPM about 10 percent of clearance applications were returned to the requesting offices, because missing or discrepant information could not be obtained telephonically before the investigation was opened.

The most common errors requiring correction before the investigation can be opened are:

- Incomplete addresses for residence, employment, and education.
- Incomplete data for delinquent debts (no explanation in comment section).
- Releases not signed, dated, or legible.
- Name on application does not exactly match name on fingerprint card.
- Date and place of birth differences between application and fingerprint card.
- Lack of cohabitant's SSN and place of birth on SSBI requests.
- If legally separated from spouse, lack of address for spouse and separation date.

In later chapters of this book, each section of the SF86 will be covered separately. Specific instructions will be provided on how to complete the form and what information to include and what to omit, as well as common errors and helpful advice.

IDENTIFICATION, PROOF OF CITIZENSHIP AND FINGERPRINTS

For initial clearances, in addition to providing appropriate identification and proof of citizenship (usually a birth certificate or passport) to the person processing your application, you will also have to have your fingerprints taken.

SCREENING OR PRE-NOMINATION INTERVIEW

As mentioned earlier, if you are being submitted for an SSBI, you may go through a screening or pre-nomination interview before you submit your SF86. The screening interview may not be an actual interview. You may only be required to complete a supplemental form that covers the same topics found at questions #16 through #30 of the SF86 but uses differently worded questions. Sometimes the supplemental form is reviewed by a security interviewer, who may ask you a few questions regarding entries you made on the form. At other times an interview of the same scope as the OPM PRSI is conducted. There appears to be little or no consistency regarding these screening interviews. The thoroughness of the interviews seems to be directly proportional to the training and experience of the interviewer, rather than any written standards. The purpose of the interview is to assist in determining the acceptability of an individual for nomination and further processing for a position requiring an SSBI.

PERSONAL SUBJECT INTERVIEW—PRSI

The PRSI is a regular part of all SSBIs and SSBI-PRs. This interview will be conducted by a federal investigator employed by OPM or a contract investigator working for OPM. The only difference is that federal investigators have gold badges and are called special agents. Contract investigators have silver badges and are called special investigators. They are required to identify themselves using their badge and credentials. Ask them for a business card at the beginning of the interview. You may want to contact them later. You should bring a photo ID issued by an agency of a state or federal government, such as a driver's license or military ID card.

If the interview is done properly, it will take between 45 to 75 minutes for an individual with only a few residences, jobs, and schools that need to be covered. If you have had extensive foreign travel, foreign contacts, or problems involving alcohol, drugs, finances, criminal conduct, etc., it will take longer.

Essentially the investigator will cover every item on your SF86 to confirm the accuracy and completeness of the information you provided (plus a few items that are not on the SF86), so bring your copy of the SF86 with you and refer to it as needed. Look at the Adjudicative Guidelines at Appendix B—all 13 guideline topics will be covered in one manner or another. Listen carefully to the questions asked by the investigator. As with the SF86, all questions are based on certain time periods. Some questions pertain to your entire life; others pertain only to the last seven or ten years or back to your 16th or 18th birthday depending on your age. For the purpose of this interview consider the seven- or ten-year time frame as being based on the date you completed the SF86. So, if you completed the SF86 on January 1, 2007, ten years includes everything between January 1, 1997 and the date of your interview.

Using the example above, if the last time you were arrested resulted in a **conviction** for petty theft on December 31, 1996, when you're asked if you've been arrested, charged or convicted of any offense within the past ten years, you can reply, "no." Be absolutely certain of the date of conviction. A person can be arrested and charged with an offense in December, but the matter may not be resolved in the court until several months later. If you were arrested and charged before January 1, 1997, and later the charge was dismissed or you were found not guilty, then you can still answer "no" to the question. Since there will be a police and possibly a court record concerning this matter, the exact dates will be in the records, and it should not become an issue. Time frames for all questions on the SF86 and the PRSI appear in Chapters 5 through 11 and at Appendix C.

Generally, resist the urge to volunteer unfavorable information about yourself that is not covered on the SF86. One exception to this is substance abuse counseling/treatment. If you answered "yes" to any question in Section 24 of the SF86 and you received drug abuse counseling/treatment, tell the investigator about it even if he forgets to ask. Otherwise, you should only answer the investigator's questions as truthfully and completely as possible. There are other times to provide more information than requested, but only when it will benefit you. The type of information you will want to volunteer is referred to as mitigating information—information that decreases the negative effect of unfavorable information. Nothing happens in isolation. Every event or circumstance occurs within the context of a multitude of other events and circumstances. Adjudicators want to know the totality of the circumstances surrounding any unfavorable information, so they can judge it within the proper context.

During the PRSI, the investigator is looking for unfavorable information about you that is not listed on the SF86, as well as details about your background and potential issue information you listed the form. It is the investigator's responsibility to ask you for details regarding anything that might be considered a security or suitability issue. These questions will cover who, what, when, where, how, how much, how many, and why. It will be to your benefit to volunteer mitigating information that is not elicited by the investigator's questions. For instance, the simple answer for not paying your debts on time is usually because your living expenses and debt repayment exceeded your income. However, if you had an addition to your family, an extended period of unemployment for yourself or your spouse, unexpected medical expenses, death in the family, divorce, separation, etc., you should volunteer this information.

If there is some unfavorable security or suitability information that you listed on your SF86 or that you otherwise anticipate being questioned about during the PRSI, look at the applicable Adjudicative Guidelines. There is usually more than one guideline that applies to a single issue. Guidelines E (Personal Conduct), H (Drug Involvement), and J (Criminal Conduct) can all apply to simple use of marijuana. If you smoked marijuana at social gatherings, you associated with persons involved in criminal activity (Guideline E), you used a controlled substance (Guideline H), and you were involved in criminal conduct (Guideline J). You should review the mitigating factors under each applicable guideline to determine which apply to your situation. It is up to you to tell the investigator about any mitigating factors. The investigator must ask an applicant why they did something illegal. Once the applicant provides a response, the investigator is not required to explore the applicant's motive any further. If the applicant was influenced by others (such as peer pressure) and if the applicant is remorseful, it is important that applicant tell the investigator. Peer pressure and remorse are mitigating factors under Guideline J—Criminal Conduct.

If the investigator fails to ask you about any unfavorable information listed on your SF86, mention the information yourself. If you don't, it will have to be addressed later and will delay your clearance.

If you have been involved in serious misconduct, had significant financial problems, or have extensive foreign connections, it would be wise to make a written explanation of the situation(s), incorporating any information related to the mitigating factors listed in each of the Adjudicative Guidelines. Take a copy of the written explanation with you to the interview and give it to the investigator. By doing this you have greatly increased the probability that all the mitigating factors will be included in the investigator's report. Often the existence of mitigating factors are not revealed until an applicant finds himself answering an adjudicator's "Letter of Intent" to deny a security clearance. If you wait until this stage of the security clearance process to introduce mitigating information, your clearance determination will take several months longer than necessary. If your written explanation of such situation(s) is lengthy (more than one page), ask the investigator to make your written statement an attachment to his report. If your situation is very serious, complicated, and requires lengthy explanation, you can ask the investigator to prepare an affidavit (based on your written statement) for you to sign and include the affidavit as an attachment to his report. After the affidavit is executed, obtain a copy from the investigator. OPM generally does not like attachments to reports, but it is the only way that you can be absolutely certain that the adjudicator will be provided all the information you gave to the investigator. This is generally not necessary for a single misdemeanor offense (including DUI), low-level recreational use of drugs followed by a reasonable period of abstinence or major life change, or a single bankruptcy without further financial problems.

Arrive promptly for your PRSI. Silence your cellular telephone. Don't bring any weapons with you into the interview room, even if you are authorized to have them. Bring anything that contains contact information on your associates and family members (i.e., address book, personal digital assistant, cellular telephone) with you to the PRSI. You may be asked to provide names and contact information on people who know you, but are not listed on your SF86, and any updated contact information on people you listed on your SF86. Also bring copies of any financial documents pertaining to bad debts (i.e., bankruptcy records, account statements, credit report, collection agency letters and other correspondence). They will help to corroborate what you are saying and to provide accurate names, addresses, and account numbers.

The investigator will explain the purpose of the interview and remind you that your participation in the interview is voluntarily. It's your choice to answer all of the investigator's questions, some of the questions, or none at all. In most instances declining to answer any question will probably result in being denied a security clearance. Only when the investigator asks a question that is obviously beyond the scope of a security investigation, can an applicant refuse to answer and still be granted a clearance. Such questions usually relate to religious beliefs, political or union affiliations, and sexual matters that are not violations of law or that would not make the applicant susceptible to blackmail. The investigator will remind you that it is a criminal offense to intentionally furnish false or misleading information.

Federal investigators have the applicant answer questions under oath or affirmation. Contract investigators have the applicant make an unsworn declaration. Both procedures carry equal weight under the law. Knowingly providing false information is a criminal offense, punishable under 10 U.S.C 1001.

During the interview (or at a later date) you may be asked to sign a general, medical, financial, or special release. Refusal to sign a release, even if you know that the record being sought does not exist, will probably result in having your clearance denied.

Occasionally at some point after the PRSI, there may be a need for a follow up contact with the investigator. This occurs when you are unable to provide needed information during the PRSI, because the need for a release arises after the PRSI, some minor matter covered during the PRSI requires clarification, or you remember some pertinent information a few days after the PRSI.

SPECIAL INTERVIEW—SPIN

There are two situations in which a SPIN will be conducted:

1. Your investigation is an SSBI or SSBI-PR and adverse information or a major discrepancy surfaces during your investigation that was not covered during the PRSI.

2. Your investigation is a NACLC (or an ANACI) and adverse information or a major discrepancy is listed on your SF86 or developed during your investigation.

The purpose of the SPIN is to afford the applicant the opportunity to refute or to confirm and provide details regarding major discrepancies and/or adverse information. Adverse information refers to the 13 criteria covered by the "Adjudicative Guidelines for Determining Eligibility for Access to Classified Information." (See Appendix B.)

The information provided in the previous section on Personal Subject Interviews applies equally to SPINs, except that only the issue(s) that triggered the SPIN will be addressed during the interview. See entries under "PRSI" in the applicable sections of Chapters 5 through 11 of this book for more information.

MILITARY APPLICANTS/ENLISTEES

All military enlistees are required to complete a Standard Form 86 for entry into the Armed Forces, even when they will later be required to complete an SF86 for a Top Secret Security Clearance. In most instances the initial SF86 will be completed at the military recruiter's office, and you will take the SF86 with you (in paper form or on a computer disk) to the Military Entrance Processing Station (MEPS). At the MEPS you are suppose to review the form, make any changes to update the form, and sign it before it is submitted. This review is often perfunctory. Sometimes you may not be given the opportunity to make any changes, or if you do provide information regarding changes, the changes may not actually be made to the form before it is submitted.

The first of two problems that usually occurs is that the military applicant often has little control over what is typed onto the SF86. Typically the applicant provides either oral or handwritten information to the recruiter for inclusion onto the SF86. For whatever reason, the recruiter completes the form for the applicant. Unfortunately when recruiters complete SF86s for the applicants, some recruiters make little effort to complete the form properly. They are not the ones who sign the form, and they have no incentive to insure its accuracy. They are rarely held accountable for incomplete or inaccurate information. This occurs because some recruiters do not understand the importance of the form or how the information is going to be used. It takes time and effort to complete the form properly. Sometimes recruiters intentionally omit information from an SF86, because they don't want any unfavorable information on the form. When it comes to security matters, recruiters have a basic conflict of interest. The main purpose of their job is to get you into the military. Some recruiters would prefer not to have to complete any forms on you that might disqualify you for enlistment into the specialty you have selected.

The second problem is if you are being submitted for a Top Secret clearance, you will be required to complete a second SF86 after you arrive at your basic training installation. If you are able to complete it accurately, it may be substantially different than your initial SF86. It is unlikely that you will actually be able to complete the SF86 accurately at basic training, unless you lived in only one location, had only one job, attended only one school in the past several years, and have memorized the names, complete addresses, and telephone numbers of all your character references. At basic training you will sometimes be given a copy of your initial SF86 from which you can extract information to complete the second SF86, but if the information on the initial SF86 is inaccurate or incomplete, it isn't very helpful. Rarely will you have other documents with you that you can use as reference materials. Additionally, at basic training you are not always given the opportunity to use the telephone to call someone to get information you can not remember or sufficient time to complete the form properly. This results in a second security form with errors and omissions that are different than on the first form. When OPM opens the investigation for the Top Secret clearance, they review any previously submitted security forms and compare that information with the SF86 submitted for the Top Secret clearance. When there are significant discrepancies between these forms, it complicates the investigation and calls into question the possibility of intentional falsification. And of course, most complications result in delays.

The second problem is magnified when a military applicant enters the Delayed Enlistment Program (DEP) several months before they actually go on active duty, since the original SF86 is submitted at the time of entry into the DEP. Many things happen (marriage, change in jobs, etc.) between the time the original SF86 is submitted and the time you must fill out the second SF86.

It is unfortunate, but many of the people military applicants rely upon to guide them through the security process do not know what needs to be entered into the security forms. They have little or no knowledge of the adjudicative criteria for granting clearances. This includes recruiters, MEPS personnel and the security personnel at basic training. It is not uncommon for security personnel at basic training to provide incorrect instructions for filling out the form.

A few military recruiters will insist on listing low-level drug use that occurred before age 16 on a security form, even though it is not required. This causes a problem when the second security form is filled out properly and does not contain the information about drug use. More often, applicants are subtly encouraged by recruiters to omit information that should be listed about illegal drug use on the original SF86, or at least minimize their use of drugs. When information about this drug use (or additional drug use) is revealed on the second SF86, during the Personal Subject Interview, or through other sources, the issue of falsification is then added to the original issue of illegal drug use.

Illegal drug use presents an excellent example of how falsification usually results in a bigger security problem than the information the applicant initially tries to hide. Although any use of illegal drugs without mitigating factors can result in a clearance denial; for most young people entering the US military, pre-service, low-level, recreational use of drugs will not present a significant problem. This is because the circumstances surrounding their use of drugs will mitigate the security concern (see the mitigating factors under Adjudicative Guidelines, Guideline H: Drug Involvement). The mere act of entering the US military usually demonstrates their intention not to use drugs in the future. They are removing themselves from the environment where drugs were used, distancing themselves from their former drug-using associates, placing themselves in an environment where they are subject to random drug testing, and hopefully they abstained from drug use at least during the period they were in the DEP.

As a practical matter, for security clearance purposes, the honesty/integrity issue raised by intentionally falsifying an SF86 is usually much more significant than the pre-service, low-level, recreational use of drugs. Military recruiters can not process applicants for some military specialties without a "drug waiver." Eligibility for drug waivers varies from service to service depending on the illegal drugs involved. Generally an applicant can always get a waiver for marijuana use. If a recruiter refuses to obtain a drug waiver for you, go to his supervisor or shop around for a different recruiter.

The Air Force is particularly restrictive regarding drug waivers. If you try to conceal drug use and it is discovered during the clearance investigation, the Air Force could court martial you for fraudulent enlistment and discharge you under less than honorable conditions. Only if your commanding officer chooses not to prosecute you and communicates that to the Air Force Central Adjudication Facility, will your security investigation be fully adjudicated and a clearance determination made. It may seem illogical, but there are situations where individuals met the standards for being granted a Top Secret security clearance but do not met the standards for the position that requires the clearance.

So, if you are planning on entering the Armed Forces in the near future, get a paper copy of the SF86 and instruction from the GSA website cited earlier in this chapter. Take the time to complete it properly yourself. Take a copy (keep the original) to the military recruiting office and insist that information from this form be used as the basis for the SF86 that the recruiter creates for you to take to the MEPS. The recruiter may obtain a credit report on you and may also check with local police departments. Make sure that any applicable data from these sources is added to your SF86 (and to your original copy). Ask the recruiter to print a copy of the SF86 he creates for you and compare it to your original. Take your original SF86 to MEPS and compare it to the form they ask you to sign. Just before you go to basic training, review your original SF86. Create an addendum on plain paper listing complete information about any new residences, jobs, schools, foreign travel, traffic citations, address changes of listed character references, etc. Take the form with you to basic training and have it available when you are required to complete a new security form.

Do not knowingly enter any incorrect information on any security form, even if you are instructed to do so by some security official. If you are a young person, you may be instructed to list the month and year of your 16th birthday as the starting date for a residence, employment, or a school—don't do it. List the actual date you began living at a residence, began an employment, or began attending a school. The SF86 requires that you list all schools, employment and residence since your 16th birthday. That does not mean that you should use your 16th birthday as the starting date for the security form. You may be told to list your parents' address for a period that you were actually living in a dormitory at a college—list the college dormitory as your residence. You may be told to omit short-term residences and employment—list them all, if they occurred during the past 10 years (or back to your 16th or 18th birthday, depending on your age). You may be told to list one of your parents as the person who can verify a residence—don't list any relatives for this purpose. You are the person who is attesting to the accuracy of the information on the form (and subjecting yourself to criminal penalties under federal law), not the person who gives you incorrect instructions.

Specific instructions concerning information that needs to be including on a security form are provided in Chapters 5 through 11 of this book.

CHAPTER 3

THE INVESTIGATIVE PROCESS

Once the request for investigation and the Standard Form 86 (including the appropriate releases) are received at OPM, the investigation is opened and assigned a case number. The case is scoped in accordance with the requirements of one of the four investigative standards (NACLC, SSBI, SSBI-PR, or PPR) described in Chapter 1. Scoping the case involves identifying the specific investigative actions required.

The case is then assigned to OPM's Federal Investigative Services (FIS) or to one of the five private companies doing investigative work for OPM. All required components of the investigation are tasked to different field offices and headquarters elements.

NATIONAL AGENCY CHECK
WITH LAW CHECKS AND CREDIT CHECK

The basic NAC and Credit Check for all investigations are handled at the OPM Headquarters element known as FIPC (Federal Investigation Processing Center) near Boyers, Pennsylvania. For SSBIs, SSBI-PRs, and PPRs the Law Enforcement Checks and other field investigative activities are dispatched to the appropriate field office based on postal ZIP codes listed on the SF86 for residences, education, employment, court actions, and arrests/charges. For NACLC some Law Enforcement Checks are done by FIPC, and some are done by field offices. Ideally all field offices and FIPC begin working on the investigation simultaneously.[39]

FIELD INVESTIGATION

---

[39] For ANACIs some law enforcement checks are done by letter inquiry by FIPC and some are done by field offices. Additionally, for ANACIs letter inquiries are sent to employers, schools, and personal references by FIPC.

If the field work on a case is assigned to FIS, only FIS field investigators will work on the case. If the field work is assigned to a contractor such as U.S. Investigative Services (USIS), only USIS field investigators will work on the case. FIS and each of the contract investigative companies have their own network of field offices. So even though there are about 7,000 investigators working for OPM, only the resources of a single field investigative entity (contractor company or FIS) will be assigned to work on your case. The only exception is for investigative work conducted outside the United States. No contractor personnel are conducting investigations for OPM outside the United States.[40] FIS personnel are doing investigative work in foreign countries where the United States has a military "Status of Forces Agreement" with the host country. In countries where there is no Status of Forces agreement, other U.S. governmental agencies conduct the investigation. So, both a contract investigative company and FIS may be involved in a single case, if overseas investigative actions are needed.

All of the contract investigative companies and FIS are large enough to have field offices in all major metropolitan areas of the United States. Typically field offices are located in large metropolitan areas and major military bases. A number of investigators will live within commuting distance of their field office. Other investigators assigned to the same office may live and work hundreds of miles away.

All field offices are assigned geographic areas of responsibility (AOR). Investigators within each field office may be assigned a portion of the field office's AOR. Consequently, more than one investigator within the same field office may work on your case, even if your home is only a few miles from your place of work or school. In major metropolitan areas or areas with high concentrations of military and defense contractor activities, more than one investigator may be assigned to cover the same area, and other investigators may have significant overlap in their assigned areas.

Some investigations are completed exactly as initially scoped, and there is no need for any coordination between investigators in different areas. These investigations are usually done in the shortest amount of time commensurate with their priority. However, in most cases, as the investigation develops, the need for additional record checks and reference interviews is identified. An investigator in one field office may send one or more case messages to investigators in other locations to advise them of the new information and the need to complete additional investigative actions. Inevitably, the more case messages and other exchanges of information between investigators, the longer an investigation will take.

---

[40] In late 2006 OPM began contracting through the US State Department for investigative support on a limited basis in some foreign countries. Training for their contract investigators was completed in spring 2007.

Likewise, the fewer field offices involved in your investigation, the greater the likelihood that your investigation will be completed sooner. This is because your investigation will not be completed until the last field office sends in its report. The more offices that are involved, the greater the likelihood that at least one of them is significantly behind in its work.

For SSBIs essentially every significant element of information you list on your SF86 will be verified (or reasonable attempts will be made to verify it), either from records or from personal references (see Chapter 1 for components of an SSBI). If information gathered from records or personal references differs substantially from information you provided on your SF86, it will be reported. Personal references from each venue (residence, employment, education), as well as general character references will be interviewed, not only to collaterally verify your activities, but also to gather information about your reliability, trustworthiness, conduct, character, and loyalty to the United States.

A Personal Subject Interview (PRSI) is a standard component of the field investigation of all SSBIs and SSBI-PRs. The Special Interview (SPIN) is not a standard component of any investigation. If there are major discrepancies or adverse information (related to the 13 adjudicative guidelines) that have not previously been addressed by the applicant in an interview, a SPIN will be assigned, and an investigator will interview the applicant specifically about the discrepancy or adverse information. SPINs can be added to SSBIs, SSBI-PRs, and NACLCs. The PRSI and SPIN are sometimes referred to simply as a Subject Interview (SI). SIs are assigned to a field investigator whose AOR covers the applicant's work location.

The following extract from *Director of Central Intelligence Directive No. 6/4, Annex B—Quality Control Guidelines for the Single Scope Background Investigation, 2 July 1998*, provides a good general outline of what investigators will cover during an SSBI:

Definition of Quality.

A quality investigation is a thorough and comprehensive collection of favorable and unfavorable information from a variety of sources, past and present, that may include employment(s), reference(s), neighborhood(s), credit, police, and the Subject.

The determination of eligibility for access to sensitive compartmented information is a discretionary determination using the whole person concept that such access is clearly in the interests of the national security. Accordingly, the investigation will be comprehensive and in such detail so as to affirmatively address unquestioned loyalty to the United States, strength of character, trustworthiness, honesty, reliability, discretion, and sound judgment, as well as freedom from conflicting allegiances and potential for coercion, and willingness and ability to abide by regulations governing the use, handling and protection of sensitive compartmented information.[41]

Conduct of the Interview

The quality of the investigation depends on the investigator's ability to elicit information from a source knowledgeable about the Subject. This is basic to the conduct of any interview. The investigator should plan and execute each interview so as to obtain the maximum amount of information from a source. Available sources should be selected from each area of coverage to ensure that pertinent information about the Subject's entire background is developed.

The investigator should conduct the interview in person and find a suitable location that protects privacy. Telephonic interviews are strongly discouraged; however, occasionally exigent circumstances may dictate that the interviews be conducted by telephone. If a telephonic interview is necessary, the report should always state why the interview was not conducted in person.

The investigator should initially advise the source of the reason/purpose for the investigation and should attempt to establish a degree of confidence in the source(s) that will promote a high level of rapport and cooperation.

The investigator should also advise the source about the Privacy Act of 1974, before completing the interview, since the source needs to understand that the Subject of the investigation has the right to review information provided by a source and has the right to know a source's identity, unless the source requests confidentiality.

Collection Requirement (Coverage)

a. For all Sources.
   Investigators should establish the duration and nature of association between the source and the Subject to assess the source's extent of knowledge. The investigator should always secure the source's full name and any other appropriate identifying data, particularly in the case of a source with a common name. All derogatory or noteworthy information concerning the Subject of the investigation that is provided by a source should be fully explored in the interview, including elicitation of the names of any corroborating sources or record information that will substantiate any derogatory testimony provided by the source. For all sources, the report should indicate what issue areas were covered and whether the information provided was favorable or unfavorable.

---

[41] DCID 6/4 concerns SCI access; however the description of an SSBI provided here applies equally to all SSBIs whether for collateral Top Secret clearances or for SCI access.

b. For References and Neighbors.

Depending on the source's degree of association, investigators should ask each reference or neighbor relevant information regarding the Subject's:

1. Family, citizenship, education, employment, residence history, and military service.
2. Reputation, character, honesty, trustworthiness, integrity, discretion, reliability, and temperament.
3. Financial stability, organizational affiliations, and whether there is a history of mental, emotional, or physical health problems.
4. Whether the Subject exhibits a pattern of excessive use of alcohol or has ever used illegal drugs or abused prescription drugs.
5. Activities which indicate a lack of discretion or demonstrate poor judgment, a character flaw, or a personality disorder.
6. Participation in criminal activity or an altercation with law enforcement agencies.
7. Travels abroad for business or pleasure and degree of contact with foreign nationals.
8. Unquestioned loyalty to the United States.

If a Subject has had access to classified information and a source is in a position to know, the investigator should ask whether the Subject properly handles classified information or has ever had a security violation. Finally, the investigator should ask if the source can recommend the Subject for a position of trust and responsibility with the US Government or, in the case of a contractor, can the Subject be trusted with classified information. The investigator should conclude the interview by asking the source to provide names of additional references.

c. Follow-up Questions.

If a source provides noteworthy or derogatory information to questions in any of the above areas of consideration, the investigator should ask follow-up questions as necessary to elicit all available information. The investigator should report as fully as possible:

1. The nature, extent, and seriousness of the conduct.
2. The motivation for and the circumstances surrounding the conduct.
3. The frequency and recency of the conduct.
4. The Subject's age and maturity at the time of the conduct.
5. Whether the conduct was voluntary or whether there was pressure, coercion, or exploitation leading to the conduct.
6. Whether the Subject has been rehabilitated or has exhibited other pertinent behavioral changes since the conduct.

If the Subject has ended the questionable conduct, the investigator should attempt to determine the motivation for positive change. The investigator should also attempt to establish whether there may be personal animosity or bias to-wards the Subject on the part of the source(s). The investigator should supply any available documentary evidence relating to the conduct in addition to the re-port of the source.

d. For Employment References.
The investigator should identify and interview the best source(s) available. These employment references should include, but are not limited to, the Sub-ject's immediate supervisor, coworker(s), and other persons with frequent pro-fessional contact. Where appropriate, the investigator should pursue the same line of inquiry as with references and neighbors. In particular, the investigator should inquire regarding:

1. Whether the Subject is willing to abide by company policies and regulations.
2. Whether the Subject appropriately safeguards the employer's proprie-tary/sensitive information.
3. Whether the Subject is financially stable.
4. Whether the Subject has a history of substance abuse, to include alcohol, and/or prescription drugs.
5. Whether the Subject has been involved in any criminal activity.
6. Whether the Subject is reliable and eligible for re-hire.

The investigator should obtain any available documentary evidence to support the report of the source(s).

e. For Subject Interviews.
The Subject is the best source of information about himself/herself. Hence, the investigator should explore with the Subject the same line of inquiry she/he pur-sues with a reference, neighborhood, and employment source(s). The investiga-tor should obtain the Subject's version of the details surrounding all issues aris-ing either in the course of the interview or in other parts of the investigation that have been completed by the time of the Subject Interview and report them com-pletely. The investigator should inquire regarding:

1. What happened and why.
2. Where, when, how, and how often it happened.
3. Who else was involved.
4. Was the conduct voluntary.

Of particular value to the adjudicator is evidence that the Subject is being contra-dictory or dissembling. If the Subject claims to have ended the conduct, the inves-tigator should attempt to determine the motivation for positive change. The inves-tigator should report only the facts.

During interviews of references, investigators will "wave the flag" and stress the importance of the investigation to national security. They will appeal to a reference's sense of patriotism and loyalty to the United States. It is often surprising what an applicant's best friend will reveal to an investigator, if the investigator is experienced and persuasive. If a personal reference is hesitant to provide unfavorable information about their friend, it's not difficult to ask the reference, "What is more important, your loyalty to your friend or your loyalty the United States and the security of our country?" How would your friends respond? If a reference is willing to provide unfavorable information, but doesn't want to be identified in the report as the source of the information, there are provisions for granting confidentiality to the reference. In such cases the information is reported without identifying the source.

No one is compelled to provide information about you. Most people feel it is their responsibility to cooperate with government security investigators; however, there are a few people who object to any government intrusion into their lives or the lives of others, regardless of the benefit to national security. If you know such people, list them as character references only if no one else is available and only after obtaining their permission.

Once all field reports have been submitted, the case is reviewed at OPM Headquarters by a case analyst to insure that all investigative requirements have been properly completed. If there are any deficiencies, additional investigative actions are tasked to one or more field offices. If there are any unresolved minor discrepancies or additional releases are needed, the applicant may be recontacted to clarify these inconsistencies or obtained the required releases.

POLYGRAPH

Senior officials from agencies that use the polygraph see it as a significant tool because of its utility in generating admissions of wrongdoing, either during the pre-test, test, or post-test period. The polygraph saves time and money, and it serves as a deterrent by eliminating some potential applicants from seeking a highly sensitive position in the first place. The polygraph examination is conducted before the background investigation, saving additional resources should the applicant be rejected as a result of polygraph admissions. According to a May 1993 NSA letter to the White House, "over 95% of the information the NSA develops on individuals who do not meet federal security clearance guidelines is derived via [voluntary admissions from] the polygraph process.[42]

Because disparities exist in the procedural safeguards employed by different agencies for those employees requiring access to highly sensitive information, full reciprocity of

---

[42] Report of the Commission on Protecting and Reducing Government Secrecy (Washington, DC: Government Printing Office, 1997).

security clearances between the agencies cannot be achieved. While the polygraph is used to screen employees at the CIA, NRO, DIA, NSA, and FBI (which resumed screening in 1993), the White House, NSC, State Department, and Congress have traditionally resisted adopting polygraph screening. Even among the agencies that use the polygraph, the scope, methods, and procedural safeguards may diverge. [43]

Agencies that Use the Polygraph for Employment Screening [44]

> Central Intelligence Agency
> Defense Intelligence Agency
> Drug Enforcement Agency
> Federal Bureau of Investigation
> National Security Agency
> National Reconnaissance Office

Polygraph examinations may be administered with the written consent of the applicant:[45]

- To assist in determining initial eligibility and continued eligibility (on a random aperiodic basis) of DoD civilian, military, and contractor personnel for access to specifically designated information protected within Special Access Programs (SAP). The scope of any polygraph examination administered for such purpose shall be limited to the counter intelligence topics (commonly referred to as a counterintelligence scope polygraph examination).[46]
- To resolve serious credible derogatory information developed in connection with a personnel security investigation of DoD civilian, military, or contractor personnel, that cannot be resolved in any other manner.
- When requested by the subject of a security clearance investigation, as a means of exculpation, with respect to allegations or evidence arising in the course of such investigation.

Polygraph examinations are used to assist in determining the eligibility of DoD personnel with their written consent for:[47]

- Assignment or detail to Central Intelligence Agency (CIA) in positions where polygraph examinations are required by the CIA.
- Employment with or assignment to the Defense Intelligence Agency (DIA) in positions that have been designated by the Director, DIA, as critical intelligence

---

[43] Ibid.

[44] Ibid.

[45] DoD Directive 5210.48, Subject: DoD Polygraph Program, December 24, 1984.

[46] Counterintelligence Scope Polygraph Examinations are fully described in Appendix 2 of DoD Regulation 5210.48, January 1985.

[47] DoD Directive 5210.48, Subject: DoD Polygraph Program, December 24, 1984.

position, provided that the scope of such examinations shall be limited to the counterintelligence topics.

- Initial or continued employment, assignment, or detail for duty with the NSA in activities that require access to sensitive cryptologic information, or to spaces where sensitive cryptologic information is produced, processed, or stored. When military personnel are assigned or detailed for duty with NSA, the scope of such examination shall be limited to the counterintelligence topics.

Polygraph examinations are conducted as a supplement to, not as a substitute for, other forms of investigation that may be required under the circumstances. Applicants for employment, assignment, or detail to positions requiring access to specifically designated information in SAPs, assignment or detail to the Central Intelligence Agency, employment in and assignment or detail to critical intelligence positions in the Defense Intelligence Agency, or employment in and assignment or detail to the National Security Agency (NSA), who refuse to take a polygraph examination will not be selected or assigned. Persons who refuse to take a polygraph examination in connection with determining their continued eligibility for access to specifically designated information in SAPs, to include incumbents of positions subsequently determined to require such access, may be denied access to the classified information in question. With the exception of the NSA, the DoD Component concerned shall ensure that such person is retained in a position of equal pay and grade that does not require such access, or arrange like employment for such individual at another DoD Component. A refusal to consent to a polygraph examination shall not be recorded in the person's personnel file or any investigative file. The person's supervisor, and in the case of a contractor employee, the person's employer, will not be informed of the refusal, unless it is necessary because the person must be reassigned to a position that does not require a polygraph examination.[48]

Generally, except for examinations to resolve serious credible derogatory information or examinations requested by clearance applicants for exculpatory purposes in connection with a security clearance investigation, polygraph examinations are primary administered to determine eligibility for special assignments or access to special categories of classified information, not for security clearances.

---

[48] DoD Regulation 5210.48, Polygraph Program, January 1985.

CHAPTER 4

ADJUDICATION & POST-ADJUDICATIVE ACTIONS

ADJUDICATION

"The 2005 federal adjudicative guidelines state that each security clearance case is to be judged on its own merits and a final decision to grant, deny, or revoke access to classified information is the responsibility of the specific department or agency. Any doubt about whether a clearance for access to classified information is consistent with national security is to be resolved in favor of national security. Executive Order 12968, which authorized the federal guidelines, makes it clear that a determination to grant clearance eligibility is a discretionary decision based on judgments by appropriately trained adjudicative staff. The guidelines, therefore, are not to be considered a simple checklist. Adjudicators are to consider available, reliable information about the person—past and present, favorable and unfavorable—in reaching an 'overall common sense' clearance eligibility determination, a process known as the 'whole person' concept.

"In making determinations of eligibility for security clearances, the federal guidelines require adjudicators to consider (1) guidelines covering 13 specific areas, (2) adverse conditions or conduct that could raise a security concern and factors that might mitigate (alleviate) the condition for each guideline, and (3) general factors related to the whole person."[49]

Although adverse information concerning conduct or conditions covered by a single criterion within one of the 13 guidelines may not be sufficient for an unfavorable determination; the applicant can be disqualified, when the information indicates a recent or recurring pattern of irresponsibility, questionable judgment, or emotionally unstable behavior.

---

[49] United States Government Accountability Office (GAO), Report to the Ranking Member, Committee on Armed Services, House of Representatives, entitled: DoD Personnel: More Consistency Needed in Determining Eligibility for Top Secret Security Clearances, GAO-01-465, April 18, 2001.

When adverse suitability information surfaces regarding an individual who currently holds a security clearance, the adjudicator must consider whether the person:

- Voluntarily reported the information
- Was truthful and complete in responding to questions;
- Sought assistance and followed professional guidance, where appropriate;
- Resolved or appears likely to favorably resolve the security concern;
- Has demonstrated positive changes in behavior and employment;
- Should have his or her access temporarily suspended pending final adjudication of the information.

If the adjudicator decides that the adverse suitability information is not serious enough to recommend denial or revocation of the clearance, the clearance may be granted or continued with a warning that future incidents of a similar nature may result in a revocation.

When the personnel security investigation uncovers no adverse security conditions, the adjudicator's task is fairly straightforward, because there is no security condition to mitigate.

ADJUDICATIVE PROCESS

Once the case analyst at OPM Headquarters is satisfied with the completed case, it is sent to the Central Adjudication Facility (CAF) of the requesting agency. There are numerous CAFs, but the largest within the Department of Defense are:

1. Defense Industrial Security Clearance Office (DISCO) in Columbus, Ohio handles cases on DoD contractor personnel and certain other federal contractors (referred to industrial cases).
2. US Army Central Adjudication Facility at Fort Meade, Maryland handles all US Army military and civilian personnel, including Army Reserves and Army National Guard.
3. Department of Navy Central Adjudication Facility in Washington, D.C. handles all US Navy and US Marine Corps military and civilian personnel, including Navy and Marine Corps Reserves.
4. Air Force Central Adjudication Facility at Bolling AFB, Maryland handles all USAF military and civilian personnel, including USAF Reserves and National Guard.

Each CAF (except DISCO) has a staff of adjudicators who review the investigative case files and grant, deny, continue, or revoke security clearances.

DEFENSE SECURITY CLEARANCE OFFICE

DISCO has a staff of case reviewers who grant and continue clearances when there is no, or minimal, derogatory information in the file, but they do not have the authority to deny or revoke clearances. If DISCO is unable to grant a clearance, they refer the case to the Defense Office of Hearings and Appeals (DOHA)[50] of the Defense Legal Services Agency. DOHA will review the case and may direct DISCO to grant or continue a security clearance. DOHA may also issue a statement of reasons (SOR) as to why it is not clearly consistent with the national interest to grant or continue a security clearance, or take interim actions, including but not limited to:

- Direct further investigation.
- Propound written interrogatories to the applicant or other persons with relevant information.
- Requiring the applicant to undergo a medical evaluation by a DoD Psychiatric Consultant.
- Interviewing the applicant.

Before DOHA makes a final decision to deny or revoke a clearance, it must provide the applicant:

- Notice of specific reasons for the proposed action (statement of reasons—SOR).
- Opportunity to respond to the reasons.
- Notice of the right to a hearing and the opportunity to cross-examine persons providing information adverse to the applicant.
- Opportunity to present evidence on his or her own behalf, or to be represented by counsel or personal representative.

If an SOR is issued and the applicant fails to respond, DOHA will direct DISCO to deny or revoke the security clearance. The SOR is actually contained within a Letter of Intent or Letter of Instructions (LOI). If the applicant chooses to answer the SOR, the answer must be received at DOHA within 20 days from the date the applicant receives the SOR. This answer can be made with or without a request for a hearing. Applicants may request an extension of time to file

---

[50] Formerly Directorate for Industrial Security Clearance Review—DISCR.

an answer to the SOR, but they must have a good reason. The applicant must submit a detailed written answer to the SOR under oath or affirmation that admits or denies each listed allegation. A general denial or similar answer is insufficient.

Should review of the applicant's answer to the SOR indicate that allegations are unfounded, or evidence is insufficient for further processing, the DOHA Department Counsel will withdrawal the SOR and direct DISCO to grant or continue the security clearance. Otherwise, the case is assigned to an Administrative Judge who will consider the case (with or without a hearing).

If there is no hearing, the DOHA Department Counsel provides the applicant with a copy of all relevant and material information (Files Of Relevant Materials—FORM) that could be presented to the Administrative Judge for a clearance decision based on the written record. The applicant has 30 days from receipt of the information to submit a documentary response setting forth objections, rebuttal, extenuation, mitigation, or explanation, as appropriate.

If a hearing is requested by the applicant or by the DOHA Department Counsel, the applicant will be notified at least 15 days in advance of the time and place of the hearing, which generally will be held at a location within a city near the applicant's place of employment or residence. The Administrative Judge may require a pre-hearing conference. The applicant must appear in person with or without counsel or a personal representative at the time and place designated by the notice of hearing. Hearings are generally open, except when the applicant requests that it be closed, or when the Administrative Judge determines that there is good cause for keeping the proceedings closed. As far in advance as practical, Department Counsel and the applicant will serve one another with a copy of any pleading, proposed documentary evidence, or other written communication to be submitted to the Administrative Judge. Department Counsel is responsible for presenting witnesses and other evidence to establish facts alleged in the SOR that have been controverted. The applicant is responsible for presenting witness or other evidence to rebut, explain, extenuate, or mitigate facts admitted by the applicant or proven by Department Counsel, and has the ultimate burden of persuasion as to obtaining a favorable clearance decision. A verbatim transcript is made of the hearing. The applicant is furnished one copy of the transcript, less the exhibits, without cost.

The administrative judge makes a written decision setting forth pertinent findings of fact, policies, and conclusions as to the allegations in the SOR, and whether it is clearly consistent with the national interest to grant or continue a security clearance. The applicant and Department Counsel are each provided a copy of the clearance decision. DOHA then directs DISCO to make appropriate notification to the applicant's employer. If the clearance is denied or revoked, the applicant is notified of appeal procedures.

NOTE: DOHA Department Counsel has the option of requesting a hearing, if you do not request a hearing in your response to the SOR. Additionally, the Administrative Judge may consider information without affording the applicant an opportunity to cross-examine the person making the statement orally, or in writing when justified (such as, confidential sources and sources who have died or are seriously ill). In such cases the applicant shall be furnished with as comprehensive and detailed a summary of the information as the national security permits. The Administrative Judge and Appeal Board may make a clearance decision either favorable or unfavorable to the applicant based on such evidence after giving appropriate consideration to the fact that the applicant did not have an opportunity to confront such evidence, but any final determination adverse to the applicant will be made only by the Secretary of Defense, or the Department or Agency Head, based on a personal review of the case record.

OTHER CENTRAL ADJUDICATION FACILITIES

The other CAFs follow the same basic procedures, except that they make denial or revocation decisions themselves, and there are no hearings. Generally, adjudicators can grant a clearance on clean cases. If there is any unfavorable information present, the case is reviewed by a senior adjudicator. Senior adjudicators can grant or continue the clearance, but if they recommend denial or revocation of the clearance, they forward the case with an SOR for review and signature of a supervisor. If there is no response to the SOR, the clearance is denied or revoked. If there is a response, the matter is reviewed by a senior supervisor or the commanding officer of the CAF who makes the final determination regarding such denials or revocations. The military CAFs do not automatically send the applicant a copy of all relevant and material information. The applicant must request it through the CAF's Freedom of Information Act Office.

Exact procedures and timelines for advising a CAF of an applicant's intention to answer/rebut an SOR and actually submitting a written rebuttal are slightly different for each CAF. Basically, the applicant has one to 15 days to advise their CAF in writing of their intention to rebut an SOR and 60 days or less to submit the written rebuttal. The US Army requires the applicant's commanding officer to attach an endorsement to the applicant's rebuttal, recommending for or against the granting of a clearance. The US Navy recommends that the commanding officer attach an endorsement. The US Air Force neither requires nor recommends an endorsement. The Army and the Air Force CAFs are allowed 60 days to review rebuttals to SORs and make a final decision regarding a clearance. The Navy CAF is allowed 30 days to make a final decision.

DISCUSSION OF ADJUDICATIONS

The DOHA website at *www.dod.mil/dodgc/doha/industrial/* has full written adjudicative decisions of all cases cited in this book. Bear in mind that what appears at this website represents only those cases referred to DOHA for adjudication where an SOR was issued, a rebuttal was received, and a determination was made that the clearance could not be granted or continued without a review by an administrative judge. The vast majority (about 94 percent) of DISCO cases are reviewed favorably by DISCO and never referred to DOHA. Ultimately one to two percent of all DISCO cases result in a security clearance being denied or revoked.

The case cited below presents a good example of the reasoning used by a DOHA Administrative Judge in reaching his decisions, particularly in the application of the "Whole Person Concept." The investigation was an SSBI. Note that the SF86 was submitted in November 2003, the PRSI was conducted sometime in 2004, but the case was not initially adjudicated until November 2005. The case was not finally adjudicated until May 31, 2006. In all likelihood the investigation took about one year, but the adjudication probably took about one and a half years. If all the information available to the Administrative Judge at the hearing had been properly presented to the security investigator and included in his report, the whole process could probably have been completed several months earlier.

No statistics are available on the number of cases where applicants quit their jobs in frustration, after waiting more than a year without receiving a clearance decision. In such situations the cases are cancelled and never completely adjudicated.

In all adjudications the judge or adjudicator looks at the "Disqualifying Conditions" that exist, then looks for potential "Mitigating Conditions." Generally if he finds that at least one mitigating condition applies, it may be sufficient to overcome the security concern of the disqualifying condition. In this case the administrative judge found (or actually the applicant presented and the judge accepted) mitigating conditions for only one disqualifying condition—drug use under Guideline H. The judge was unable to find mitigation for Guideline E—Personal Conduct (unwillingness to comply with rules and regulations, specifically falsifying the SF86), the related criminal aspect of falsification, and the underlying criminal offense of illegal drug use under Guideline J, so he used the "Whole Person" concept to mitigate these disqualifying conditions.

The parenthetical citations (i.e., E2.A5.1.2.2) in the written decision presented below (and in other written decisions at DOHA's website) refer to paragraph numbers in DoD Directive 5220.6. The Adjudicative Guidelines are reprinted in DoD Directive 5220.6 and follow the paragraph numbering sequence within that document. However, DoD Directive 5220.6 contains an older version of the Adjudicative Guidelines, not the new one published in December 2005.

CASE NUMBER: 05-09958.h1
Drugs; Personal Conduct; Criminal Conduct
05/31/2006

SF 86 was submitted in November 2003. On November 3, 2005, a Statement of Reasons (SOR) was issued to Applicant. On November 11, 2005, Applicant responded to the SOR allegations, and requested a hearing. The case was assigned to an Administrative Judge on January 30, 2006. A notice of hearing was issued on February 24, 2006, and a hearing was held on March 16, 2006. One government exhibit and five applicant exhibits were admitted into evidence. One government witness, an investigator, testified. The Applicant and one witness testified on behalf of the Applicant. The transcript was received on April 7, 2006.

Applicant is a 26-year-old employee of a major defense contractor working as an engineer/scientist. The issues in the case involve Applicant's occasional use of marijuana during a period of less than a year when he was in college in 2001-2002, and his failure to report that use at Question 27 concerning drug use on his application for a top secret security clearance (SF 86) filed in November 2003. That question requires an affirmative answer if drugs were used in the past seven years after age 16. He did not report the drug use as he feared loss of his clearance that would jeopardize his employment if he revealed the conduct.

In 2004 Applicant voluntarily gave information to a security investigator with the Office of Personnel Management admitting his drug use during the period alleged. The number of uses was vague ranging from five to ten but no more than a maximum of fifteen. The agent credited him with candor and honesty in his admission and his regret for the drug use and the omission on the SF 86. No written statement was taken by the agent.

Applicant has no intention of using drugs in the future and has not done so since 2002. He has no contact with the people with whom he used marijuana while in college. He was married in September, 2005, is active in his church, owns his own home, and is a responsible citizen. His wife is employed in a responsible corporate position and they are planning on children in the near future. His hobbies are sports and reading.

Applicant has two college degrees including a Master's degree in engineering which he received in 2003. He started working on a Ph.D. but has deferred it because of the time demands of his job. While in college he traveled abroad on a fellowship doing medical research on cancer treatment. He has received numerous awards as a student including the outstanding graduate student in his department and for various achievements during the past two years from his employer.

Applicant is highly regarded by his supervisors and colleagues who testified for him or submitted letters of support illustrating his work ethic, trustworthiness, and skills in his field. He has held a security clearance since his employment in September 2003. He very much regrets his conduct in using drugs and his failure to report it on his SF 86.

The government has cited Disqualifying Condition (DC) 1 under Guideline H concerning drug involvement as relevant to the proposed denial of a security clearance for the Applicant. Drug involvement is always a security concern because it raises questions about a person's willingness or ability to protect classified information. Any drug abuse is a condition that may be disqualifying. The following definition is provided: "Drug abuse is the illegal use of a drug . . ." (E2.A8.1.1.3). Possible Mitigating Conditions that might be applicable are that the drug involvement was not recent (E2.A8.1.3.1.), and there is a demonstrated intent not to abuse any drugs in the future. (E2.A8.1.3.3.) Applicant has not used drugs since 2002 and is unlikely to use them in the future. The mitigating conditions are applicable.

Because Applicant deliberately falsified his security clearance application, disqualifying conditions under Guideline E (Personal Conduct) and Guideline J (Criminal Conduct) were alleged. Under Guideline E, conduct involving untrustworthiness, unreliability, or unwillingness to comply with rules and regulations could indicate the person may not properly safeguard classified information. (E2.A5.1.1.) Specifically, the deliberate omission, concealment, or falsification of relevant and material facts from a person security application could raise a security concern and may be disqualifying. (E2.A5.1.2.2.)

Under Guideline J, the government alleged Applicant's deliberate falsification of his SF 86 as a violation of 18 U.S.C. § 1001 and the underlying illegal use of drugs as a criminal offense. It is a criminal offense to knowingly and willfully make any materially false, fictitious, or fraudulent statement or representation or knowingly make or use a false writing in any matter within the jurisdiction of the executive branch of the Government of the United States. 18 U.S.C. § 1001. Information is material if it would affect a final agency decision or, if incorrect, would impede a thorough and complete investigation of an applicant's background. ISCR Case No. 01-06870, 2002 WL 32114535 (App. Bd. Sep. 13, 2002). An applicant's failure to accurately admit his drug use would impede a thorough security investigation and affect a final agency decision.

The Government established each of the allegations under Guidelines E and J alleged in the SOR. None of the mitigating conditions listed under Guideline E apply, however I will evaluate his behavior in terms of the "whole person concept." An applicant may mitigate criminal conduct security concerns by demonstrating the factors leading to the violation are not likely to recur (E2.A10.1.3.4.) and there is clear evidence of successful rehabilitation (E2.A10.1.3.6.). I conclude both of these mitigating conditions apply.

In all adjudications the protection of our national security is of paramount concern. Persons who have access to classified information have an overriding responsibility for the security concerns of the nation. The objective of the security clearance process is the fair-minded, commonsense assessment of a person's trustworthiness and fitness for access to classified information. The "whole person" concept recognizes we should view a person by the totality of their acts and omissions. Each case must be judged on its own merits taking into consideration all relevant circumstances, and applying sound judgment, mature thinking, and careful analysis.

Applicant was a young college student when he used drugs. He applied for a security clearance shortly after his college graduation, and he failed to report his drug usage. However, he fully admitted his wrongdoing when interviewed by the OPM investigator. Applicant is an impressive person of talent and strong motivation who holds a responsible position in his company. He has a bright future. His drug use was relatively infrequent and occurred during his college years. He has grown out of it and will not use drugs again. At the hearing, I was impressed by his contrition, his unequivocal acceptance of responsibility for his actions, and his promise that he would be truthful and remain free of drugs in the future. In evaluating Applicant's conduct personal and criminal conduct under Guidelines E and J and the whole person concept, I find for Applicant.

After considering all the evidence in its totality, and as an integrated whole to focus on the whole person of Applicant, I conclude Applicant's record of conduct justifies a finding that it is clearly consistent with the national interest to grant a security clearance to him.

In applying the standards listed in the Adjudicative Guidelines, adjudicators may also use the Adjudicator's Desktop Reference (ADR), a computer program developed by the Defense Personnel Security Research Center (PERSEREC) for additional guidance. The ADR contains an older version of the Adjudication Guidelines and extensive background information on the relevance and applicability of suitability issue information. PERSEREC anticipates updating their ADR in the near future and it will be available to the public on the internet.

APPEALS

Military and DoD Civilian applicants whose clearances are denied or revoked by a CAF have the choice of submitting a written appeal (with supporting documents) directly to their CAF's Personnel Security Appeal Board (PSAB), or requesting a personal appearance before a DOHA Administrative Judge. Procedures and timelines for the appeal process differ slightly for each military service. Generally an appellant has 10 days from the receipt of the final denial or revocation notice to submit a request to DOHA for a personal appearance before an Administrative Judge and 30 to 60 days to submit a written appeal directly to the PSAB.

Applicants who choose to appear before a DOHA Administrative Judge are permitted to explain their case (with or without an attorney or personal representative) and submit supporting documents, but it is not a hearing. There are no witnesses, other than the applicant, and there is no cross-examination. The DOHA Administrative Judge evaluates all the information presented and makes a clearance recommendation to the CAF's PSAB.

PSABs are composed of three members at the minimum military grade of O-5 or civilian grade of GS-14. If the appellant is an O-6 or GS-15 or higher, at least one member of the board will be equivalent or senior in grade to the appellant. One of the three members of the PSAB will be a permanent board member and serve as the board president. This person will have a thorough knowledge of and experience in the field of personnel security. One of the three board members will be an attorney, unless the board has access to legal counsel, and not more than one member will be from the security field. CAF officials may not be board members, nor may they communicate with board members regarding any open case. Appeals are decided by majority vote of the board members. PSABs render final determinations and notify the appellant in writing through the appellant's local command. Notification occurs within 60 days of the receipt of the written appeal or 30 days of receipt of the recommendation of the DOHA Administrative Judge (if there was a personal appearance). The written notification will provide the reasons that the PSAB either sustained or overturned the original determination of the CAF. PSAB decisions are final.

For DISCO cases, when a DOHA Administrative Judge issues a security clearance decision, the applicant or Department Counsel may appeal the Administrative Judge's clearance decision by filing a written notice of appeal with the Appeal Board within 15 days of the date of the Administrative Judge's clearance decision. A notice of cross-appeal may be filed with the Appeal Board within 10 days of receipt of the notice of appeal. In these cases appeals go before an Appeal Board of three administrative judges. No new evidence is received or considered by the Appeal Board. Except for rare circumstances where there were procedural errors, an Appeals Board's decision is final. Approximately 20 to 30 percent of the security clearance decisions issued by DOHA Administrative Judges are appealed.

After filing a timely notice of appeal, a written appeal brief must be received by the Appeal Board within 45 days of the date of the Administrative Judge's clearance decision. The appeal brief must state the specific issue or issues being raised, and cite specific portions of the case record supporting any alleged error. A written reply brief, if any, must be filed within 20 days of receipt of the appeal brief. A copy of any brief filed must be served upon the applicant or Department Counsel, as appropriate. The Appeal Board issues a written clearance decision addressing the material issues raised on appeal. A copy of the Appeal Board's written clearance decision is provided to the parties. The Appeal Board has the authority to:

- Affirm the decision of the Administrative Judge;
- Remand the case to an Administrative Judge to correct an identified error. If the case is remanded, the Appeal Board will specify the action to be taken on remand; or
- Reverse the decision of the Administrative Judge, if correction of identified error mandates such action.

NOTE: There are provisions in DoD Directive 5220.6 that allow an applicant whose clearance was initially denied or revoked and whose clearance was granted or reinstated after appeal to file a claim for lost earnings due to the initial denial or revocation; however, to be successful it is necessary to show gross negligence on the part of the Department of Defense.

An applicant whose security clearance has been finally denied or revoked by the DOHA is barred from reapplication for one year from the date of the initial unfavorable clearance decision. A reapplication for a security clearance must be made initially by the applicant's employer to the DISCO and is subject to the same processing requirements as those for a new security clearance application. The applicant shall thereafter be advised he is responsible for providing the Director, DOHA, with a copy of any adverse clearance decision together with evidence that circumstances or conditions previously found against the applicant have been rectified or sufficiently mitigated to warrant reconsideration.

NOTE: The adjudication and appeal process described above applies only to security clearances; it does not apply to special access authorizations. At some CAFs adjudication of security clearances and special access authorizations are done concurrently. At other CAFs it is a bifurcated process. There are appeal procedures for those who are denied a special access authorization; however, there is no absolute right to appeal. There have been rare instances where people have been granted a Top Secret security clearance but denied SCI access. When this occurs it is almost always due to some foreign connection (see DCID 6/4, Annex D for SCI appeal procedures).

DIFFERENCES BETWEEN DOD CONTRACTOR AND DOD CIVILIAN/MILITARY ADJUDICATIONS

At first glance it may seem that DoD contractor personnel have greater proce- dural protections and administrative remedies than DoD civilian and military personnel, because of their right to a hearing. But a hearing is an adversarial process in which the government is represented by an attorney experienced in security clearance matters, and the applicant may not be able to afford equal representation. When contractor personnel appeal their cases, they can not in- troduce new evidence that was not considered by the Administrative Judge; whereas, DoD civilian and military personnel can submit new evidence and the PSAB can take an entirely fresh look at the case and make what they believe to be the appropriate decision, without regard for the lower-level decision. Lastly, in contractor cases, either party (the applicant or the DOHA attorney) can ap- peal the decision of a DOHA Administrative Judge, but in military/civilian cases only the applicant has the right to appeal to a PSAB.

FREEDOM OF INFORMATION & PRIVACY ACTS

The Defense Security Service privacy policy can be found at *www.dss.mil/contactus/privacy.htm*. The Office of Personnel Management pri- vacy policy is at *www.opm.gov/html/privacy.asp*. Both agencies will release copies of investigative case files to former Subjects of their investigations with certain limitations.

Because each investigation is unique, it is difficult to provide a comprehen- sive list of information that might be redacted from your investigative file be- fore it is released to you. The most common redacted information falls into one of these three general areas:

- Information that pertains to another person and release of which would, constitute a violation of their privacy.
- Information that is currently and properly classified.
- Information that may tend to identify a source to whom DSS or OPM granted an express promise of confidentiality.

Copies of open investigations will not be released until the case is closed. In certain instances, medical information may be withheld. In those cases you can request that the medical information be sent to a physician of your choice, so the physician can explain the information to you.

REQUESTS FOR INVESTIGATIVE RECORDS

OPM INVESTIGATIONS
To obtain a copy of your background investigation conducted by OPM, mail your request to:

FOI/P, OPM-FIPC
P.O. Box 618
1137 Branchton Road
Boyers, PA 16018-0618

Your request must include your hand written signature and all of the following information:

- Full name
- Social Security Number
- Date of birth
- Place of birth
- Current home address (a Post Office Box is not acceptable; the records are sent by certified mail and require your signature [sic]).

Alternatively, you may FAX your hand signed request to telephone number 724-794-4590.

DSS INVESTIGATIONS

To obtain a copy of your DSS investigation, you must send a written request containing the following:

- Full current name
- Any other names you may have used in the past
- Date of Birth
- Social Security Number
- An originally notarized signature
- A brief description of the records you are seeking
- Any other information that you believe may be useful in searching for records pertaining to you
- Whether you want someone else to receive the records on your behalf (include name and address of the other party)

Mail your request to:

Defense Security Service
Privacy Act Branch
938 Elkridge Landing Road
Linthicum, MD 21090-2917

Please note, that due to privacy concerns, facsimile and electronic mail requests for investigative files are **not** accepted by DSS. Only originally signed and properly notarized requests will be accepted via postal mail.

You may be required to pay for postage. Questions can be emailed to foia.questions@dss.mil.

Additionally, due to the transfer of the personnel security investigations function to the Office of Personnel Management (OPM) on February 20, 2005 any requests for investigations completed after February 20, 2005, should be mailed to the OPM. DSS only maintains those personnel security investigations completed by DSS agency prior to the February 20, 2005, transfer.

PART II

SECURITY CLEARANCE

APPLICATION FORM

CHAPTER 5

PERSONAL IDENTIFYING INFORMATION & CITIZENSHIP

PERSONAL IDENTIFYING INFORMATION

SECURITY FORM: **Sections 1 through 7** of the SF86 are very straight forward and require little explanation. For *Other Names Used* you do not have to list a diminutive name, such as Ken for Kenneth, Al for Albert, Joe for Joseph, etc., unless there are records that identify you that way or there are people who would not recognize you by your real name. If you have been known by any other names, you should list the names and the dates that you were known by these other names.

APPLICABLE ADJUDICATIVE GUIDELINES
There are no applicable guidelines for Sections 1 through 7, other than Guideline E: Personal Conduct as it relates to providing full, frank and truthful answers to all lawful questions in connection with a personnel security or trustworthiness determination by the government.

NACLC: Your personal identifying information (PID) will be used as the basis for conducting the NACLC.

SSBI/SSBI-PR
Personal Subject Interview: You will be asked to verify the information in Sections 1 through 7. If you were known by any other names, you will be asked to explain the name changes, and you may be asked to provide documentation of legal name changes, if the name changes occurred due to reasons other than adoption, marriage, or divorce.

Field Investigation: During all records checks and reference interviews, you PID will be verified or corroborated to the extent possible. A check of Bureau of Vital Statistics records is conducted when any discrepancy is found to exist.

U.S. CITIZENSHIP

Note: The following information is based on Title 8 U.S. Code, Section 1401, 3 January 2005.

Birth Within The United States

Applicants born in the United States are U.S. citizens at birth, regardless of the citizenship or nationality of the parents (unless born to foreign diplomatic staff). A birth certificate is considered evidence of citizenship.

Birth In An Outlying Possession Of The United States

Applicants born in an outlying possession of the United States, such as Puerto Rico, Guam, the Northern Mariana Islands, the U.S. Virgin Islands, and the Panama Canal Zone (before it was returned to Panama), are U.S. citizens, if one parent was a U.S. citizen who lived in the U.S. or one of its outlying possessions for a continuous period of one year any time prior to the birth of the applicant.

Through Birth Abroad To Two United States Citizens.

An applicant is a U.S. citizen, if both the applicant's parents were U.S. citizens at the time of the applicant's birth, **and** at least one of applicant's parents lived in the United States prior to the applicant's birth.

Through Birth Abroad To One United States Citizen.

An applicant is a U.S. citizen if:

1. one of the applicant's parents was a U.S. citizen at the time of the applicant's birth and;
2. the applicant's citizen parent lived at least 5 years in the United States before the applicant's birth and;

3. at least 2 of these 5 years in the United States were after the applicant's citizen parent's 14th birthday (Note: If the applicant was born before November 14, 1986, their U.S. citizen parent must have lived in the U.S. for at least 10 years and 5 of those years were after their 14th birthday. Different rules apply for those born before December 24, 1952).

Or if:

1. one of the applicant's parents was a U.S. citizen who lived in the U.S. or one of its outlying possessions continuously for one year prior to the applicant's birth and;
2. the other parent was a U.S. national, but not a citizen of the U.S. prior to the applicant's birth.

THROUGH ADOPTION BY A U.S. CITIZEN PARENT

If you were a foreign national adopted by a U.S. citizen parent and immigrated to the United States prior to age 18, your parents should have applied for, and received, a Certificate of Citizenship for you. If you were adopted and did not reach the age of 18 until after February 27, 2001, U. S. Citizenship was conferred to you by operation of law (automatically), under the Child Citizenship Act of 2000 (Public Law 106-395). A Certificate of Citizenship would not be issued to you, unless requested.

SECURITY FORM: Section 8—Citizenship.

1. If known, list your birth mother's maiden name at *Item 8b*, otherwise list "unknown." If your were adopted, use the *comment section* to list your adoptive mother's maiden name.
2. If you were born in the United States (and your parents were not foreign diplomats), check the top box at *Item 8a*.
3. If you were born outside the United States, check the middle box at *Item 8a*.
   a. If at least one of your parents was a U.S. citizen at the time of your birth, your birth should have been registered with a U.S. consulate or embassy in the foreign country, and a State Department Form 240 (Report of Birth Abroad of a Citizen of the United States) was issued to your parents. A copy of the form was filed with the U.S. State Department under the name of the parents. The State Department Form 240 is proof of citizenship. Parents occasionally obtain a passport or a Certificate of Citizenship for their child as additional proof of citizenship. Provide the appropriate information at *Item 8c* under *State Department Form 240— Report of Birth Abroad of a Citizen of the United States* and/or informa-

tion regarding a current or previous *U.S. Passport* and/or information regarding a *Certificate of Citizenship.*

b. If both of your parents were citizens of a foreign country at the time of your birth, complete the appropriate blocks under *Item 8c* for *Naturalization Certificate* or *Citizenship Certificate.* If either of your parents became a Naturalized U.S. citizen before your 18th birthday, you were automatically eligible to become a U.S. citizen derivatively due to one of your parent's Naturalization. If this is the case and your parent requested it, you would have been issued a Certificate of Citizenship by the Immigration and Naturalization Service—INS.[51] If neither of your parents became a Naturalized citizen before your 18th birthday, then you would have had to go through the naturalization process yourself and been issued a Certificate of Naturalization. Look closely at whatever documentation you have. The name of the certificate appears across the top part of the form. Two or three numbers appear on the form—a certificate number, a former INS (or CIS) Registration number, and sometimes a petition number. The INS or CIS Registration number begins with the letter "A." The Certificate of Naturalization number usually has more digits than the petition number and neither has any alphabetic characters. A Certificate of Citizenship number sometimes begins with the letters "A" or "AA." These certificates were issued by U.S. District Courts and by INS. You will need to provide the city and state where the certificate issued, the certificate number, and the date the certificate was issued.

c. If you were a foreign national adopted by a U.S. citizen parent and you have a Certificate of Citizenship, provide the city and state where the certificate was issued, the certificate number, and the date the certificate was issued at *Item 8c.* If you were a foreign national adopted by a U.S. citizen parent and do not have a Certificate of Citizen but have U.S. citizenship under the Child Citizenship Act of 2000, explain this in the *Continuation Space* on Page 9 of the SF86 (or in the *comment section* of the electronic version of the form) along with the adoption location, adoption certificate number, and adoption date.

4. You must enter a response at *Item 8d, Dual Citizenship.* You should enter either the name of a country or "None." If you have dual citizenship, if you were born outside the United States, or if one (or both) of your parents was a foreign citizen at the time of your birth, see the section on dual citizenship below and the section on Foreign Connections in Chapter 8.

---

[51] INS is now known as the US Bureau of Citizenship and Immigration Services—CIS.

DUAL CITIZENSHIP. If you were born in a foreign country be aware that not all countries confer citizenship based **solely** on birth within the territory of the country. Some of these countries are Australia, Canada, France, Ireland, Mexico, New Zealand and almost all Central American and South American countries. However, if one of your parents was a citizen of the country where you were born, there are many more countries that will consider you a citizen of that country. Like the United States, many countries consider you a citizen of their country, if one of your parents was a citizen of that country at the time of your birth, regardless of where you were born. Often it depends on which parent was a citizen of the other country. Some countries confer citizenship matrilineally and some patrilineally. Do not list another country in Item d (Dual Citizenship), unless you are sure you have dual citizenship. One way to find out is to go to www.opm.gov/extra/investigate/IS-01.pdf and view the document, "Citizenship Laws of the World." Another way is to contact the country's embassy in Washington, DC. **Do not tell them you are inquiring about possible dual citizenship because of a security clearance application, and try not to give them identifying information about yourself.**

If you have ever had a passport (current or expired) from another country, and you have not renounced your foreign citizenship by communicating directly with a government agency of that country (such as an embassy), you are probably still a citizen of the other country. With few exceptions, everyone immigrating to the United States must enter this country using a passport issued by their native country. So if you immigrated to the U.S. by yourself or with your parents, you probably traveled on a foreign passport. If you were young, you may have been included in your mother's passport. Becoming a naturalized citizen of the United States or obtaining U.S. citizenship derivatively through the naturalization of one of your parents rarely has any affect on your previous citizenship. The act of raising your hand and taking an oath of allegiance to the United States during your naturalization ceremony has no practical effect on your prior citizenship. The laws of some countries state that voluntarily accepting foreign citizenship results in loss of their citizenship. These laws have no affect, unless you tell them you accepted U.S. citizenship.

If you know or determine that you have foreign citizenship, **do not** take any action to renounce it. As a person who is applying for a security clearance or who already has a security clearance, you do not want to attract the attention of a foreign embassy or consulate to yourself. If any action is necessary with regard to your foreign citizenship, you will be told what to do by a representative of the U.S. Government.

ALIEN. *Item 8e* does not apply to people applying for a security clearance. It is only used for Aliens applying for Limited Access Authorizations or only for employment purposes.

APPLICABLE ADJUDICATIVE GUIDELINES

GUIDELINE C: FOREIGN PREFERENCE

Paragraph 9. *The Concern.* When an individual acts in such a way as to indicate a preference for a foreign country over the United States, then he or she may be prone to provide information or make decisions that are harmful to the interests of the United States.

Paragraph 10. *Conditions that could raise a security concern and may be disqualifying include:*

(a) exercise of any right, privilege or obligation of foreign citizenship after becoming a U.S. citizen or through the foreign citizenship of a family member. This includes but is not limited to:

(1) possession of a current foreign passport;

(2) military service or a willingness to bear arms for a foreign country;

(3) accepting educational, medical, retirement, social welfare, or other such benefits from a foreign country;

(4) residence in a foreign country to meet citizenship requirements;

(5) using foreign citizenship to protect financial or business interests in another country;

(6) seeking or holding political office in a foreign country;

(7) voting in a foreign election;

(b) action to acquire or obtain recognition of a foreign citizenship by an American citizen;

(c) performing or attempting to perform duties, or otherwise acting, so as to serve the interests of a foreign person, group, organization, or government in conflict with the national security interest;

(d) any statement or action that shows allegiance to a country other than the United States: for example, declaration of intent to renounce United States citizenship; renunciation of United States citizenship.

Paragraph 11. *Conditions that could mitigate security concerns include:*

(a) dual citizenship is based solely on parents' citizenship or birth in a foreign country;

(b) the individual has expressed a willingness to renounce dual citizenship;

(c) exercise of the rights, privileges, or obligations of foreign citizenship occurred before the individual became a U.S. citizen or when the individual was a minor;

(d) use of a foreign passport is approved by the cognizant security authority;

(e) the passport has been destroyed, surrendered to the cognizant security authority, or otherwise invalidated;

(f) the vote in a foreign election was encouraged by the United States Government.

NACLC: If you were not born in the United States, your citizenship will be verified through State Department or CIS records. If you immigrated to the United States, it could result in a SPIN (Special Interview) for foreign connections (see Chapter 8). If during the period of investigation you were outside the United States for six months or more or were involved in any criminal conduct abroad, an Interpol records check will be conducted.[52]

Note: Everyone must present proof of citizenship to the security manager at their company, government organization, or military unit for verification at some point before their initial security clearance investigation is requested.

SSBI/SSBI-PR:

Personal Subject Interview: If you were born outside the United States or have a parent who held foreign citizenship, be prepared to discuss the source of your citizenship, your parent's current or former foreign citizenship, and any possible dual citizenship. If you were formerly a citizen of another country or hold dual citizenship, be prepared to discuss all passports you have held, any other right or privilege of foreign citizenship you may have received, and the degree of loyalty or allegiance you may feel toward the other country.

Field Investigation: During all records checks and reference interviews, your citizenship will be corroborated to the extent possible.

---

[52] OPM Federal Investigative Notice No. 05-01, dated March 1, 2005.

EXAMPLES OF CLEARANCE ADJUDICATION

CASE NUMBER: 02-11843.h1
Foreign Influence; Foreign Preference
01/08/2004

Applicant, a native of the Republic of China (Taiwan), became a United States (U.S.) Naturalized citizen in 1987. In 1996, she acquired a Taiwanese passport, primarily to prove her identity in Taiwan in connection with the sale of an apartment purchased by her parents in her name in 1977. She traveled to Taiwan in 1997 and 1999 on that foreign passport. Since learning the use of the foreign passport was inappropriate, she used her U.S. passport exclusively. Concerns of foreign preference are mitigated by her recent surrender of her expired foreign passport and her application to renounce Taiwanese citizenship. There is little risk of foreign influence presented by the Taiwanese citizenship and/or residency of close family members as they are neither agents of a foreign government nor in positions where they are likely to be exploited. Clearance is granted.

CASE NUMBER: 03-12416.h1
Foreign Preference; Foreign Influence
09/30/2004

Applicant has dual U.S. and Saudi Arabian citizenship. Applicant has passports issued by both countries. Applicant does not want to renounce his Saudi Arabian citizenship nor surrender his Saudi Arabian passport, in accordance with the "Money Memo". Applicant lives in Saudi Arabia with his parents, his wife and child. Applicant's father is a Saudi Arabian citizen, and Applicant's mother is a U.S. citizen living in Saudi Arabia. Applicant has not mitigated the foreign preference and foreign influence security concerns. Applicant has not complied with the passport surrender requirements of the "Money Memo". Clearance is denied.

CASE NUMBER: 03-02041.h1
Foreign Influence
08/23/2004

Applicant was born in Egypt but is now a naturalized U.S. citizen. His parents, siblings, wife, and her parents are all citizens of Egypt. His wife is now a permanent resident alien in the U.S., but one sister lives in Canada, and the rest of Applicant's family and his in-laws live in Egypt. Applicant travels to Egypt frequently, owns property there to use when he visits, and wants to retain his Egyptian citizenship for cultural reasons. He has failed to present information to mitigate the resulting security concerns under Guideline B (Foreign Influence). Clearance is denied.

CASE NUMBER: 02-28472.h1
Foreign Preference; Foreign Influence
08/23/2004

Applicant is a 45-year-old naturalized citizen of the United States employed by a defense contractor. Applicant is entitled to dual citizenship with Trinidad and Tobago, her country of birth, and retained and used her passport from that country for her personal convenience. Applicant's maternal grandmother and her husband's parents and siblings are citizens and residents of Trinidad and Tobago. Applicant has since surrendered her foreign passport. All Applicant's immediate family members live in this country and all are naturalized citizens of the United States, or are applying for citizenship. All Applicant's financial interests are in this country. Considering the extent of Applicant's ties to the United States, Applicant has mitigated the security concerns arising from her dual citizenship and possible foreign influence. Clearance is granted.

CASE NUMBER: 02-17178.h1
Foreign Preference; Foreign Influence
09/30/2004

Applicant is a 60-year-old professor of aeronautical engineering who seeks a security clearance. Applicant has an expired Israeli passport, and holds dual U.S. and Israeli citizenship. Applicant has not surrendered his Israeli passport. Applicant has family members who are citizens of and resident in Israel, including his daughter who is a member of the Israeli military. Applicant did not mitigate the foreign preference or the foreign influence security concerns. Clearance is denied.

Note: In August 2000 an Assistant Secretary of Defense issued what is now known as the "Money Memorandum," regarding possession and/or use of a foreign passport and Adjudicative Guideline C. The memo reads, ". . . the guideline requires that any clearance be denied or revoked unless the applicant surrenders the foreign passport or obtains official approval for its use from the appropriate agency of the United States Government."[53]

---

[53] Memorandum from Arthur L. Money, Assistant Secretary of Defense for Command, Control, Communications, and Intelligence; Subject: Guidance to DoD Central Adjudicative Facilities (CAF) Clarifying the Application of the Foreign Preference Adjudicative Guideline; dated August 16, 2000.

CHAPTER 6

RESIDENCE, EDUCATION, & EMPLOYMENT

RESIDENCE

SECURITY FORM: **Section 9—Where You Have Lived.**

Begin with your current residence. List the correct physical address and the month and year you actually began living there. If it would be difficult to find this residence based only on the address, include information in the *comment section* describing the physical location of the residence.

In the block *Name of Person Who Knows You* do not list an immediate family member or other close relative, unless there is no one else you can list. If you can, list a neighbor who has known you for most of the time you have been at this residence. If none of your neighbors know you, list a friend, schoolmate or coworker who lives in the same city and who has visited you at your current residence. If no one fits this description and you rent, list your apartment manager, property manager, or landlord. Include their address and telephone number.

Unless you have lived at the same place for entire period of the investigation, you will need to enter one or more previous addresses. Regardless of what the security form indicates, the period for an SSBI is 10 years or back to 18th birthday, whichever is shorter (or back to your 16th birthday if you are under 20 years of age).

Even though the period of investigation for an SSBI-PR and NACLC is back to the date of the prior investigation or five years, list all residences within the past seven years as indicated on the security form. If you are under 25 years of age, list your residences back to your 18th birthday. If you are under 20 years of age, include residences back to your 16th birthday.

Note: If you are young and only required to list information back to your 18th or 16th birthday, do not use the month and year of your 18th or 16th birthday as the starting date for a residence—list the actual dates of the residence.

You should list all residences for the entire investigative period. This includes dormitories at school and temporary residence of 30 days or more (such as hotels or as a houseguest at another person's residence).

If you moved out of one residence and into another residence in the same month, list the same month and year you left one residence as the starting date for the second residence. You need to list a *Name of Person Who Knew You*, including their address and telephone number for each residence within the past five years. Use the guidelines listed above for selecting this person. If you have trouble remembering your neighbors, use the internet and go to an internet website such as *www.whitepages.com/10001/find_neighbors*. You can use this website in conjunction with *www.maps.google.com* to locate the nearest cross street for more neighbors. Use any name you recognize as a former neighbor on your SF86.

If you are unable to provide an accurate date, enter your best guess for the month and year and indicate in the *comment section* that the beginning and/or ending date is an approximation. If you don't remember the address of a former residence, but you remember the name of a neighbor, try the website: *www.whitepages.com/10001/person*. Enter as much of your former neighbor's name as you remember, plus the Zipcode or city and state. The address listed for your former neighbor may jog your memory. If this doesn't work, try going through your old financial records (including tax returns, cancelled checks, bank and credit card statements, etc), educational records, employment records, and old correspondence. If you are still unable to provide an address, use words like "street number and name unrecalled" in the field for street address and include any information you can about the location of the residence in the *comment section*.

Most investigators dislike the neighborhood component of an investigation, because people rarely list a neighbor on their security form. And even if they list a neighbor, the requirement is for interviews of two neighbors at each location. Investigators typically make repeated trips to the general areas of your past and present residences, attempting to catch two of your neighbors at their homes. There is nothing to prevent you from providing a name and contact information for a second neighbor in the *comment section* of the SF86. This will allow the investigator to telephone both neighbors and schedule appointments to see them at a time and location convenient to your neighbors. Otherwise the investigator walks around the neighborhood knocking on doors. *(See the section on Character References in Chapter 7 for more information about listing references on your SF86.)*

If you don't know two people by name that lived immediately around you at a prior residence, you should anticipate that the investigator will have difficulty obtaining two neighborhood references. If there are two people you know who live within a block or two of your residence, list one at the appropriate block of Question #9 and list the other one at Question #12, *People Who Know You Well.*

APPLICABLE ADJUDICATIVE GUIDELINES
See Adjudicative Guideline E at the end of this chapter, since it applies equally to residence, education, and employment. Financial issues related to residences are fully covered in Chapter 10 and under Adjudicative Guideline F.

NACLC: Law enforcement agency records in all jurisdictions where you have resided for the past five years will be reviewed.

SSBI/SSBI-PR
Personal Subject Interview: Expect to be asked about others who lived with you, such as family members, cohabitants, house sharers, dormitory roommates, and long term houseguests. Other questions will include those designed to elicit information directly related to Adjudicative Guideline E and F. Accordingly, expect to be asked about evictions, failure to pay rent on time, unpaid debts (i.e., rent, damages, utilities) at the time you moved, complaints about your conduct by landlord or neighbors, and any contact you may have had with police at your residence. *(See Chapter 2, page 23 for PRSI guidance.)*

Field Investigation (SSBI): Confirmation of all residences for the last three years through appropriate interviews with neighbors and through records reviews. Law enforcement agency records in all jurisdictions where you have resided during the period of investigation (generally 10 years), except that law enforcement agency records checks at former residences of less than six months duration may be excluded.

Field Investigation (SSBI-PR): Interviews of two neighbors in the vicinity of the subject's most recent residence of six months or more. Confirmation of current residence regardless of length. Law enforcement agency records in all jurisdictions where you have resided since your last investigation will be reviewed, except that law enforcement agency records at former residences of less than six months duration may be excluded.

(See Chapter 3, page 34 for questions generally asked of all sources, references, and neighbors.)

EDUCATION

SECURITY FORM: Section 10—Where You Went to School.

Begin with the school you are currently attending or the last school you attended within the past seven years for NACLCs and SSBI-PRs and ten years for SSBIs. If you haven't attended any school within the past seven or ten years, list the last post-secondary school you attended regardless of how long ago you went there.

Note: Do not list a military service school, unless the school is authorized to grant an Associates, Bachelors, Masters or Doctorate Degree. Do not list the Defense Language Institute, unless you actually received a college degree from the DLI. You will list all attendance at military service schools and degree granting military educational institutions that you attended in the employment section of the SF86, if you were assigned to the schools as a federal employee or active duty service member. If in doubt, see the section on Employment in this chapter for further information.

For an SSBI you will also need to enter all previous secondary (high school) and post-secondary schools you attended within the past 10 years. Regardless of what the security form indicates, the period for an SSBI is 10 years or back to 18th birthday, whichever is shorter (or back to your 16th birthday if you are under 20 years of age).

Even though the period for an SSBI-PR and NACLC is back to the date of the prior investigation or five years, list all schools you attended within the past seven years as indicated on the security form. If you are under 25 years of age, list schools back to your 18th or 16th birthday, as appropriate.

You must list all schools attended for the entire period. This includes any school where you were enrolled, regardless of whether you attended for only one day. For correspondence schools, extension courses, and other distance learning (such as online computer courses) list the address where records are maintained. Indicate in the comment section that you were enrolled in a distance learning program.

If you are unable to provide an accurate date, enter your best guess for the month and year and indicate in the *comment section* that the beginning or ending date is an approximation. If you don't remember the address of the school, use an internet search engine like *www.google.com* or an internet directory like *www.whitepages.com/10001/business* to find it. If you are still unable to provide a street number or street name, use the words "street number and name unrecalled" in the field for street address and include any information you can about the location of the school in the *comment section*. If you attended a school intermittently, use inclusive dates and use the *comment section* to provide as much specific information as possible.

In the block *Name of Person Who Knew You* do not list an immediate family member or other close relative, unless there is no one else you can list. Do not use the name of a school dean, principal, or registrar that you obtained from a directory or the internet. List the person with whom you had the most contact at the school and for whom you have a current address and telephone number, preferably someone who knew you for the entire time you were at the school. In order of preference you should list schoolmates who were also roommates or dormitory neighbors (that you did not list at Question #9), other schoolmates, fellow fraternity or sorority members, sports teammates, fellow club members or club faculty advisors, thesis advisor, guidance counselors, coaches, foreign language teachers, and other teachers. If you anticipate that the investigator will have difficulty finding a second educational reference at a school you attended within the past three years, use the *comment section* to provide the name and contact information for the second educational reference. Try to list home addresses and telephone numbers for your references. The investigator can easily get the telephone number of the school himself. If your investigation is being conducted in the middle of the summer or at Christmas break, it may be impossible for the investigator to contact your educational references, if you don't list their home addresses and home telephone numbers. *(See the section on Character References in Chapter 7 for more information about listing references on your SF86.)*

You need to list a *Name of Person Who Knew You*, including an address and telephone number for each school you attended during the past three years. Obtaining references at a school that you no longer attend can be a problem for investigators. Students are transient. After a year has passed, teachers usually only remember the best and the worst students. If you were involved in ROTC or in extra-curricular activities at school, such as sports, music, student government, etc., list a staff member at the school, such as a sports coach, faculty advisor for student counsel, band director, or military science instructor who knew you. The SF86 instructions state not to list any references at schools you attended more than three years ago; however, it is recommended that you list someone at schools you attended four to seven years ago, if you attended the schools full-time for six months or more and if your SF86 is for an SSBI. Use the *comment section* for this, if necessary.

APPLICABLE ADJUDICATIVE GUIDELINES
See Adjudicative Guideline E at the end of this chapter, since it applies equally to residence, education, and employment. Financial issues related to education are fully covered in Chapter 10 and under Adjudicative Guideline F.

NACLC: Law enforcement agency records in all jurisdictions where you have physically attended school for six months or more during the past five years will be reviewed.[54]

SSBI/SSBI-PR
Personal Subject Interview: You will be asked to verify all the information you provided on your SF86 regarding education. Other questions will include those designed to elicit information directly related to Adjudicative Guidelines E and F. Accordingly, expect to be asked about academic and disciplinary problems encountered at these schools, as well as any educational debts. If you were unemployed while attending school, you will be asked how you paid for your education and living expenses. *(See Chapter 2, page 23 for PRSI guidance.)*

Field Investigation: For SSBIs corroboration of most recent or most significant claimed attendance, degree, or diploma. Interviews of appropriate educational sources if education is a primary activity during the most recent three years. Law enforcement agency records (including campus police) at all schools physically attended for six months or more within the basic period of investigation (generally 10 years). Additionally, direct or collateral personal coverage to verify any significant education activities during years 4 through 7.[55] Except for law enforcement agency records, there is no standard SSBI-PR coverage for education. *(See Chapter 3, page 34 for questions generally asked of all sources, references and neighbors.)*

EMPLOYMENT

SECURITY FORM: Section 11—Your Employment Activities.
Unless you had only one period of employment or unemployment within the past 7 to 10 years, you will need to enter one or more previous periods of employment/unemployment. Regardless of what the security form indicates, the

---

[54] Additionally for ANACIs, letter inquiries are sent to current and past schools to confirm the subjects' background claims and to obtain information about their basic suitability for employment.

[55] OPM Federal Investigative Notice No. 97-02, July 29, 1997.

period of investigation for an SSBI is 10 years or back to 18th birthday, whichever is shorter (or back to your 16th birthday if you are under 20 years of age). Even though the period of investigation for an SSBI-PR and NACLC is back to the date of the prior investigation or five years, list all periods of employment/unemployment within the past seven years as indicated on the security form. If you are under 25 years of age, list all periods of employment/unemployment back to your 18th or 16th birthday, as appropriate.

You must list separately (in reverse chronological order) each period of employment, self-employment, and unemployment. Begin with your current employment/self-employment/unemployment in *block #1* and work backwards. This includes jobs where you may have only worked for one day and part-time jobs, even though you had other employment that covered the same time period. You must include separate entries for all part-time employment (including National Guard and military reserve components), temporary duty locations of 90 days or more away from your primary workplace, and each permanent military assignment.

If you are civilian, list *Your Position Title*. If you are military, list your *Military Rank*. Investigators don't need to know that you are an amphibious tank gunner; they need to know how to identify you to other military personnel (i.e., Private Jones, Captain Smith, Sergeant Baker), since first names are used so infrequently in the military.

Provide the name and telephone number of your **immediate** supervisor. If your supervisor is at a different location than you, provide your supervisor's address. If you are a military officer attending a military service school, list your company commander or equivalent, even though you out rank him or her. If you are active duty military attending a civilian college or university for degree completion or graduate studies and you do not have a military supervisor that you contact regularly in person, list your thesis advisor, department chairman or some other person who is monitoring your academic performance.

For the *Employer/Verifier Name/Military Duty Location* and *Employer/Verifier's Street Address*, list the organization and location where your personnel file is maintained. If your physical job location is elsewhere, list your work address in the *Street Address of Job Location* block. List your immediate supervisor's name in the *Supervisor's Name & Street Address* block. If your supervisor is not located at the address you list for your *Street Address of Job Location,* list his or her address in the *Supervisor's Name & Street Address* block.

For most entries in this section, you will only enter one address, but for some three different addresses may be needed. For instance, the immediate supervisor of a Special Agent in Charge (SAC) of an OPM field office is usually located at regional headquarters some distance from the field office, and the SAC's official personnel file is located at OPM Headquarters near Boyer, PA.

In this case the address of OPM Headquarters would be listed in the *Employer's/Verifier's Street Address* block, the address of the field office would be listed in the *Street Address of Job Location* block, and the Regional Director's name and address would be listed in the *Supervisor's Name & Street Address* block.

If you are using the paper version of the SF86 and you are or were self-employed, enter the appropriate dates, enter 6 in the block for *code*, list business name under *Employer/Verifier Name*, and list your position title (i.e., consultant, plumber, store proprietor, financial planner, etc.), business address, and telephone number. Use the *comment section* to list the name, address and telephone number of an individual who can verify your period of self-employment, such as a business/professional associate or a client who has known you for a long time. If you are using an electronic version of the SF86, you will be prompted for this information. In either case use the *comment section* to provide a name and contact information for a second individual who can verify your period of self-employment.

If you are using the paper version of the SF86 and you are or were unemployed, enter the appropriate dates, enter 7 in the block for *code* and the word "unemployed" under *Employer/Verifier Name*, and in the block for *Supervisor's Name & Street Address* enter the name, address, and telephone number of a person who can verify your activities during the period of unemployment. If you are using an electronic version of the SF86, you will be prompted for this information.

Previous Periods of Activity. These fields are used to list employment at the same place on different occasions. Say for instance, you currently work for Lockheed Martin in Sunnyvale, CA and have been there since 01/2005. You previously worked for Lockheed Martin at the same location from 01/2003 to 03/2004. You would enter the previous period of employment at Lockheed Martin directly under the current period of employment within block #1. Include the telephone number of your previous supervisor(s) in the *comment section*.

If you attended a degree granting school (i.e., US Naval Postgraduate School, Defense Intelligence School, War College, Stanford University, etc.) as a paid federal employee (military or civilian) and your duty location was at the school, list it under employment and education. As indicated above, in the employment section list the organization to which you were assigned and if different, list the school as the job location and your supervisor's location.

If you are young and only required to list information back to your 18th or 16th birthday, do not use the month and year of your 18th or 16th birthday as the starting date for a period of employment—list the actual date. You may use the month and year of your 18th or 16th birthday as the starting date for a period of unemployment.

You must list **all periods of federal civilian service**, regardless of how long ago it occurred.

If you don't remember the name of a former supervisor, you can enter "name unrecalled." If you are certain that your former immediate supervisor is no longer at your former place of employment, list your second tier supervisor or anyone else that is still there that had any supervisory authority over you. If you anticipate that the investigator will have difficulty finding two employment references at any place you worked for six months or more during the past seven years, use the *comment section* to provide name(s) and contact information for former work associates. This is particularly helpful when you know the name, home address and telephone number of former work associates at a defunct business, at a business with very high personnel turnover, or at a place where company policy prohibits interviews of company employees during work hours. *(See the section on Character References in Chapter 7 for more information about listing references on your SF86.)*

If you are unable to provide an accurate date, enter your best guess for the month and year and indicate in the *comment section* that the beginning or ending date is an approximation. If you don't remember the address of an employer, try using an internet directory like *www.whitepages.com/10001/business* or an internet search engine like *www.google.com* to find it. If you don't remember the name of a previous employer, look at your W-2 forms in your old income tax records. You can also ask to review your personnel file at your current employer. Hopefully there will be a copy of your employment application form in the file listing your previous jobs. If you are still unable to provide a name, a street number or street name, use words like "construction company— name unrecalled, street number and name unrecalled" in the field for employer and street address. Include any information you can about the identity of the employer and its location in the *comment section*.

SECURITY FORM: Section 22—Your Employment Record.

For SSBIs you must include information going back 10 years or back to your 18th birthday, whichever is shorter (or back to your 16th birthday is you are under 20 years of age). Basically, you should answer "yes" to question 22, if you left a job after having a supervisor suggest that you leave, left after a disagreement with your supervisor, or if you left without giving appropriate notice of your intention to leave (job abandonment). Use the *comment section* to provide a brief explanation, such as: "No notice voluntary quit after disagreement with manager, Richard Jones" or "Asked to leave by supervisor, John Wilson, due to substandard work performance" or "Fired for repeated tardiness by department manager, Jane Smith." Try to include the name of the person who terminated or suggested you terminate your employment.

APPLICABLE ADJUDICATIVE GUIDELINES

GUIDELINE K: HANDLING PROTECTED INFORMATION

Paragraph 33. *The Concern.* Deliberate or negligent failure to comply with rules and regulations for protecting classified or other sensitive information raises doubt about an individual's trustworthiness, judgment, reliability, or willingness and ability to safeguard such information, and is a serious security concern.

Paragraph 34. *Conditions that could raise a security concern and may be disqualifying include:*

(a) deliberate or negligent disclosure of classified or other protected information to unauthorized persons, including but not limited to personal or business contacts, to the media, or to persons present at seminars, meetings, or conferences;

(b) collecting or storing classified or other protected information in any unauthorized location;

(c) loading, drafting, editing, modifying, storing, transmitting, or otherwise handling classified reports, data, or other information on any unapproved equipment including but not limited to any typewriter, word processor, or computer hardware, software, drive, system, gameboard, handheld, "palm" or pocket device or other adjunct equipment;

(d) inappropriate efforts to obtain or view classified or other protected information outside one's need to know;

(e) copying classified or other protected information in a manner designed to conceal or remove classification or other document control markings;

(f) viewing or downloading information from a secure system when the information is beyond the individual's need to know;

(g) any failure to comply with rules for the protection of classified or other sensitive information;

(h) negligence or lax security habits that persist despite counseling by management;

(i) failure to comply with rules or regulations that results in damage to the National Security, regardless of whether it was deliberate or negligent.

Paragraph 35. *Conditions that could mitigate security concerns include:*

(a) so much time has elapsed since the behavior, or it happened so infrequently or under such unusual circumstances that it is unlikely to recur or does not cast doubt on the individual's current reliability, trustworthiness, or good judgment;

(b) the individual responded favorably to counseling or remedial security training and now demonstrates a positive attitude toward the discharge of security responsibilities;

(c) the security violations were due to improper or inadequate training.

Also see Adjudicative Guideline E at the end of this chapter, since it applies equally to residence, education, and employment.

NACLC: As a minimum, all investigations will include checks of law enforcement agencies having jurisdiction where the subject has worked within the last five years. Generally, if you are or were employed by the U.S. Armed Forces or an agency of the federal government, an employment records check will be conducted.[56] A SPIN may be conducted for any listed or developed unfavorable employment information.

SSBI/SSBI-PR

Personal Subject Interview: You will be asked to verify all information listed on your SF86 regarding employment and unemployment during the basic period of investigation. Other questions will include those designed to elicit information directly related to Adjudicative Guideline E and Guideline K. Accordingly you should expect to be asked the reason you left each employment, if there were any allegations of misconduct or dishonesty against you, and whether you had any disciplinary action taken against you (i.e., counseling statements, letters of reprimand, suspensions, etc.). *(See Chapter 2, page 23 for PRSI guidance.)*

Field Investigation (SSBI): Verification of all employments for the past seven years; personal interviews of sources (supervisors, coworkers, or both) for each employment of six months or more; corroboration through records and/or sources of all periods of unemployment exceeding sixty days; verification of all prior federal and military service, including discharge type. For military members, all service within one branch of the armed forces will be considered as one employment, regardless of assignments. A check of appropriate

---

[56] Additionally for ANACIs, letter inquiries are sent to current and past employers to confirm the subjects' background claims and to obtain information about their basic suitability for employment.

criminal history records covering all locations where, for the last ten years, the Subject has been employed for six months or more. If no employment exceeds six months, local agency checks will be performed as deemed appropriate.

Field Investigation (SSBI-PR): Verification of all employment since the last investigation. Attempts to interview a sufficient number of sources (supervisors, coworkers, or both) at all employments of six months or more. For military members, all service within one branch of the armed forces will be considered as one employment, regardless of assignments. A check of appropriate criminal history records covering all locations where, during the period covered by the reinvestigation, the subject has been employed for six months or more. If no employment exceeds six months, local agency checks will be performed as deemed appropriate.

(See Chapter 3, page 34 for questions generally asked of all sources and employment references.)

EXAMPLES OF CLEARANCE ADJUDICATION

CASE NUMBER: 02-30080.h1
Personal Conduct; Criminal Conduct
05/05/2005

Applicant was charged with various minor crimes between 1994 and 1998. He omitted some of the arrests from his March 2002 security questionnaire (SF 86). Applicant also falsely stated in that SF 86 and on a resume he gave his employer that he holds a masters degree. The record supports a finding that Applicant's omissions were deliberate falsifications. As such, they were also in violation of §18 U.S.C. 1001. Clearance is denied.

CASE NUMBER: 04-07350.h1
Personal Conduct; Criminal Conduct
01/26/2006

Applicant was terminated from two jobs under adverse conditions—misuse of government equipment and repeated attendance problem. She deliberately falsified her employment application for a defense contractor and a statement to a Defense Security Service agent by not disclosing these job terminations. Applicant failed to mitigate security concerns raised under Guidelines E and J. Clearance is denied.

CASE NUMBER: 03-19311.h1
Personal Conduct
01/30/2006

Applicant's rule violations began in 1995 when he was counseled to stay away from a former girlfriend for arguments and disagreements with her in the workplace. After several women subordinates complained about his inappropriate touching during work hours in November 1999, he was counseled and indicated in response to the Statement of Reasons (SOR) that he stopped the behavior. The 22 count court-martial filed in February 2002, that he admitted to in April 2002, provides considerable evidence that proves he continued his invasive actions toward women from May 1999 to November 2001. Applicant's rule violations and deliberate omissions of his military and criminal records have not been mitigated. Clearance is denied.

CASE NUMBER: 04-05021.h1
Personal Conduct; Sexual Behavior
05/12/2006

Applicant seeks a security clearance as a requirement for his position as a security officer for a defense contractor. In 1996, Applicant was terminated as a corrections officer for violating his department's sexual harassment policy and related misconduct on the job. In 2001, he resigned from his position as chief security officer from a cruise ship lines following allegations of sexual harassment. Further, at the time of the alleged misconduct on the cruise ship lines, he was married and he did not want his wife to find out what had happened. This raised personal conduct and sexual behavior concerns. Applicant has mitigated these concerns as a result of significant life style changes and also by having informed his wife of his past. Clearance is granted.

APPLICABLE ADJUDICATIVE GUIDELINES

GUIDELINE E: PERSONAL CONDUCT

Paragraph 15. *The Concern.* Conduct involving questionable judgment, lack of candor, dishonesty, or unwillingness to comply with rules and regulations can raise questions about an individual's reliability, trustworthiness and ability to protect classified information. Of special interest is any failure to provide truthful and candid answers during the security clearance process or any other failure to cooperate with the security clearance process.

The following will normally result in an unfavorable clearance action or administrative termination of further processing for clearance eligibility:

(a) refusal, or failure without reasonable cause, to undergo or cooperate with security processing, including but not limited to meeting with a security investigator for subject interview, completing security forms or releases, and cooperation with medical or psychological evaluation;

(b) refusal to provide full, frank and truthful answers to lawful questions of investigators, security officials, or other official representatives in connection with a personnel security or trustworthiness determination.

Paragraph 16. *Conditions that could raise a security concern and may be disqualifying also include:*

(a) deliberate omission, concealment, or falsification of relevant facts from any personnel security questionnaire, personal history statement, or similar form used to conduct investigations, determine employment qualifications, award benefits or status, determine security clearance eligibility or trustworthiness, or award fiduciary responsibilities;

(b) deliberately providing false or misleading information concerning relevant facts to an employer, investigator, security official, competent medical authority, or other official government representative;

(c) credible adverse information in several adjudicative issue areas that is not sufficient for an adverse determination under any other single guideline, but which, when considered as a whole, supports a whole-person assessment of questionable judgment, untrustworthiness, unreliability, lack of candor, unwillingness to comply with rules and regulations, or other characteristics indicating that the person may not properly safeguard protected information;

(d) credible adverse information that is not explicitly covered under any other guideline and may not be sufficient by itself for an adverse determination, but which, when combined with all available information supports a whole-person assessment of questionable judgment, untrustworthiness, unreliability, lack of candor, unwillingness to comply with rules and regulations, or other characteristics indicating that the person may not properly safeguard protected information. This includes but is not limited to consideration of:

(1) untrustworthy or unreliable behavior to include breach of client confidentiality, release of proprietary information, unauthorized release of sensitive corporate or other government protected information;

(2) disruptive, violent, or other inappropriate behavior in the workplace;

(3) a pattern of dishonesty or rule violations;

(4) evidence of significant misuse of Government or other employer's time or resources;

(e) personal conduct or concealment of information about one's conduct, that creates a vulnerability to exploitation, manipulation, or duress, such as (1) engaging in activities which, if known, may affect the person's personal, professional, or community standing, or (2) while in another country, engaging in any activity that is illegal in that country or that is legal in that country but illegal in the United States and may serve as a basis for exploitation or pressure by the foreign security or intelligence service or other group;

(f) violation of a written or recorded commitment made by the individual to the employer as a condition of employment;

(g) association with persons involved in criminal activity.

Paragraph 17. *Conditions that could mitigate security concerns include:*

(a) the individual made prompt, good-faith efforts to correct the omission, concealment, or falsification before being confronted with the facts;

(b) the refusal or failure to cooperate, omission, or concealment was caused or significantly contributed to by improper or inadequate advice of authorized personnel or legal counsel advising or instructing the individual specifically concerning the security clearance process. Upon being made aware of the requirement to cooperate or provide the information, the individual cooperated fully and truthfully;

(c) the offense is so minor, or so much time has passed, or the behavior is so infrequent, or it happened under such unique circumstances that it is unlikely to recur and does not cast doubt on the individual's reliability, trustworthiness, or good judgment;

(d) the individual has acknowledged the behavior and obtained counseling to change the behavior or taken other positive steps to alleviate the stressors, circumstances, or factors that caused untrustworthy, unreliable, or other inappropriate behavior, and such behavior is unlikely to recur;

(e) the individual has taken positive steps to reduce or eliminate vulnerability to exploitation, manipulation, or duress;

(f) association with persons involved in criminal activities has ceased or occurs under circumstances that do not cast doubt upon the individual's reliability, trustworthiness, judgment, or willingness to comply with rules and regulations.

Note: If there is any unfavorable information related to a period of residence, education or employment/unemployment not covered under Guideline E (above), it would be covered by the applicable adjudicative guideline related to the unfavorable information (i.e., criminal, financial, drugs, alcohol, etc.).

CHAPTER 7

CHARACTER REFERENCES, SPOUSE/FORMER SPOUSE, RELATIVES, AND ASSOCIATES

CHARACTER REFERENCES

SECURITY FORM: Section 12—People Who Know You Well.

As indicated in the instructions to the SF86 you should, "List three people who know you well and live in the United States. They should be good friends, peers, colleagues, roommates, etc., whose combined association with you covers as well as possible the last 7 years. Do not list you spouse, former spouse, or other relative, and try not to list anyone who is listed elsewhere on this form." They should all be U.S. Citizens. Investigators refer to these individuals as Listed Character References.

Most applicants should **not** list their closest three friends. Only the first Listed Character Reference should be a close friend—someone who has known you well for at least the past three years and can point the investigator in the direction of your other close friends. Ideally this friend will know you from some social activity outside of work, such as religious activities, sports, clubs, or other organizations.

Bear in mind the overall personal reference requirements for your type of investigation (see the section on Investigations in Chapter 1). For an SSBI the minimum requirements are:

- 2 educational references at each school attended for the past three years,
- 2 neighbors at each residence for the past three years,
- 2 employment references at each place of employment (of six months or more) for the past seven years, and
- 4 social references (at least two of whom must be developed social references, who are not listed anywhere on the SF86).

To the extent possible you should provide names and contact information to fulfill all the reference coverage needed to complete your investigation (except for the two "developed social references"). **There should be at least two people who know you socially, who are not listed anywhere on your SF86**.

The easiest place for investigators to get the two required developed social references is your current or former place of employment and/or your school (if you are currently a full-time student). Therefore, do not list anywhere on your SF86 at least two of your closest coworkers or current schoolmates, who can be easily identified and contacted by the investigator. If you don't have any social contact with people you know at work or school, think of at least two people who know you socially through religious activities, clubs, sports, or organizations, who can be easily identified and contacted by the investigator, and do not list them anywhere on your SF86.

The second Listed Character References should be a neighbor at the most recent residence of six months or more.

The third Listed Character Reference can be a neighbor at a prior residence (if you lived there less than seven years ago), faculty member or schoolmate at a school you attended in the past three years, or anyone with whom you have had at least monthly contact with over the past seven years or with whom you had at least monthly contact with between three to seven years ago. If you were outside the United States for more than a few months anytime during the period of investigation, try to list at least one person who is in the United States and with whom you had repeated contact in the foreign country.

If you are a young person, try not to list your parents' friends or associates. It is acceptable to list people who are much older than you are, if you had substantial contact with them outside of work or school—such as a scout leader, baseball coach, or youth pastor, but not a family dentist, doctor or financial advisor. Listing someone such as an FBI agent or a police officer is not particularly helpful, unless they know you well, and they know who your friends are. It is better to list a friend than the parent of a friend.

If you've moved in the past few years and you don't recall the addresses and telephone numbers of your former friends and associate at your previous location, try an internet directory like *www.whitepages.com/10001/person*.

Applicable Adjudicative Guidelines
See the applicable Adjudicative Guidelines at the end of this chapter, since they apply equally to character references, spouse/former spouse, relatives, and associates.

NACLC: There is no standard NACLC coverage for this section.[57]

SSBI/SSBI-PR

Personal Subject Interview: You will be asked to verify all the information you provided in this section of your security form, and you will be expected to provide information regarding any address or telephone number changes. If it appears to the investigator that your listed character references do not provide the appropriate coverage for your case, you may be asked to provide names and contact information for other potential references.

Field Investigation: There is no requirement to interview character references you listed on your security form. **For SSBIs** there is a requirement to interview "four references, of whom at least two are developed; to the extent practicable, all should have social knowledge of the Subject and collectively span at least the last seven years." **For SSBI-PRs** there is a requirement to interview "two character references who are knowledgeable of the Subject; at least one will be a developed reference. To the extent practical, both should have social knowledge of the Subject and collectively span the entire period of the reinvestigation. As appropriate, additional interviews may be conducted, including with cohabitants and relatives." *(See Chapter 3, page 34 for questions generally asked of all sources, references, and neighbors.)*

SPOUSE/FORMER SPOUSE

SECURITY FORM: Section 13—Your Spouse.

Check only one box in this section that describes your current marital status. Unless you check box #1 in this section, you must enter information at either *Item 13a* or *13b* or both. There is no time limit for information required in this section. If you have been married several times, information regarding all your former spouses should be entered, regardless of how long ago your marriage ended. If you do not know the current address of a former spouse and you were unable to find it by using a website like *www.whitepages.com/10001/person*, then list your former spouse's last known address and explain this in the *comment section*.

APPLICABLE ADJUDICATIVE GUIDELINES

See the applicable Adjudicative Guidelines at the end of this chapter, since they

---

[57] For ANACIs letter inquiries are sent to personal references to confirm the subjects' background claims and to obtain information about their basic suitability for employment.

apply equally to character references, spouse/former spouse, relatives, and associates.

NACLC: There is no standard NACLC coverage for this section; however, if your current spouse was born or resides outside the United States or has foreign citizenship, it could result in a SPIN for foreign connections (see Chapter 8, page 99).

SSBI/SSBI-PR

Personal Subject Interview: You will be asked to verify all information in this section. Be prepared to discuss any criminal or notorious conduct by your current or former spouse that could reflect unfavorably upon you. Be prepared to discuss the underlying reason for any divorce, if it was related to one of the 13 Adjudicative Guidelines, such as your misconduct, use of alcohol or drugs, cruel or violent conduct, mental or emotional problems, financial problems, or acts of disloyalty to the United States. If the reason for a divorce was very personal in nature and not related to one of the 13 Adjudicative Guidelines, such as alienation of affection or sexual incompatibility, you can tell the investigator that you and your spouse's marital expectations were different and those differences had nothing to do with security or suitability issues. If you initiated the divorce because of your spouse's misconduct or other problem, you should say so and provide as much or as little information as you chose. If your former spouse's misconduct could possibly reflect adversely on you, it would be wise to provide as much information as necessary. You may be asked about any financial obligation you have to a former spouse. *(See Chapter 2, page 23 for PRSI guidance.)*

Field Investigation: All former spouses will be interviewed, if the divorce occurred within the period of investigation. They will be asked the same questions asked of other character references, plus questions regarding satisfaction of any financial obligations, such as payment of child or spousal support. There is no requirement to interview a current spouse; however, in rare circumstances a current spouse may be interviewed when absolutely necessary to resolve an issue or verify some past activity. *(See Chapter 3, page 34 for questions generally asked of all sources, references, and neighbors.)*

Additional Investigation: For an SSBI a National Agency Check is conducted on the applicant's current spouse. For an SSBI-PR a National Agency Check is conducted on the applicant's current spouse, unless one was conducted during a prior investigation.

RELATIVES AND ASSOCIATES

SECURITY FORM: Section 14—Your Relatives And Associates.

As indicated in the instructions to the SF86 you should list ". . . the full names, correct code, and other requested information for each of your relatives or associates, **living or dead**, specified below." Read the SF86 list of relatives and associates closely.

Remember to include "Other Relatives" (Code 17) and "Other Associates" (Code 18)—foreign national relatives and associates, not listed for Codes 1 through 16, with whom you or your spouse are bound by affection, obligation, or close and continuing contact. You do not have to list Other Relatives or Other Associates who are deceased.

If you are sharing a residence or living with someone you did not list as one of your relatives or associates, you should list them and use Code 19. If you are undergoing an SSBI or SSBI-PR and you have a spouse-like relationship with this person, you should identify them as a cohabitant and provide their Social Security Number, so a National Agency Check can be conducted on them at the same time your NAC is being conducted.

If you are unable to obtain all the information for a relative or associate who must be listed in this section, you should enter "unknown" in the appropriate fields. In the *comment section*, you should include a reason why you entered "unknown" in any data field, such as "no contact in over 10 years."

SECURITY FORM: Section 15—Citizenship of Your Relatives and Associates.

This section originally only pertained to your immediate family (mother, father, brother, sister, child and current spouse) and any current cohabitant (spouse-like relationship) who are not U.S. Citizens. On the computer versions of the SF86, the program will ask for this information automatically if you list any of your family or associates as having been born in a foreign country. In which case you will only have to add information regarding their citizenship or Resident Alien status.

If you are using a paper version of the SF86, you need to indicate the person's relationship to you (i.e., Mother), the person's full name, and date of birth, as well as information regarding their citizenship or Resident Alien status.

For U.S. Citizens list their Naturalization Certificate number and insert the number 1—Naturalization Certificate in the block for *Document Code* or list their Citizenship Certificate number and insert the number 2—Citizenship Certificate in the block for *Document Code*. In the *Additional Information* block list the agency that issued the certificate and the date and location where the certificate was issued. It is recommended that you also list their former Alien Registration (also known as INS Registration) number. Look at whatever documentation they have closely. The name of the certificate appears across the top part of the form. Two or three numbers appear on the form—a certificate number, former INS (or CIS) Registration number, and sometimes a petition number. The INS Registration number begins with the letter A. The Certificate of Naturalization number usually has more digits than the petition number and neither has any alphabetical characters. These certificates are issued by US District Courts and by the CIS (former INS). A Certificate of Citizenship number may also begin with the letters "A" or "AA."

For U.S. Citizens born outside the United States who don't have a Citizenship Certificate, but at least one parent was a U.S. Citizen at the time, enter 4—Other for *Document Code* and "Born abroad of U.S. Citizen parent" in the block for *Additional Information*. If they have a State Department form 240, enter "SD Form 240" in the block *Certificate/Registration #*. If this situation applies to a cohabitant, list full name, date of birth and place of birth for your cohabitant's mother and father in the *comment section*. This is needed to verify your cohabitant's U.S. citizenship through State Department records.

For foreign citizens who are Resident Aliens (have a "Green Card") of the United States, list their Alien Registration number and insert the number 3—Alien Registration in the block for *Document Code*. In the *Additional Information* block, list the date and place they originally entered the United States (port of entry) as an immigrant or refugee.

For all other foreign citizens residing in the United States, enter 4—Other for *Document Code* and provide an explanation in the block for *Additional Information*.

For foreign citizens who reside outside the United States, it is not necessary to provide any additional information.

APPLICABLE ADJUDICATIVE GUIDELINES
See the applicable adjudicative guidelines at the end of this chapter, since they apply equally to character references, spouse/former spouse, relatives, and associates.

NACLC: There is no standard NACLC coverage for these sections of the SF86; however, if a family member or associate was born outside the United States, resides in a foreign country, or has foreign citizenship, it could result in an SPIN (Special Interview) for foreign connections (see Chapter 8, page 99).

SSBI/SSBI-PR

Personal Subject Interview: You will be asked to verify all the information in these sections of your SF86. If any of the people listed in this section reside in a foreign country or hold foreign citizenship, be prepared to provide as much information as you can about your contact with them and their employ-ment/activities. Although you are not responsible for the actions of others, if a close relative or associate has been involved in any criminal or notorious con-duct, including participation in extremist activities, expect to be questioned about their activities and the degree to which you can be influenced by them. *(See Chapter 2, page 23 for PRSI guidance.)*

Field Investigation: There is no requirement to interview your listed rela-tives and associates. If you were unemployed and living with a relative or close associate during any portion of the investigative period, that person may be in-terviewed primarily to verify your activities during that period. All reference interviews will include questions regarding your degree of contact with foreign nationals. *(See Chapter 3, page 34 for questions generally asked of all sources, references, and neighbors.)*

Additional Investigation: For SSBIs a National Agency Check is con-ducted on a person with whom the applicant currently has a spouse-like rela-tionship (commonly referred to as a cohabitant). Citizenship or legal status of all foreign-born immediate family members is verified. For SSBI-PRs a Na-tional Agency Check is conducted on the applicant's current cohabitant, unless one was previously conducted during a prior investigation. Citizenship or legal status of all foreign-born immediate family members is verified, unless verified during a prior investigation.

APPLICABLE ADJUDICATIVE GUIDELINES

GUIDELINE A: ALLEGIANCE TO THE UNITED STATES

Paragraph 3. *The Concern.* An individual must be of unquestioned allegiance to the United States. The willingness to safeguard classified information is in doubt if there is any reason to suspect an individual's allegiance to the United States.

Paragraph 4. *Conditions that could raise a security concern and may be disqualify-ing include:*

(a) involvement in, support of, training to commit, or advocacy of any act of sabo-tage, espionage, treason, terrorism, or sedition against the United States of America;

(b) association or sympathy with persons who are attempting to commit, or who are committing, any of the above acts;

(c) association or sympathy with persons or organizations that advocate, threaten, or use force or violence, or use any other illegal or unconstitutional means, in an effort to:

(1) overthrow or influence the government of the United States or any state or local government;

(2) prevent Federal, state, or local government personnel from performing their official duties;

(3) gain retribution for perceived wrongs caused by the Federal, state, or local government;

(4) prevent others from exercising their rights under the Constitution or laws of the United States or of any state.

Paragraph 5. *Conditions that could mitigate security concerns include:*

(a) the individual was unaware of the unlawful aims of the individual or organization and severed ties upon learning of these;

(b) the individual's involvement was only with the lawful or humanitarian aspects of such an organization;

(c) involvement in the above activities occurred for only a short period of time and was attributable to curiosity or academic interest;

(d) the involvement or association with such activities occurred under such unusual circumstances, or so much times has elapsed, that it is unlikely to recur and does not cast doubt on the individual's current reliability, trustworthiness, or loyalty.

GUIDELINE B: FOREIGN INFLUENCE

Paragraph 6. *The Concern.* Foreign contacts and interests may be a security concern if the individual has divided loyalties or foreign financial interests, may be manipulated or induced to help a foreign person, group, organization, or government in a way that is not in U.S. interests, or is vulnerable to pressure or coercion by any foreign interest. Adjudication under this Guideline can and should consider the identity of the foreign country in which the foreign contact or financial interest is located, including, but not limited to, such considerations as whether the foreign country is known to target United States citizens to obtain protected information and/or is associated with a risk of terrorism.

7. *Conditions that could raise a security concern and may be disqualifying include:*

(a) contact with a foreign family member, business or professional associate, friend, or other person who is a citizen of or resident in a foreign country if that contact creates a heightened risk of foreign exploitation, inducement, manipulation, pressure, or coercion;

(b) connections to a foreign person, group, government, or country that create a potential conflict of interest between the individual's obligation to protect sensitive information or technology and the individual's desire to help a foreign person, group, or country by providing that information;

(c) counterintelligence information, that may be classified, indicates that the individual's access to protected information may involve unacceptable risk to national security;

(d) sharing living quarters with a person or persons, regardless of citizenship status, if that relationship creates a heightened risk of foreign inducement, manipulation, pressure, or coercion;

 (f) failure to report, when required, association with a foreign national;

(g) unauthorized association with a suspected or known agent, associate, or employee of a foreign intelligence service;

(h) indications that representatives or nationals from a foreign country are acting to increase the vulnerability of the individual to possible future exploitation, inducement, manipulation, pressure, or coercion;

(i) conduct, especially while traveling outside the U.S., which may make the individual vulnerable to exploitation, pressure, or coercion by a foreign person, group, government, or country.

Paragraph 8. *Conditions that could mitigate security concerns include:*

(a) the nature of the relationships with foreign persons, the country in which these persons are located, or the positions or activities of those persons in that country are such that it is unlikely the individual will be placed in a position of having to choose between the interests of a foreign individual, group, organization, or government and the interests of the U.S.;

(b) there is no conflict of interest, either because the individual's sense of loyalty or obligation to the foreign person, group, government, or country is so minimal, or the individual has such deep and longstanding relationships and loyalties in the U.S., that the individual can be expected to resolve any conflict of interest in favor of the U.S. interest;

(c) contact or communication with foreign citizens is so casual and infrequent that there is little likelihood that it could create a risk for foreign influence or exploitation;

(d) the foreign contacts and activities are on U.S. Government business or are approved by the cognizant security authority;

(e) the individual has promptly complied with existing agency requirements regarding the reporting of contacts, requests, or threats from persons, groups, or organizations from a foreign country;

GUIDELINE E: PERSONAL CONDUCT

Paragraph 15. *The Concern.* Conduct involving questionable judgment, lack of candor, dishonesty, or unwillingness to comply with rules and regulations can raise questions about an individual's reliability, trustworthiness and ability to protect classified information. . . .

Paragraph 16. *Conditions that could raise a security concern and may be disqualifying also include:*

(g) association with persons involved in criminal activity.

Paragraph 17. *Conditions that could mitigate security concerns include:*

(e) the individual has taken positive steps to reduce or eliminate vulnerability to exploitation, manipulation, or duress;

(f) association with persons involved in criminal activities has ceased or occurs under circumstances that do not cast doubt upon the individual's reliability, trustworthiness, judgment, or willingness to comply with rules and regulations.

EXAMPLES OF CLEARANCE ADJUDICATION

CASE NUMBER: 02-16593.h1
Foreign Influence
02/25/2005

Applicant is a naturalized citizen of the U.S. He came to the U.S. as a college student from the People's Republic of China (PRC). Applicant has a Ph.D. in nuclear physics. Both of his children are residents and citizens of the U.S. His parents, two brothers, and a sister are citizens and residents of PRC. He provides approximately $2,000.00 per year in financial support to his retired parents. None of his relatives are involved with the Chinese government. He is not vulnerable to foreign influence because of his strong attachment to the U.S.—extensive personal, professional, and economic ties—and because his family is not in a position to be exploited in a way that could force Applicant to choose between loyalty to these family members and his loyalty to the U.S. Clearance is granted.

CASE NUMBER: 04-10936.h1

Foreign Influence
04/13/2006

Applicant is a naturalized United States citizen who was born in the People's Republic of China (PRC). Concerns were raised because his parents, brother, friends and extended family members are citizens of and reside in the PRC. Applicant maintains frequent contact with his immediate family members who reside in the PRC. Security concerns under foreign influence remain. Clearance is denied.

CASE NUMBER: 05-02878.h1
Foreign Influence
01/27/2006

The Applicant is a native born American. His parents fled Lebanon in 1976 because of that country's civil war. His parents are dual nationals who reside in Lebanon. His father "runs a hospital . . . funded by the Catholic Church." His mother is "a homemaker." The Applicant's 17 year old brother is also a dual national. He lives with the Applicant's parents, but will return to the U.S. to attend college when he is emancipated at age 18. The Applicant's sister is a dual national, residing with the Applicant in the U.S. She is a college student. The Applicant's very elderly grandparents are citizens and residents of Lebanon, as are his aunts and uncles, one uncle being a dual national with the U.S. None of the Applicant's foreign relatives are connected with a foreign government or the subject of coercion vis-a-vis the Applicant. Clearance is granted.

CASE NUMBER: 04-12732.h1
Foreign Influence
02/21/2006

Applicant was born and raised in Iran. He attended college and graduate school in the U.S. and, after completing his education, chose to remain in the U.S. He married an Iranian born national he met in the U.S., and they have two children. He is employed as a software engineer for a defense contractor. His parents, two sisters, and one brother-in-law are resident citizens of Iran. He successfully mitigated foreign influence concerns regarding his brother-in-law, but was unable to mitigate concerns for his remaining immediate family members in Iran. Clearance is denied.

CASE NUMBER: 04-08738.h1
Foreign Influence
01/17/2006

Applicant's foreign contacts include his spouse, his mother and nine siblings who are citizens of Viet Nam. His spouse is a Resident Alien of the U.S. and has applied for U.S. citizenship. His mother and siblings reside in Viet Nam. They are all farmers. These foreign contacts do not pose a security risk. Clearance is granted.

CASE NUMBER: 05-01707.h1
Foreign Influence
03/31/2006

Applicant married a Russian citizen who is a permanent resident of the U.S. She maintains close ties with her parents and her daughter who are citizens and residents of Russia, but Applicant has little or no contact with his wife's Russian relatives. Applicant has strong ties to the U.S. and would not compromise national security. Applicant mitigated the security concerns relating to possible foreign influence. Clearance is granted.

CHAPTER 8

MILITARY SERVICE, FOREIGN CONNECTIONS/TRAVEL, & SELECTIVE SERVICE

MILITARY SERVICE

SECURITY FORM: Section 16—Your Military History & Section 19—Your Military Record.

Section 16—Select a "yes" or "no" response to questions 16a and 16b. If you answered "yes" to either question or you served in a foreign military, provide the requested information. Unless you completed a period of U.S. military service prior to 1970, your *Service/Certificate* # will be your Social Security Number. List service in different branches of the U.S. military separately. List service in different components (active duty, reserve, and National Guard) separately. If you had a break in service within the same branch and component, list each period separately. There is no time limit to this section.

Section 19—Select a "yes" or "no" response to question 19. If you answered "yes", list the month and year of discharge and the type of discharge (i.e., dishonorable discharge, general discharge, bad conduct discharge). There is no time limit to this section. If you were subject to court martial or other disciplinary proceedings under the Uniform Code of Military Justice in conjunction with your discharge, this action must also be listed at *Question 23—Your Police Record*. If possible provide a name and contact information in the *comment section* for anyone who can corroborate the circumstances surrounding your discharge.

APPLICABLE ADJUDICATIVE GUIDELINES

GUIDELINE C: FOREIGN PREFERENCE

Paragraph 9. *The Concern.* When an individual acts in such a way as to indicate a preference for a foreign country over the United States, then he or she may be prone to provide information or make decisions that are harmful to the interests of the United States.

Paragraph 10. *Conditions that could raise a security concern and may be disqualifying include:*

(a) exercise of any right, privilege or obligation of foreign citizenship after becoming a U.S. citizen or through the foreign citizenship of a family member. This includes but is not limited to:

(2) military service or a willingness to bear arms for a foreign country. . . .

(c) performing or attempting to perform duties, or otherwise acting, so as to serve the interests of a foreign person, group, organization, or government in conflict with the national security interest;

(d) any statement or action that shows allegiance to a country other than the United States. . . .

Paragraph 11. *Conditions that could mitigate security concerns include:*

(c) exercise of the rights, privileges, or obligations of foreign citizenship occurred before the individual became a U.S. citizen or when the individual was a minor. . . .

GUIDELINE J: CRIMINAL CONDUCT

Paragraph 30. *The Concern.* Criminal activity creates doubt about a person's judgment, reliability and trustworthiness. By its very nature, it calls into question a person's ability or willingness to comply with laws, rules and regulations.

Paragraph 31. *Conditions that could raise a security concern and may be disqualifying include:*

(b) discharge or dismissal from the Armed Forces under dishonorable conditions.

Paragraph 32. *Conditions that could mitigate security concerns include:*

(a) so much time has elapsed since the criminal behavior happened, or it happened under such unusual circumstances that it is unlikely to recur or does not cast doubt on the individual's reliability, trustworthiness, or good judgment;

(b) the person was pressured or coerced into committing the act and those pressures are no longer present in the person's life;

(c) evidence that the person did not commit the offense;

(d) there is evidence of successful rehabilitation; including but not limited to the passage of time without recurrence of criminal activity, remorse or restitution, job training or higher education, good employment record, or constructive community involvement.

Note: For dishonorable discharges, see the note at the end of Chapter 9 regarding the Smith Act.

NACLC: If you had prior service in the U.S. military, your prior military service record will be reviewed regardless of how long ago it occurred. If you received less than an honorable discharge from the military or had prior service in a foreign military, it could result in a SPIN regarding the military discharge or foreign preference.

SSBI/SSBI-PR

Personal Subject Interview: Be prepared to discuss all periods of military service. You will be asked to verify all information in this section of your SF86. You will be asked the reason each period of service ended, and if there were any allegations of misconduct or dishonesty against you. If you received less than an Honorable Discharge, be prepared to explain the circumstances surrounding your discharge. *(See Chapter 2, page 23 for PRSI guidance.)*

Field Investigation: For SSBIs if your military service occurred within the past seven years, it will be treated like any other period of employment. For SSBI-PRs if your last period of military service ended after your last investigation, it will be treated like any other period of employment. (See Chapter 6, page 72.)

EXAMPLES OF CLEARANCE ADJUDICATION

CASE NUMBER: 03-11112.h1
Criminal Conduct
12/08/2005

As a result of a general court-martial, Applicant was dismissed from the U.S. Air Force after being convicted of four specifications of conduct unbecoming an officer by making false official statements in Dec 86 (twice), Aug 88, and Oct 88. Applicant failed to mitigate criminal conduct security concerns. The dismissal of an officer from the service is the equivalent of a dishonorable discharge. It is a separation from the service under dishonorable conditions, and the Department of Defense is prohibited from granting Applicant a clearance absent a waiver of 10 U.S.C. § 986.(Smith Act). Clearance is denied.

CASE NUMBER: 04-04805.h1
Criminal Conduct; Financial; Personal Conduct
08/17/2005

Applicant, a 35-year-old employee of a defense contractor and former sergeant, was discharged under other than honorable conditions in 2001 for misuse of a government credit card, and making false official statements, and forgery to cover up the original offense. While he omitted several details of the offenses on his SF 86, the omissions were minor and he made a full effort to report them on the form, in his interview, and at the hearing. He has since taken private employment with two companies holding a security clearance. His first work concerned rebuilding the Pentagon after 9/11. He has successfully rehabilitated himself, is financially secure, and cares for two daughters as a single father. The security concerns have been mitigated. Clearance is granted.

CASE NUMBER: 05-00374.h1
Personal Conduct
01/30/2006

The Army instituted a Special Court-Martial based on Applicant's second violation of its fraternization rules. He was found guilty of two violations and received a bad conduct discharge after eight years of service. Subsequent to his discharge, he violated private company policy on one occasion when he opened an inappropriate e-mail, causing problems with co-workers computers. Based on his otherwise favorable work history, he mitigated the government's concerns under Guideline E. Clearance is granted

CASE NUMBER: 97-0172.h1
Foreign Preference
08/13/1997

A dual citizen of the United States and a foreign nation since birth, Applicant was raised in the foreign country and served in its military. His recent exercise of his United States citizenship is undermined by his continued use of his foreign passport in preference to his United States passport and his willingness to again serve in the foreign military if required. Clearance is denied.

CASE NUMBER: 99-0062.h1
Foreign Preference; Foreign Influence
09/15/1999

Applicant, born and raised in Israel, is a dual citizen of Israel and the United States since becoming a US citizen through naturalization in 1973. Required to obtain an Israeli passport in order to exit the country during a visit to see his mother in 1977, Applicant has used his United States passport when traveling to all other nations. Foreign military service was completed prior to his US citizenship. He is willing to renounce his foreign citizenship if necessary to obtain his clearance. Family members who are resident citizens of Israel do not raise sufficient foreign influence concerns to warrant denial of access. Clearance is granted.

FOREIGN CONNECTIONS/TRAVEL

SECURITY FORM: Section 17—Your Foreign Activities and Section 18—Foreign Countries You Have Visited.

Section 17—Enter a "yes" or "no" response to questions 17a, 17b, 17c, and 17d. If you answered "yes" to any of these question, you must enter a complete explanation for your "yes" response(s) in the *Continuation Space* at the end of the paper version of the SF86 or in the *comment section* of the electronic SF86.

If you have a bank account in a foreign country or own foreign stocks directly, you should answer "yes" to question 17a. If you own foreign stocks as part of a U.S. mutual fund or have a bank account with a foreign owned bank in the United States, you may answer "no" to question 17a. Basically, if you have ever received any money or other compensation from a foreign source (other than gift from friend or relative) or have any financial asset in a foreign country, you should answer "yes" to question 17a and/or 17b.

If you had any contact with foreign government officials, other than official U.S. Government business, routine visa applications, or border crossings, you should answer "yes" to question 17c. If you were ever stopped, detained or questioned for any reason by foreign law enforcement, security or intelligence personnel, you should answer "yes" to question 17c.

If you currently have a foreign passport or if you had a foreign passport that expired within the past seven years, you must answer, "yes" to question 17d.

Section 18—As indicated in the instructions on the SF86 for this section, "List foreign countries you have visited, except on travel under official Government orders, beginning with the most current (#1) and working back 7 years. (Travel as a government dependent or contractor must be listed.) . . . **Include** short trips to **Canada** or **Mexico.** If you lived near a border and made numerous short (one day or less) trips to the neighboring country, you do not need to list each trip. Instead, provide the time period, the code, the country, and a note ("Many Short Trips"). Do not repeat travel covered in Sections 9, 10, or 11."

However, it is necessary to list travel to other countries during periods that you lived abroad. For example, if you were stationed with the U.S. Armed Forces or attended a college in Germany, you should have listed that information under residence and employment, or residence and education. Trips you made to the Czech Republic, Belgium, France, Poland, etc., during that time, must be listed in Section 18, if those trips occurred within the past seven years. If you made numerous trips to neighboring countries while living in a foreign country, you may summarize them in same manner as for Canada and Mexico, but you must specify each country. Use the comment section to explain all such travel. Additionally, you must identify the purpose of travel as either: Business, Pleasure, Education, and Other. "Other" can include such purposes as attending a funeral, child adoption, medical treatment, etc. and will also require a brief explanation.

APPLICABLE ADJUDICATIVE GUIDELINES

GUIDELINE B: FOREIGN INFLUENCE

Paragraph 6. *The Concern.* Foreign contacts and interests may be a security concern if the individual has divided loyalties or foreign financial interests, may be manipulated or induced to help a foreign person, group, organization, or government in a way that is not in U.S. interests, or is vulnerable to pressure or coercion by any foreign interest. Adjudication under this Guideline can and should consider the identity of the foreign country in which the foreign contact or financial interest is located, including, but not limited to, such considerations as whether the foreign country is known to target United States citizens to obtain protected information and/or is associated with a risk of terrorism.

Paragraph 7. *Conditions that could raise a security concern and may be disqualifying include:*

(a) contact with a foreign family member, business or professional associate, friend, or other person who is a citizen of or resident in a foreign country if that contact creates a heightened risk of foreign exploitation, inducement, manipulation, pressure, or coercion;

(b) connections to a foreign person, group, government, or country that create a potential conflict of interest between the individual's obligation to protect sensitive information or technology and the individual's desire to help a foreign person, group, or country by providing that information;

(c) counterintelligence information, that may be classified, indicates that the individual's access to protected information may involve unacceptable risk to national security;

(e) a substantial business, financial, or property interest in a foreign country, or in any foreign-owned or foreign-operated business, which could subject the individual to heightened risk of foreign influence or exploitation;

(f) failure to report, when required, association with a foreign national;

(g) unauthorized association with a suspected or known agent, associate, or employee of a foreign intelligence service;

(h) indications that representatives or nationals from a foreign country are acting to increase the vulnerability of the individual to possible future exploitation, inducement, manipulation, pressure, or coercion;

(i) conduct, especially while traveling outside the U.S., which may make the individual vulnerable to exploitation, pressure, or coercion by a foreign person, group, government, or country.

Paragraph 8. *Conditions that could mitigate security concerns include:*

(a) the nature of the relationships with foreign persons, the country in which these persons are located, or the positions or activities of those persons in that country are such that it is unlikely the individual will be placed in a position of having to choose between the interests of a foreign individual, group, organization, or government and the interests of the U.S.;

(b) there is no conflict of interest, either because the individual's sense of loyalty or obligation to the foreign person, group, government, or country is so minimal, or the individual has such deep and longstanding relationships and loyalties in the U.S., that the individual can be expected to resolve any conflict of interest in favor of the U.S. interest;

(c) contact or communication with foreign citizens is so casual and infrequent that there is little likelihood that it could create a risk for foreign influence or exploitation;

(d) the foreign contacts and activities are on U.S. Government business or are approved by the cognizant security authority;

(e) the individual has promptly complied with existing agency requirements regarding the reporting of contacts, requests, or threats from persons, groups, or organizations from a foreign country;

(f) the value or routine nature of the foreign business, financial, or property interests is such that they are unlikely to result in a conflict and could not be used effectively to influence, manipulate, or pressure the individual.

GUIDELINE C: FOREIGN PREFERENCE

Paragraph 9. *The Concern.* When an individual acts in such a way as to indicate a preference for a foreign country over the United States, then he or she may be prone to provide information or make decisions that are harmful to the interests of the United States.

Paragraph 10. *Conditions that could raise a security concern and may be disqualifying include:*

(a) exercise of any right, privilege or obligation of foreign citizenship after becoming a U.S. citizen or through the foreign citizenship of a family member. This includes but is not limited to:

(1) possession of a current foreign passport;

(2) military service or a willingness to bear arms for a foreign country;

(3) accepting educational, medical, retirement, social welfare, or other such benefits from a foreign country;

(4) residence in a foreign country to meet citizenship requirements;

(5) using foreign citizenship to protect financial or business interests in another country;

(6) seeking or holding political office in a foreign country;

(7) voting in a foreign election;

(b) action to acquire or obtain recognition of a foreign citizenship by an American citizen;

(c) performing or attempting to perform duties, or otherwise acting, so as to serve the interests of a foreign person, group, organization, or government in conflict with the national security interest;

(d) any statement or action that shows allegiance to a country other than the United States: for example, declaration of intent to renounce United States citizenship; renunciation of United States citizenship.

Paragraph 11. *Conditions that could mitigate security concerns include:*

(a) dual citizenship is based solely on parents' citizenship or birth in a foreign country;

(b) the individual has expressed a willingness to renounce dual citizenship;

(c) exercise of the rights, privileges, or obligations of foreign citizenship occurred before the individual became a U.S. citizen or when the individual was a minor;

(d) use of a foreign passport is approved by the cognizant security authority;

(e) the passport has been destroyed, surrendered to the cognizant security authority, or otherwise invalidated;

(f) the vote in a foreign election was encouraged by the United States Government.

Note: In August 2000 an Assistant Secretary of Defense issued what is now known as the "Money Memorandum" regarding possession and/or use of a foreign passport and Adjudicative Guideline C. The memo reads, ". . . the guideline requires that any clearance be denied or revoked unless the applicant surrenders the foreign passport or obtains official approval for its use from the appropriate agency of the United States Government."[58]

GUIDELINE E: PERSONAL CONDUCT

Paragraph 15. *The Concern.* Conduct involving questionable judgment, lack of candor, dishonesty, or unwillingness to comply with rules and regulations can raise questions about an individual's reliability, trustworthiness and ability to protect classified information. . . .

Paragraph 16. *Conditions that could raise a security concern and may be disqualifying also include:*

(e) personal conduct or concealment of information about one's conduct, that creates a vulnerability to exploitation, manipulation, or duress, such as . . . (2) while in another country, engaging in any activity that is illegal in that country or that is legal in that country but illegal in the United States and may serve as a basis for exploitation or pressure by the foreign security or intelligence service or other group. . . .

Paragraph 17. *Conditions that could mitigate security concerns include:*

(a) the individual made prompt, good-faith efforts to correct the omission, concealment, or falsification before being confronted with the facts;

(e) the individual has taken positive steps to reduce or eliminate vulnerability to exploitation, manipulation, or duress;

GUIDELINE L: OUTSIDE ACTIVITIES

Paragraph 36. *The Concern.* Involvement in certain types of outside employment or activities is of security concern if it poses a conflict of interest with an individual's security responsibilities and could create an increased risk of unauthorized disclosure of classified information.

Paragraph 37. *Conditions that could raise a security concern and may be disqualifying include:*

(a) any employment or service, whether compensated or volunteer, with:

---

[58] Memorandum from Arthur L. Money, Assistant Secretary of Defense for Command, Control, Communications, and Intelligence; Subject: Guidance to DoD Central Adjudicative Facilities (CAF) Clarifying the Application of the Foreign Preference Adjudicative Guideline; dated August 16, 2000.

(1) the government of a foreign country;

(2) any foreign national, organization, or other entity;

(3) a representative of any foreign interest;

(4) any foreign, domestic, or international organization or person engaged in analysis, discussion, or publication of material on intelligence, defense, foreign affairs, or protected technology;

(b) failure to report or fully disclose an outside activity when this is required.

Paragraph 38. *Conditions that could mitigate security concerns include:*

(a) evaluation of the outside employment or activity by the appropriate security or counterintelligence office indicates that it does not pose a conflict with an individual's security responsibilities or with the national security interests of the United States;

(b) the individual terminates the employment or discontinued the activity upon being notified that it was in conflict with his or her security responsibilities.

NACLC: There is no standard NACLC coverage for this section; however, if you answered "yes" to questions 17a, 17b, 17c, or 17d or listed travel to a country like Cuba or North Korea, it could result in a SPIN for foreign preference, personal conduct, or outside activities.

Additional NAC Coverage: If you lived in a foreign country for more than six months or there is any information that suggests that you were involved in criminal activity overseas within the period of investigation, an Interpol records check will be conducted.[59]

SSBI/SSBI-PR

Personal Subject Interview: You will be asked to verify all your responses in Section 17 of the SF86. Any "yes" response will be thoroughly explored. If you have foreign financial assets, you should estimate their value and indicate what they represent as a percentage of your net worth.

You will be asked to verify all foreign travel listed at Section 18 of your SF86 and questioned about any unlisted travel, including official travel on Government orders and military deployments. Be prepared to discuss your mode of travel, how you paid for the travel, identity of traveling companions, and others who can verify your travel.

---

[59] OPM Federal Investigative Notice No. 05-01, March 1, 2005.

If you traveled extensively while living in a foreign city, be prepared to discuss other cities in that country you visited, as well as other countries you visited during that time period. For example, when asked about these trips, you can summarize them as "Trips of one to three days duration to numerous cities throughout Germany and the neighboring countries of Belgium, France, Austria, and Poland for sightseeing."

Be prepared to provide information regarding any foreign nationals with whom you have any continuing contact. This information will include their name, citizenship, date of birth, address, occupation, employer (or school name if a student), and the nature and frequency of your contact with them. You are only expected to provide as much of the information as you know about the other person. You do not need to contact them to obtain the information. (See Chapter 2, page 23 for PRSI guidance.)

Field Investigation: Attempts will be made to verify and develop all foreign travel, financial interests, associates and activities directly or indirectly through routine personal and record sources.

EXAMPLES OF CLEARANCE ADJUDICATION

CASE NUMBER: 05-02741.h1
Foreign Influence; Foreign Preference
03/31/2006

Applicant is a dual citizen of the U.S. and Sudan. He was born in Sudan and naturalized as a U.S. citizen in June 2000. He has not exercised his Sudanese citizenship since becoming a U.S. citizen. His mother, two siblings, father-in-law, mother-in-law, and half-brother are citizens and residents of Sudan. He co-owns property worth about $100,000 in Sudan. He has provided virtually no information about his family ties or property interests in Sudan. Applicant has refuted the allegation of foreign preference, but he has not mitigated the security concerns based on foreign influence. Clearance is denied.

CASE NUMBER: 02-11404.h1
Foreign Preference; Foreign Influence
08/30/2004

Security concerns remain over Applicant's foreign preference activated by his dual citizenship and his decision to retain a foreign passport: he stated that he would not relinquish the foreign passport even though current Department of Defense policy requires it. However, he has mitigated the allegations of foreign influence. Although his father and sister are citizens of Sweden, there is no evidence that they have ties to the government, or could be exploited by a foreign power in a way that would force him to choose between his ties to them and to the United States (U.S.). Clearance is denied.

CASE NUMBER: 02-10909.h1
Foreign Preference; Foreign Influence
10/05/2004

After security concerns arose over Applicant's foreign preference because of her dual citizenship, she voluntarily chose to comply with the Department of Defense policy requirements and destroyed her foreign passport in January 2004. After she became a naturalized United States (U.S.) citizen in April 2000, she obtained a U.S. passport in June 2000 and used it on subsequent travel to Peoples Republic of China ("China"). Although she has relatives who are citizens of China, they are elderly and do not have ties to the government; there is no evidence they are in a position to be exploited by a foreign power in a way that could force Applicant to choose between loyalty to them and the U.S. She has mitigated the allegations of foreign preference and influence. Clearance is granted.

CASE NUMBER: 02-23235.h1
Personal Conduct
08/23/2004
Applicant rebutted security concerns over personal conduct issues resulting solely from her travel to Cuba in February 2000 as that isolated incident of poor judgment fails to demonstrate "a pattern of dishonesty or rule violations." This personal conduct concern is superseded by her good judgment in fully disclosing this irregular travel to Cuba in security clearance applications both in October 2000 and again in April 2002 and by her subsequent history of her excellent conduct on the job where Applicant is highly regarded. Since being granted a clearance in 2001, Applicant has displayed good judgment and reliability in her handling of classified information. Clearance is granted.

SELECTIVE SERVICE

SECURITY FORM: Section 20—Your Selective Service Record.

If you answer "yes" to question 20a and 20b, enter your Selective Service Registration Number in the "Registration Number" block. If you don't know your registration number, either telephone the Selective Service at 847-688-6888 or 847-688-2576 or visit their website at *www.sss.gov* and select the "Verify a Registration" link to get your registration number.

If you answer "yes" to question 20a, but "no" to question 20b, provide a reason in the "Legal Exemption Explanation" block. Legal exemptions include, not becoming a permanent resident of the United States until after your 26th birthday and joining the U.S. Armed Forces before or within 30 days of your 18th birthday. If you entered military service more than a month after your 18th birthday and did not register with Selective Service when required (within 30 days of your 18th birthday), your failure to register as required will generally not be an issue. If this situation applies to you and you are in the military, indicate in the Legal Exemption Explanation block that you are currently serving in the U.S. Armed Forces. If you were discharged from the U.S. Armed Forces before your 26th birthday and you did not previously register, you are required to register immediately after being discharged.

Almost all male citizens and non-citizens (living in the United States) are required to register, if they are between 18 and 26 years of age, including illegal aliens, legal permanent residents, and refugees. The general rule is that if a male non-citizen takes up residency in the U.S. before his 26th birthday, he must register with Selective Service. For more information about who must register and legal exemptions go to the Selective Service website at *www.sss.gov* and select the "registration info" link.

APPLICABLE ADJUDICATIVE GUIDELINES

GUIDELINE E: PERSONAL CONDUCT

Paragraph 15. *The Concern.* Conduct involving questionable judgment, lack of candor, dishonesty, or unwillingness to comply with rules and regulations can raise questions about an individual's reliability, trustworthiness and ability to protect classified information. . . .

Paragraph 16. *Conditions that could raise a security concern and may be disqualifying include:*

(c) credible adverse information in several adjudicative issue areas that is not sufficient for an adverse determination under any other single guideline, but which, when considered as a whole, supports a whole-person assessment of questionable judgment, untrustworthiness, unreliability, lack of candor, unwillingness to comply with rules and regulations, or other characteristics indicating that the person may not properly safeguard protected information.

(d) credible adverse information that is not explicitly covered under any other guideline and may not be sufficient by itself for an adverse determination, but which, when combined with all available information supports a whole-person assessment of questionable judgment, untrustworthiness, unreliability, lack of candor, unwillingness to comply with rules and regulations, or other characteristics indicating that the person may not properly safeguard protected information. This includes but is not limited to consideration of:

(3) a pattern of dishonesty or rule violations.

Paragraph 17. *Conditions that could mitigate security concerns include:*

(a) the individual made prompt, good-faith efforts to correct the omission, concealment, or falsification before being confronted with the facts;

(b) the refusal or failure to cooperate, omission, or concealment was caused or significantly contributed to by improper or inadequate advice of authorized personnel or legal counsel advising or instructing the individual specifically concerning the security clearance process. Upon being made aware of the requirement to cooperate or provide the information, the individual cooperated fully and truthfully;

(c) the offense is so minor, or so much time has passed, or the behavior is so infrequent, or it happened under such unique circumstances that it is unlikely to recur and does not cast doubt on the individual's reliability, trustworthiness, or good judgment.

NACLC: There is no standard NACLC coverage for this section.

SSBI/SSBI-PR

Personal Subject Interview: You will be asked to verify the information you provided in this section. If you failed to register when required, you will be questioned about it.

Field Investigation: There is no standard field investigative coverage for this section.

EXAMPLES OF CLEARANCE ADJUDICATION

CASE NUMBER: 04-04139.h1
Alcohol; Personal Conduct
03/16/2006

Applicant's consumption of alcohol led to his arrest for minor in possession of alcohol in 1995, disorderly conduct in 1998, public drinking in 1999, and driving under the influence in 2002. Over the three years since the DUI, he has demonstrated maturity in fulfilling his obligations as an employee for a defense contractor and as a provider for his fiancée and their two-year-old daughter. While he continues to drink beer on occasion, he does so responsibly and exhibits no signs of an alcohol problem. Alcohol consumption concerns are mitigated. Applicant's failure to comply with his legal obligation to register for the Selective Service was unintentional. Clearance is granted.

CASE NUMBER: 03-02799.h1
Criminal Conduct; Personal Conduct
07/26/2004

In 1981, when he was 18 years old, Applicant deliberately violated federal law by failing to register for the draft with the U.S. Selective Service System because he found such registration morally repugnant and against his conscience. Applicant defends his decision and would undoubtedly refuse to register if ordered to do so today. Applicant failed to mitigate the criminal conduct and personal conduct security concerns raised by his conduct. Clearance is denied.

CHAPTER 9

MENTAL HEALTH, POLICE RECORDS, & DRUG USE

MENTAL HEALTH

SECURITY FORM: Section 21—Your Medical Record.

You should include information in this section of the SF86 going back a full seven years, even if it occurred before your 16th birthday.

Question 21 on the SF86 can be confusing. On the paper version of the SF86 you will see that there are two parts to this question. On the electronic versions you will only see the first part of the question, unless you answer "yes" to the first part. If you answer "yes" to the first part, the second part will then appear. The first part of Question 21 asks, "In the last 7 years, have you consulted with a mental health professional (psychiatrist, psychologist, counselor, etc.) or have you consulted with another health care provider about a mental health related condition?" If you have consulted with a mental health professional for any reason, you should answer, "yes" (this includes marital, family, relationship, and grief counseling). Also, if you consulted any other health care provider (i.e., family doctor, nurse practitioner, etc.) regarding a mental health related condition, you should answer, "yes."

The term "mental health professional" means someone licensed to provide mental health counseling or treatment. This includes but is not limited to Marriage, Family, and Child Counselors (MFCC), Marriage and Family Therapists (MFT), Licensed Clinical Social Workers (LCSW), Licensed Psychologists, and psychiatrists (medical doctors with a clinical specialty in psychiatry). You do not have to include counseling from a clergyman, unless he or she is also a mental health professional. Nor do you have to include counseling from unlicensed graduate students working at a college or university counseling center, unless you had contact with their licensed supervisor.

The second part of the question then asks, "If you answered 'Yes,' provide the dates of treatment and the names and address of the therapist or doctor below, unless the consultation(s) involved only marital, family, or grief counseling, not related to violence by you."

There is no exception for "relationship" counseling, even though the nature of the counseling is no different than marital or family counseling. When in doubt, list it. You should list marital or family counseling, if one of the reasons that you sought counseling was because you became physically violent (i.e., physically hurting or damaging a person, animal or object). You should also list any counseling where your treatment included the prescription of drugs for depression, anxiety, bipolar disorder or ADHD. For instance, if you received counseling and were prescribed an anti-depressant for an extended period of time following the death of a loved one, this goes beyond normal grief counseling and should be listed.

This section should not be of concern for most people who have had mental health counseling, particularly if the counseling is not current. See the adjudicative guidelines below for an explanation of what is and what is not a security concern.

If you provide information in the second part of Question 21, you should contact the offices or facilities where you received the counseling/treatment and ask if they have their own form for authorizing the release of patient information. If they have their own form, obtain copy (in person or by fax) and take it with you to your PRSI or SPIN. This alone may reduce the time involved in your investigation by two weeks or more. If possible you should provide name and contact information in the *comment section* for at least one person (other than the psychologist) who knows about your condition and treatment.

APPLICABLE ADJUDICATIVE GUIDELINES

GUIDELINE I: PSYCHOLOGICAL CONDITIONS

Paragraph 27. *The Concern.* Certain emotional, mental, and personality conditions can impair judgment, reliability, or trustworthiness. A formal diagnosis of a disorder is not required for there to be a concern under this guideline. A duly qualified mental health professional (e.g., clinical psychologist or psychiatrist) employed by, or acceptable to and approved by the U.S. Government, should be consulted when evaluating potentially disqualifying and mitigating information under this guideline. No negative inference concerning the standards in this Guideline may be raised solely on the basis of seeking mental health counseling.

Paragraph 28. *Conditions that could raise a security concern and may be disqualifying include:*

(a) behavior that casts doubt on an individual's judgment, reliability, or trustworthiness that is not covered under any other guideline, including but not limited to emotionally unstable, irresponsible, dysfunctional, violent, paranoid, or bizarre behavior;

(b) an opinion by a duly qualified mental health professional that the individual has a condition not covered under any other guideline that may impair judgment, reliability, or trustworthiness;

(c) the individual has failed to follow treatment advice related to a diagnosed emotional, mental, or personality condition, e.g. failure to take prescribed medication.

Paragraph 29. *Conditions that could mitigate security concerns include:*

(a) the identified condition is readily controllable with treatment, and the individual has demonstrated ongoing and consistent compliance with the treatment plan;

(b) the individual has voluntarily entered a counseling or treatment program for a condition that is amenable to treatment, and the individual is currently receiving counseling or treatment with a favorable prognosis by a duly qualified mental health professional;

(c) recent opinion by a duly qualified mental health professional employed by, or acceptable to and approved by the U.S. Government that an individual's previous condition is under control or in remission, and has a low probability of recurrence or exacerbation;

(d) the past emotional instability was a temporary condition (e.g., one caused by a death, illness, or marital breakup), the situation has been resolved, and the individual no longer shows indications of emotional instability;

(e) there is no indication of a current problem.

Note: Refusal to sign a medical release, like any other refusal or failure to cooperate with security processing will probably result in termination of the investigation and denial of the clearance as covered in Guideline E—Personal Conduct (see Appendix B, page B-8). Also see the provisions of the Smith Act at the end of this chapter.

NACLC: There is no standard NACLC coverage for this section; however, any entry other than that related only to marital, family, or grief counseling may result in a SPIN, an interview of the mental health/medical practitioner, and a review of the pertinent records.

SSBI/SSBI-PR

Personal Subject Interview: You will be asked to verify the information you provided in this section. Be prepared to provide details of **any** mental health counseling within the past seven years (even if it precedes your 16th birthday), including who, when, how often, where, and why, as well as diagnosis, medications prescribed, and referrals to other practitioners. You may be asked to sign a medical release. *(See Chapter 2, page 23 for PRSI guidance.)*

Field Investigation : Interviews of all references will include questions regarding possible mental health problems and mental health treatment. Efforts will be made to corroborate any listed or developed mental health issues. If there was counseling (other than that related only to marital, family, or grief counseling) and if a release was obtained from the applicant, an interview of the mental health/medical practitioner will be conducted and the pertinent medical records will be reviewed.

EXAMPLES OF CLEARANCE ADJUDICATION

CASE NUMBER: 02-05768.h1
Mental
01/08/2004
Thirty-year-old Applicant abused marijuana on a continuing basis from about 1989 until January 1999. During the period September 1996 until February 1997 his marijuana use occurred about once each day. In February 1997, Applicant was admitted to a hospital following a *manic episode*, initially thought to have been caused by poor quality marijuana. In fact, the *manic episode* was eventually diagnosed as a bipolar disorder, a condition that may indicate a defect in judgment, reliability, or stability. Applicant was hospitalized for about one month, treated with mood stabilizing medication, and discharged to outpatient care. His continuing monthly treatment with a psychologist and psychiatrist for therapy and medication supervision (four different drugs) to manage his bipolar symptoms has satisfied all questions and doubts as to his security eligibility and suitability. The personality disorder is under control or in remission, and has a low probability of recurrence or exacerbation if he continues to follow medical advice relating to treatment of the condition. Clearance is granted.

CASE NUMBER: 02-17574.h1
Mental
01/18/2006

In March of 2005, a Licensed Clinical Psychologist issued a provisional diagnosis of the Applicant. She averred that the Applicant was most likely suffering from a Paranoid Personality Disorder, which "condition definitely causes significant defects or likely defects in judgment and reliability," and "is not now in remission." At the Applicant's December 15, 2005, hearing, the same Clinical Psychologist observed the Applicant's demeanor, and reiterated her provisional diagnosis. She averred that the Applicant's condition impacted her reliability, stability, and was continuing in nature. Mitigation is not shown. Clearance is denied.

CASE NUMBER: 01-04783.h1
Criminal Conduct; Mental
02/28/2003

Although the Applicant's past criminal conduct is not recent, his related mental disorder, which is currently in remission, is of security significance. On three separate occasions, in June of 1997, in October of 1998, and more recently in October of 2000, the Applicant failed to take his prescribed medications. Each failure led to psychotic episodes which required hospitalization. If he goes off his medication again, there is "a 95% likelihood" of another such episode. In light of his recent history, it is too soon to conclude that the Applicant will not again cease taking his medication, thereby becoming psychotic and a security risk. Clearance is denied.

POLICE RECORDS

SECURITY FORM: Section 23—Your Police Record.

Questions 23a, 23b, and 23d pertain to your entire life. Questions 23e and 23f require information covering the past seven years, unless your investigation is an SSBI in which case you must enter all information for the past **ten years**. These questions are not limited by your age (i.e., if you are 18 years old you must go back to either to age 8 or 11 depending on the type of investigation involved). Read the instructions to this section carefully, as well as each of the questions "a" through "f." Note that questions a, b, c, and d use the words "charge(d)" or "convicted." Question "f" uses the words "arrested, charged or convicted" and includes "detentions" involving traffic citations where the fine was $150[60] or more and any traffic citation involving drugs or alcohol.

When you are issued a traffic citation and released after you sign it, you were "detained." A detention is not an arrest; however, the traffic citation results in being "charged" with the traffic offense and if you pay the fine or bail forfeiture, it is a "conviction." Consequently all traffic violations are covered under Question "f," but you are permitted to exclude those with fines less than $150. All traffic citations involving alcohol or drugs must be listed regardless of the amount of the fine or how long ago they occurred.

As a practical matter if you were taken into custody by a peace officer, you were arrested. If your freedom was only temporarily restricted by a police officer, you were detained. In some jurisdictions there are laws that provide for exceptions to this general rule. For instance California Penal Code Section 849(b)(2) provides that a person arrested for intoxication only, may be released from custody when no further proceedings are desirable. A person arrested for public intoxication, then released from custody after signing a citation promis-

---

[60] There is a possibility that in the near future the $150 exception for traffic fines may be increased to $300.

ing to appear in court, was arrested. A person arrested for public intoxication and released without signing a citation, was detained. In this situation the original arrest is actually reclassified as civil protective custody or detention not amounting to an arrest. Technically in this case, the matter does not have to be listed on the SF86; however, since the police will have a record of the matter, it is better to disclose it in the comment section of the SF86.

There are situations where people are arrested but never charged. This usually occurs when the local public prosecutor's office (who receives the arrest report) doesn't believe there is enough evidence to take the matter before a court or doesn't feel it is worth the effort to prosecute the matter. This is different from the situation when an *information* (criminal complaint or petition) is filed with the court, but the prosecutor later files a *nolle prosequi* declaring his intention not to prosecute the case in whole or in part or when the charge is later dismissed. If you were charged with a felony offense or any offense involving alcohol, drugs, firearms, or explosives and the charge is later dismissed or not prosecuted, you must list it on your SF86, no matter how long ago it occurred.

Felony offenses are generally defined as those offenses for which a person can be sent to prison for one year or more. It doesn't matter that a person's actual sentence didn't include any jail or prison time, as long as the offense carried a possible penalty of one year or more in prison. If you were arrested for a felony more than 7 years ago (10 years for an SSBI) but never charged, you do not have to list it on your SF86. Likewise, if you were arrested more than 7 years ago (10 years for an SSBI) for an offense that involved alcohol, drugs, firearms, or explosives but never charged, you do not have to list it.

Say you were arrested by local police for a misdemeanor offense six years ago, spent a night in the county jail, released on bail the next morning, and the charge was dismissed at court. In preparation for filling out your SF86 you go to the police department that arrested you, and they have no record of your arrest. You also check with the court that dismissed the charge against you, and they no longer have any record of the case. Do you list this matter on your SF86 or not? The answer is yes—you should list it; it is the truthful thing to do. Bear in mind that there may be a booking record at the county sheriff's office where you were jailed for the night and arrest information would have been forwarded to the FBI, as well as to a state-level criminal record center. Likewise, if your case was "sealed" or "expunged" by the court, the court record and possibly the local police record may not be available to a security investigator; however, the arrest was probably reported to the FBI and a state-level criminal record center. FBI records are rarely affected by court expunction orders.

In many jurisdictions criminal justice records of juveniles can only be released to designated criminal justice and investigative agencies. For example in California the presiding judge of each county court system issues a TNG Order designating agencies that may routinely receive juvenile probation and court records. If OPM is not listed on the TNG Order, it must petition the presiding judge of the county court system for access to a specific record. Just because there is a law restricting access to juvenile justice records in your jurisdiction or because your military recruiter wasn't given any information about your juvenile arrest during his police records checks on you, do not assume that juvenile justice records are beyond the reach of security investigators.

Question 23e applies to all military disciplinary proceedings under the Uniform Code of Military Justice. This includes Summary Courts Martial, Special Courts Martial, General Courts Marital, and all non-judicial punishment under Article 15 of the Uniform Code of Military Justice (variously referred to as NJP, Captain's Mast, Office Hours, Summarized Article 15, Company Grade Article 15, and Field Grade Article 15) that occurred within the past 7 years (10 years for an SSBI).

If you answered "yes" to any of these questions, you should list name and contact information in the *comment section* for anyone who knows about these matters, preferably someone who can corroborate what happened.

APPLICABLE ADJUDICATIVE GUIDELINES

GUIDELINE J: CRIMINAL CONDUCT

Paragraph 30. *The Concern.* Criminal activity creates doubt about a person's judgment, reliability and trustworthiness. By its very nature, it calls into question a person's ability or willingness to comply with laws, rules and regulations.

Paragraph 31. *Conditions that could raise a security concern and may be disqualifying include:*

(a) a single serious crime or multiple lesser offenses;

(b) discharge or dismissal from the Armed Forces under dishonorable conditions;

(c) allegation or admission of criminal conduct, regardless of whether the person was formally charged, formally prosecuted or convicted;

(d) individual is currently on parole or probation;

(e) violation of parole or probation, or failure to complete a court-mandated rehabilitation program.

Paragraph 32. *Conditions that could mitigate security concerns include:*

(a) so much time has elapsed since the criminal behavior happened, or it happened under such unusual circumstances that it is unlikely to recur or does not cast doubt on the individual's reliability, trustworthiness, or good judgment;

(b) the person was pressured or coerced into committing the act and those pressures are no longer present in the person's life;

(c) evidence that the person did not commit the offense;

(d) there is evidence of successful rehabilitation; including but not limited to the passage of time without recurrence of criminal activity, remorse or restitution, job training or higher education, good employment record, or constructive community involvement.

NACLC: Law Enforcement records are reviewed for all listed criminal and traffic offenses. If full disposition of the matter is not reflected in the Law Enforcement record, court records are reviewed. Even though routine state or local law enforcement records checks are only conducted in jurisdictions where you lived, worked, or attended school for the last five years, a standard component of the National Agency Check (NAC) is a review of FBI records. The FBI maintains a database of arrest information submitted to them by state and local police agencies. Consequently if you are undergoing a NACLC and you moved away from one jurisdiction six years ago, arrest information from that jurisdiction will probably have been forwarded to the FBI and will show up in your NAC results. Any arrest can result in a SPIN.

SSBI/SSBI-PR

Personal Subject Interview: You will be asked to verify accuracy and completeness of information in this section of your SF86. If you listed any offenses on your SF86 or disclose any offenses during your interview that you did not list on your SF86, be prepared to provide detailed information about the matter. If you didn't list it on your SF86 and you were required to list it, you will be asked why you failed to list it. "I forgot" might work for a traffic citation, but it generally doesn't work for an arrest that resulted in being fingerprinted, photographed, and held in a jail cell (unless of course you have been in jail numerous times and you listed most of them). *(See Chapter 2, page 23 for PRSI guidance.)*

Field Investigation: Records of all criminal justice agencies (law enforcement and courts) where listed and developed arrest information (including detentions for traffic citations with fines of $150 or more) might exist are reviewed for details regarding the arrest and the disposition of the case. Interviews of all references will include questions regarding possible criminal conduct. Any indication of criminal conduct contained in any record that is review will be reported. Effort will be made to corroborate any listed or developed criminal conduct.

EXAMPLES OF CLEARANCE ADJUDICATION

CASE NUMBER: 05-04499.h1
Personal Conduct; Criminal Conduct
06/12/2006

Applicant was a Postal Service employee for eight years. Between May 1999 and May 2000 it appears Applicant on multiple occasions took cash (totaling $737.84) from her drawer that she had received in payment for postage sold to customers. The theft was discovered during an inventory, and she admitted she stole the money to pay her personal expenses. Applicant was charged with misappropriating $1,000 or less (a misdemeanor). She pled guilty, and was placed on two years probation. She served 120 days home confinement and paid a $500 fine. Although she was only charged with a misdemeanor, her conduct consisted of multiple individual thefts, spanned a one-year period of time, and exhibited an extreme breach of trust. Clearance is denied.

CASE NUMBER: 02-17626.h1
Criminal Conduct
07/15/2004

Applicant was arrested five times within three years as a result of domestic disputes with his bipolar wife. Applicant mitigated criminal conduct security concerns by getting his wife the medical and psychiatric help she needed and by learning coping skills through a domestic violence treatment program. Clearance is granted.

CASE NUMBER: 02-30630.h1
Criminal Conduct, Alcohol
02/02/2005

Applicant engaged in underage drinking, and was caught driving under the influence (DUI) within six months of getting his driver's license at age 16. Following the dissolution of his first marriage in 1994/95, Applicant began frequenting dance clubs looking for female companionship, often drinking to intoxication. A 1996 DUI had little impact on his behavior, and in February 1999 he caused an accident involving personal injury while driving drunk. He was convicted of felony aggravated battery but spent only 30 days in jail. Applicant began to appreciate the consequences of drinking and driving. Remarried and in a stable lifestyle since May 2000, Applicant continues to consume alcohol, but in moderation with no evidence of adverse impact on his judgment, reliability, and trustworthiness. His abusive drinking is sufficiently of the past to mitigate the alcohol consumption concerns. Clearance is granted.

ILLEGAL DRUG ACTIVITY

SECURITY FORM: Section 24—Your Use Of Illegal Drugs And Drug Activity.

It is important to recognize that any admission of illegal drug activity on your SF86, can not be used in any criminal proceeding against you.

Question 24a asks about **illegal use** of controlled substances and illegal use of prescription drugs within the past seven years or since your 16th birthday (whichever is shorter). The question is written in such a way as to exclude legal use of controlled substances (such as the use of a controlled substance in a country where it is not prohibited by law).

Question 24b asks about illegal use of controlled substances **at any time** while employed as law enforcement officer, prosecutor, or courtroom official; while possessing a security clearance; or while in a position directly and immediately affecting the public safety.

Question 24c asks about illegally buying, selling, manufacturing, trafficking, producing, transferring, shipping, or receiving controlled substance for your own intended profit or that of another in the past seven years. This is a full seven-year question with no exception for people under 23 years of age, but it is limited to illegal drug related activities a person engages in for profit.

If you responded "yes" to questions 24a or 24b, you should list inclusive dates, identify the drugs and indicate the number times the drug was used. If you frequently used a drug, instead of listing a number you can indicate frequency, such as daily, twice a week, monthly, etc. If you responded "yes" to question 24c, it would be best to use the *comment section* and indicate: "Request interview regarding question 24c."

If you answered "yes" to any of these questions, you should list name and contact information in the *comment section* for two people who know about these matters, preferably people who can corroborate what happened.

APPLICABLE ADJUDICATIVE GUIDELINES

GUIDELINE H: DRUG INVOLVEMENT

Paragraph 24. *The Concern.* Use of an illegal drug or misuse of a prescription drug can raise questions about an individual's reliability and trustworthiness, both because it may impair judgment and because it raises questions about a person's ability or willingness to comply with laws, rules, and regulations.

(a) Drugs are defined as mood and behavior altering substances, and include:

(1) Drugs, materials, and other chemical compounds identified and listed in the Controlled Substances Act of 1970, as amended (e.g., marijuana or cannabis, depressants, narcotics, stimulants, and hallucinogens), and (2) inhalants and other similar substances;

(b) drug abuse is the illegal use of a drug or use of a legal drug in a manner that deviates from approved medical direction.

Paragraph 25. *Conditions that could raise a security concern and may be disqualifying include:*

(a) Any drug abuse (see above definition);

(b) testing positive for illegal drug use;

(c) illegal drug possession, including cultivation, processing, manufacture, purchase, sale, or distribution; or possession of drug paraphernalia;

(d) diagnosis by a duly qualified medical professional (e.g., physician, clinical psychologist, or psychiatrist) of drug abuse or drug dependence;

(e) evaluation of drug abuse or drug dependence by a licensed clinical social worker who is a staff member of a recognized drug treatment program;

(f) failure to successfully complete a drug treatment program prescribed by a duly qualified medical professional;

(g) any illegal drug use after being granted a security clearance;

(h) expressed intent to continue illegal drug use, or failure to clearly and convincingly commit to discontinue drug use.

Paragraph 26. *Conditions that could mitigate security concerns include:*

(a) the behavior happened so long ago, was so infrequent, or happened under such circumstances that it is unlikely to recur or does not cast doubt on the individual's current reliability, trustworthiness, or good judgment;

(b) a demonstrated intent not to abuse any drugs in the future, such as:

(1) dissociation from drug-using associates and contacts;

(2) changing or avoiding the environment where drugs were used;

(3) an appropriate period of abstinence;

(4) a signed statement of intent with automatic revocation of clearance for any violation;

(c) abuse of prescription drugs was after a severe or prolonged illness during which these drugs were prescribed, and abuse has since ended;

(d) satisfactory completion of a prescribed drug treatment program, including but not limited to rehabilitation and aftercare requirements, without recurrence of abuse, and a favorable prognosis by a duly qualified medical professional.

NACLC: There is no standard NACLC coverage for this section; however, any "yes" response to one of the questions in this section may result in a SPIN.

SSBI/SSBI-PR

Personal Subject Interview: You will be asked to verify the information you provided in this section. Be prepared to provide details of **any** drug involvement you listed on your SF86.

If you received any counseling or treatment for substance abuse within the past seven years (or since your 16th birthday, whichever is shorter), you will be asked to identify who provided the treatment and to sign a release authorizing the interview of the counselor and review medical records. In such cases you should contact the office or facility where you received the counseling/treatment and ask if they have their own form for authorizing the release of patient information. If they have their own form, obtain a copy (in person or by fax) and take it with you to your PRSI or SPIN. This alone may reduce the time involved in your investigation by two weeks or more. *(See Chapter 2, page 23 for PRSI guidance.)*

Field Investigation: Interviews of all references will include questions regarding possible use of illegal drugs and misuse of other chemical substances (i.e., prescription drugs, solvents, glues, etc.). Any indication of substance abuse contained in any record that is reviewed will be reported. Effort will be made to corroborate any listed or developed substance abuse. If there was substance abuse counseling and a release was obtained from the applicant, an interview of the substance abuse counselor will be conducted and the pertinent treatment records will be reviewed.

EXAMPLES OF CLEARANCE ADJUDICATION

CASE NUMBER: 05-09958.h1
Drugs; Personal Conduct; Criminal Conduct
05/31/2006

Applicant mitigated personal conduct concerns for his failure to reveal on his November 2003 security clearance application (SF 86) occasional drug use during a period of less than a year while in college ending in August 2002. He voluntarily revealed the drug use to an investigator in 2004. The drug use is mitigated for passage of time. Criminal conduct and personal conduct allegations also mitigated through whole person analysis. Clearance is granted. (*See the section on Adjudications in Chapter 4, for a more thorough discussion of this case.*)

CASE NUMBER: 02-00380.h1
Drugs
12/09/2003

Applicant is a 30 year old employee of a defense contractor. Applicant used marijuana with varying frequency, at times daily, from approximately 1995 to May 2001. He used it to help him relax. He purchased marijuana an unknown amount of times. Applicant used psilocybin mushrooms once in 1992, LSD three times between 1992 and 1995, and cocaine about 24 times from July through December 2000. He purchased cocaine once. Applicant last used an illegal drug (marijuana) in May 2001, about a week before he filled out his security clearance application (SF86). In his response to the SF86, applicant stated that prior to obtaining his current employment, he did not consider the impact drug use might have on his career. Now that he knows drug use is incompatible with his career plans, he is motivated to abstain from any future use. In both a signed, sworn statement that he gave to the Defense Security Service (DSS) in July 2001, and in his response to the SF86, applicant stated that he did not intend to use illegal drugs in the future. Applicant's approximately two years of abstinence, together with his credibly stated intention not to use illegal drugs in the future, is sufficient to overcome the Government's case under Guideline H. Clearance is granted.

CASE NUMBER: 04-03281.h1
Drugs; Personal Conduct; Criminal Conduct
04/18/2006

As a teenager, Applicant abused marijuana with varying frequency from approximately 1998 to November 2000, and tried LSD in 1999. His illegal drug involvement led to criminal arrests for drug abuse in May 1999, July 2000 and November 2000. Despite an intent to refrain from illegal drugs in the future, he smoked marijuana twice in 2003. His illegal drug involvement is mitigated by his change to a drug-free lifestyle, but criminal conduct and personal conduct concerns persist where he falsely denied on his security clearance application that he had used any illegal drugs since age 16. Clearance is denied.

CASE NUMBER: 04-07769.h1
Drugs; Personal Conduct
01/23/2006

Applicant is a software engineer for a defense contractor. She used a variety of illegal drugs from 1997 to 2003. She used illegal drugs after being granted an interim security clearance, and associated with individuals involved in criminal activities. In 2003, she stopped using illegal drugs, changed her life style, stopped associating with drug users, and sought help from a therapist. Applicant has mitigated security concerns about her prior drug use. Clearance is granted.

NOTE: SMITH ACT (Title 10 U.S.C. § 986) as amended essentially states that:

After October 30, 2000, the Department of Defense may not grant or renew a security clearance for an officer or employee of the Department of Defense; a member of the Army, Navy, Air Force, or Marine Corps who is on active duty or is in an active status; or an officer or employee of a contractor of the Department of Defense, if that person:

(1) Has been convicted in any court of the United States of a crime and sentenced to imprisonment for a term exceeding one year *and was incarcerated as a result of that sentence for not less than a year.*

(2) Is an unlawful user of, or is addicted to, a controlled substance (as defined in section 102 of the Controlled Substances Act (21 U.S.C. § 802).

(3) Is mentally incompetent, as determined by a mental health professional approved by the Department of Defense.

(4) Has been discharged or dismissed from the Armed Forces under dishonorable conditions.

Exceptions—In a meritorious case, the Secretary of Defense or the Secretary of the military department concerned may authorize an exception for a person described in paragraph (1) or (4), *if there are mitigating factors. Any such waiver may be authorized only in accordance with standards and procedures prescribed by, or under the authority of, an Executive order or other guidance issued by the President.*[61]

---

[61] Authority to grant a waiver has been delegated to the directors of the Defense Office of Hearings and Appeals, National Security Agency, Defense Intelligence Agency, and Washington Headquarters Services.

CHAPTER 10

ALCOHOL, PRIOR INVESTIGATIONS, & FINANCES

ALCOHOL

SECURITY FORM: Section 25—Your Use of Alcohol.

This is a full seven-year question and not limited by your age. The question asks, "In the last 7 years, has your use of alcoholic beverages (such as liquor, beer, wine) resulted in any alcohol-related treatment or counseling (such as for alcohol abuse or alcoholism)?" This includes situations where you were directed by a court or other authority (i.e., school, employer, military) to attend an alcohol course following an alcohol related arrest or incident.

If you sought counseling on your own or attended Alcoholics Anonymous meetings on your own within the past seven years, list it. If you received alcohol counseling or treatment through an Employee Assistance Program, you must list it.

If you list any information in this section, you should contact the offices or facilities where you received the counseling/treatment (except Alcoholics Anonymous) and ask if they have their own form for authorizing the release of patient information. If they have their own form, obtain a copy (in person or by fax) and take it with you to your PRSI or SPIN. This alone may reduce the time involved in your investigation by two weeks or more. You should also list name and contact information in the *comment section* for anyone who knows about this matter (other than the counselor), preferably someone who can corroborate your consumption of alcohol.

APPLICABLE ADJUDICATIVE GUIDELINES

GUIDELINE G: ALCOHOL CONSUMPTION

Paragraph 21. *The Concern.* Excessive alcohol consumption often leads to the exercise of questionable judgment or the failure to control impulses, and can raise questions about an individual's reliability and trustworthiness.

Paragraph 22. *Conditions that could raise a security concern and may be disqualifying include:*

(a) alcohol-related incidents away from work, such as driving while under the influence, fighting, child or spouse abuse, disturbing the peace, or other incidents of concern, regardless of whether the individual is diagnosed as an alcohol abuser or alcohol dependent;

(b) alcohol-related incidents at work, such as reporting for work or duty in an intoxicated or impaired condition, or drinking on the job, regardless of whether the individual is diagnosed as an alcohol abuser or alcohol dependent;

(c) habitual or binge consumption of alcohol to the point of impaired judgment, regardless of whether the individual is diagnosed as an alcohol abuser or alcohol dependent;

(d) diagnosis by a duly qualified medical professional (e.g., physician, clinical psychologist, or psychiatrist) of alcohol abuse or alcohol dependence;

(e) evaluation of alcohol abuse or alcohol dependence by a licensed clinical social worker who is a staff member of a recognized alcohol treatment program;

(f) relapse after diagnosis of alcohol abuse or dependence and completion of an alcohol rehabilitation program;

(g) failure to follow any court order regarding alcohol education, evaluation, treatment, or abstinence.

Paragraph 23. *Conditions that could mitigate security concerns include:*

(a) so much time has passed, or the behavior was so infrequent, or it happened under such unusual circumstances that it is unlikely to recur or does not cast doubt on the individual's current reliability, trustworthiness, or good judgment;

(b) the individual acknowledges his or her alcoholism or issues of alcohol abuse, provides evidence of actions taken to overcome this problem, and has established a pattern of abstinence (if alcohol dependent) or responsible use (if an alcohol abuser);

(c) the individual is a current employee who is participating in a counseling or treatment program, has no history of previous treatment and relapse, and is making satisfactory progress;

(d) the individual has successfully completed inpatient or outpatient counseling or rehabilitation along with any required aftercare, has demonstrated a clear and established pattern of modified consumption or abstinence in accordance with treatment recommendations, such as participation in meetings of Alcoholics Anonymous or a similar organization and has received a favorable prognosis by a duly qualified medical professional or a licensed clinical social worker who is a staff member of a recognized alcohol treatment program.

NACLC: There is no standard NACLC coverage for this section; however, a "yes" response to this question may result in a SPIN and you will be asked to provide written authorization for the interview of the counselor and the review of your patient records.

SSBI/SSBI-PR

Personal Subject Interview: You will be asked to verify the information you provided in this section. Be prepared to provide details of any alcohol counseling or treatment you listed on your SF86 or admit during the interview. You will be asked if you consume (or previously consumed) alcohol and if so, the frequency and amount of consumption. If you received any counseling or treatment for alcohol use within the past seven years, you will be asked to sign a release authorizing the interview of the counselor and review of medical records. If you have consumed alcohol and you are underage, you will be asked if you intend to continue drinking alcohol while underage. *(See Chapter 2, page 23 for PRSI guidance.)*

Field Investigation: Interviews of all references will include questions regarding alcohol use. Any indication of alcohol abuse contained in any record that is reviewed will be reported. Effort will be made to corroborate and obtain details of any listed or developed alcohol abuse, whether chronic or episodic. If there was alcohol counseling and a release was obtained from the applicant, an interview of the alcohol counselor will be conducted and the pertinent treatment records will be reviewed.

EXAMPLES OF CLEARANCE ADJUDICATION

CASE NUMBER: 02-16274.h1
Alcohol
04/29/2005

Applicant was twice convicted of alcohol related driving offenses in 1984 and 1997. Part of the sentence following his second conviction required him to attend an outpatient alcohol treatment program, which he did from November 1998 to April 1999. He stopped drinking for six to eight months after completing this program and began drinking again. In June 2003, he self-referred to an intensive outpatient alcohol treatment program and has been alcohol free for one year. Additionally, he has held a top secret clearance for 25 years while making substantial and significant contributions to the defense industry. He has successfully mitigated security concerns pertaining to past alcohol consumption. Clearance is granted.

CASE NUMBER: 04-09648.h1
Alcohol
05/16/2006

Applicant's periodic excessive consumption of alcohol resulted in four alcohol-related incidents within a five year period between 1998 and 2003. He was routinely abusing alcohol without realizing it, for his alcohol tests registered between .133% (in 1998) and .23% (in 2003). Since his last alcohol-related incident in 2003, and after completion of a second DUI program, Applicant reconsidered his options and focused on positive endeavors and eliminated his stressors, and at the same time, developed a diminished interest in alcohol. While he has not abstained from further alcohol consumption, he has reduced it to the point where he now drinks more responsibly. Applicant has successfully mitigated and overcome the government's case. Clearance is granted.

CASE NUMBER: 04-08975.h1
Alcohol
03/03/2006

Applicant has a long history of excessive consumption of alcohol, resulting in hospitalization for detoxification in August 1994, July 2002, March 2003, July 2003, and the Spring of 2004, and a conviction for Driving Under the Influence of Alcohol in 2000. Applicant was diagnosed as alcohol dependent and obtained treatment on several occasions, but later resumed drinking alcohol to excess. He has been abstinent for over one year, and is dedicated to living alcohol-free hereafter. Applicant failed to mitigate the security concerns arising from his alcohol consumption. Clearance is denied.

PRIOR INVESTIGATIONS

SECURITY FORM: Section 26—Your Investigations Record.

This section only pertains to employment or security clearance investigations conducted by the federal government.

For question 26a everyone who entered the U.S. Armed Force (including Reserves and National Guard) before 2000 was investigated by DoD, even though they may not have been granted a security clearance. Prior to 2000, all military and defense contractor personnel who received a security clearance from DoD were investigated by DoD. DoD civilians were often granted Confidential and Secret clearances by DoD based on an OPM National Agency Check with Inquiries (NACI). DoD also previously conducted security clearance investigations for the U.S. Coast Guard and certain State Department contractors.

The FBI only conducts background investigations on prospective U.S. Justice Department employees, Justice Department employees who need a security clearance, individuals being considered for a Presidential appointment, and a very limited number of prospective Department of Energy officials who will occupy "Positions of a High Degree of Importance or Sensitivity." There are a few other federal agencies that conduct their own employment or security clearance investigations.[62]

In the past the OPM conducted employment and security clearance investigations for most other federal agencies, including employment investigations of DoD civilians being placed in non-critical, non-sensitive positions. In 2000 OPM began conducting a portion of DoD security clearance investigations. In 2004 they began processing almost all DoD background and security clearance investigations. In 2005 the entire investigative staff of DSS transferred to OPM.

For most DoD investigations conducted between 2000 and 2004 it is difficult to know whether the investigation was conducted by DoD or OPM. Your security manager should be able to obtain this information for you.

Only employees and contractors of the Department of Energy are granted "Q" or "L" clearances. DoD issues Confidential, Secret, and Top Secret clearance. DoD also grants Sensitive Compartmented Information (SCI) access authorizations. Since the Single Scope Background Investigation (SSBI) was implemented in December 1991, everyone who was the subject of a favorably completed SSBI was eligible to be considered for SCI access, however, very few were actually granted an SCI access authorization. If you were "read on" to SCI, you know it, and there will be no question in your mind about it.

Question 26b asks if you have **ever** been debarred from federal employment and have **ever** had a security clearance or access authorization denied, suspended, or revoked. In this case the term "access authorization" refers to SCI or SAP or other DoD classified information where a formal "access authorization" was denied, suspended, or revoked. It also pertains to DOE "L" and "Q" Access Authorizations, since within DoE the term Access Authorization has the same meaning as security clearance. Question 26b does not pertain to access to DoD "collateral" classified information. There are situations where individuals were granted a Top Secret clearance, but had an access authorization, such as SCI,

---

[62] The following departments/agencies have statutory or delegated authority to conduct background investigations: Central Intelligence Agency; Department of State; Department of the Treasury; Internal Revenue Service; Bureau of Engraving and Printing; Federal Bureau of Investigation; National Security Agency; Defense Intelligence Agency; U.S. Agency for International Development; Department of Homeland Security; Bureau of Customs and Border Protection; U.S. Secret Service; Small Business Administration; Broadcasting Board of Governors; Department of Justice—Bureau of Alcohol, Tobacco, Firearms, and Explosives; U.S. Postal Service; Tennessee Valley Authority; National Reconnaissance Office; and Peace Corps. Even though these agencies have authority to conduct their own investigations, some of them request OPM to conduct all or part of their investigations.

denied. There are also situations where cleared individuals have their access to collateral classified material suspended, but never actually have their clearance suspended. Only the security clearance granting authority (usually a Central Adjudication Facility) has the right to suspend, deny or revoke a security clearance. However, others in a position of authority, such as military commanding officers have the authority to suspend a cleared individual's access to classified information. This usually occurs at the same time that a report of unfavorable information is forwarded to the CAF recommending the clearance be suspended and a security investigation initiated. Sometimes the CAF determines that the report does not contain sufficient information to suspend the clearance and may chose not to initiate an investigation. In which case appropriate notifications are made and the individual's access is reinstated. It is also possible that a person could have an SCI access authorization suspended, but not have their security clearance suspended. If you are unsure about any clearance or access suspension action against you, list it on your SF86 and provide an explanation in the *comment section*. The agency that suspends, denies, or revokes a clearance or access authorization is usually not the same agency that conducted the clearance investigation.

Also list in the *comment section* name and contact information in the for anyone who knows about this matter, preferably someone who can corroborate what happened.

APPLICABLE ADJUDICATIVE GUIDELINES

GUIDELINE K: HANDLING PROTECTED INFORMATION

Paragraph 33. *The Concern.* Deliberate or negligent failure to comply with rules and regulations for protecting classified or other sensitive information raises doubt about an individual's trustworthiness, judgment, reliability, or willingness and ability to safeguard such information, and is a serious security concern.

Paragraph 34. *Conditions that could raise a security concern and may be disqualifying include:*

(a) deliberate or negligent disclosure of classified or other protected information to unauthorized persons, including but not limited to personal or business contacts, to the media, or to persons present at seminars, meetings, or conferences;

(b) collecting or storing classified or other protected information in any unauthorized location;

(c) loading, drafting, editing, modifying, storing, transmitting, or otherwise handling classified reports, data, or other information on any unapproved equipment including but not limited to any typewriter, word processor, or computer hardware, software, drive, system, gameboard, handheld, "palm" or pocket device or other adjunct equipment;

(d) inappropriate efforts to obtain or view classified or other protected information outside one's need to know;

(e) copying classified or other protected information in a manner designed to conceal or remove classification or other document control markings;

(f) viewing or downloading information from a secure system when the information is beyond the individual's need to know;

(g) any failure to comply with rules for the protection of classified or other sensitive information;

(h) negligence or lax security habits that persist despite counseling by management;

(i) failure to comply with rules or regulations that results in damage to the National Security, regardless of whether it was deliberate or negligent.

Paragraph 35. *Conditions that could mitigate security concerns include:*

(a) so much time has elapsed since the behavior, or it happened so infrequently or under such unusual circumstances that it is unlikely to recur or does not cast doubt on the individual's current reliability, trustworthiness, or good judgment;

(b) the individual responded favorably to counseling or remedial security training and now demonstrates a positive attitude toward the discharge of security responsibilities;

(c) the security violations were due to improper or inadequate training.

GUIDELINE E: PERSONAL CONDUCT

Paragraph 15. *The Concern.* Conduct involving questionable judgment, lack of candor, dishonesty, or **unwillingness to comply with rules and regulations** can raise questions about an individual's reliability, trustworthiness and ability to protect classified information. . . .

Paragraph 16. *Conditions that could raise a security concern and may be disqualifying also include:*

(d) credible adverse information that is not explicitly covered under any other guideline and may not be sufficient by itself for an adverse determination, but which, when combined with all available information supports a whole-person assessment of questionable judgment, untrustworthiness, unreliability, lack of candor, unwillingness to comply with rules and regulations, or other characteristics indicating that the person may not properly safeguard protected information. This includes but is not limited to consideration of:

(1) untrustworthy or unreliable behavior to include breach of client confidentiality, release of proprietary information, unauthorized release of sensitive corporate or other government protected information;

(3) a pattern of dishonesty or rule violations;

(f) violation of a written or recorded commitment made by the individual to the employer as a condition of employment;

Paragraph 17. *Conditions that could mitigate security concerns include:*

(c) the offense is so minor, or so much time has passed, or the behavior is so infrequent, or it happened under such unique circumstances that it is unlikely to recur and does not cast doubt on the individual's reliability, trustworthiness, or good judgment;

(d) the individual has acknowledged the behavior and obtained counseling to change the behavior or taken other positive steps to alleviate the stressors, circumstances, or factors that caused untrustworthy, unreliable, or other inappropriate behavior, and such behavior is unlikely to recur.

NACLC: A check of DCII (Defense Clearance and Investigations Index), SII (Security and Investigations Index), and JPAS (Joint Personnel Adjudications System) records are a standard part of a NACLC. These records contain listings of investigations and security clearance actions conducted by OPM and DoD. Having been debarred from federal employment or having had a security clearance or access authorization denied, suspended, or revoked may result in a SPIN.

SSBI/SSBI-PR

Personal Subject Interview: You will be asked to verify all information in this section. Be prepared to provide details surrounding the suspension, revocation, or denial of a security clearance or access authorization and any debarment from federal service. Be prepared to discuss details surrounding any suspension of access, security violation, or mishandling of classified, sensitive, or proprietary material. *(See Chapter 2, page 23 for PRSI guidance.)*

Field Investigation: Interviews of all references will include general questions regarding the handling of classified, sensitive, personal, or proprietary information. Any indication of mishandling protected information contained in any record that is review will be reported. Effort will be made to corroborate and obtain details of any listed or developed security clearance/access problems and mishandling of privileged or protected information.

EXAMPLES OF CLEARANCE ADJUDICATION

CASE NUMBER: 02-07444.h1
Personal Conduct
01/27/2004

While Applicant failed to reveal on his security form in 2002 that his security clearance was revoked in November 1991, his security officials advised he was only required to document the previous ten years and indeed the form specifically requires any military disciplinary record only for the past seven year. Further, he was never informed of the revocation as he was honorably discharged in October 1991. Any personal conduct concern is superseded by his subsequent long history of outstanding conduct on the job where Applicant is highly regarded for his integrity and honesty overall. He also has highly favorable references. Clearance is granted.

CASE NUMBER: 03-08519.h1
Security Violations
03/28/2006

Applicant's three security violations (failing to secure a DoD Approved Closed Area) between December 2001 and July 17, 2002 are aggravated by the fact they constitute a pattern of adverse conduct that is not isolated. Though the first security violation is extenuated by the lack of an adequate security briefing, the other two incidents are not assuaged by any of the mitigating conditions. Applicant was found not to be culpable for the last violation, but she admitted she was the last person in the secured area. The lack of security violations since July 2002 weighs in Applicant's favor but does not satisfy her ultimate burden of persuasion under the security violations guideline. Clearance is denied.

CASE NUMBER: 02-28059.h1
Security Violations: Personal Conduct
03/30/2006

Applicant, with several years of experience handling classified information, gave communications security (COMSEC) hardware loaded with material classified secret to an employee at work in June 2001 without verifying this person's clearance or need-to-know. In February 2002, Applicant loaded secret information onto a work computer that had not been approved for the storage of classified information and then sent the file over an unencrypted (unclassified) intranet at work. In May 2002, Applicant failed to properly document the receipt of a classified fax before shredding it in an unapproved shredder. His pattern of gross negligence in the handling of classified information is not mitigated where he continues to make excuses for his noncompliance with security regulations. Clearance is denied.

FINANCES

SECURITY FORM: Section 27—Your Financial Record.

These are all full seven-year questions and not limited by your age. You may think you have an unblemished credit record, but something may appear on your credit report that you were unaware of. You are entitled to one free credit report every 12 months from each of the three nationwide consumer credit reporting agencies– Equifax, Experian, and TransUnion. As mentioned in Chapter 2, it is extremely important for you to know what appears in all three of these reports prior to completing this section of the SF86. You can go online to *www.annualcreditreport.com/cra/index.jsp* and get a free copy of your credit reports.

If you had a Chapter 13 bankruptcy within the past seven year and had it converted to a Chapter 7 bankruptcy, you should list both bankruptcy actions on your SF86. In most cases wage garnishments occur because of an unsatisfied court judgment . However, in some states, child support and spousal support payments are automatically collected through wage garnishments. Also, if you are in the Armed Forces and become excessively delinquent on your credit account with military exchange services (i.e., AAFES or NAVEX) or owe any money to your military branch, it will probably be collected by wage garnishment (without a court order), even if the indebtedness was no fault of yours. These all need to be listed on your SF86 with an explanation in the *comment section*.

If you answered "yes" to any of the Section 27 questions, you will need to indicate month and year the action occurred, type of action (i.e., BK13, BK7, Garnishment, Tax Lien, Judgment, Repossession), dollar amount involved, the name used to identify you in the action, and the name and address of the court, plaintiff, and/or government agency involved.

SECURITY FORM: Section 28—Your Financial Delinquencies.

Question 28a is a full seven-year question and not limited by your age. This question asks about previously delinquent debts that were more than 180 days delinquent when they were paid off or were more than 180 days delinquent when you resumed making regular payments that were satisfactory to the creditor. Question 28b concerns only debts that are more than 90 days delinquent as of the date you complete your SF86.

If you responded "yes" to question 28a or 28b, list the date the debt was incurred. For current or former delinquent debts related to revolving credit accounts, such as credit cards, list the date the account was opened and in the comment section indicated the date the account became delinquent. If the debt has been paid off, list the date the debt was satisfied. Also list the amount that is currently delinquent or the amount that was formerly delinquent, as well as the other identifying information requested.

If you have any past due debts, the best thing you can do is to get completely caught up on your payments. Say you have a credit card account that you haven't made a payment on for five months. If immediately before you complete your SF86, you pay the credit card company (or collection agency handling the account) the total amount of the past due payments including the fees and penalties, you do not have to list it on your SF86. If you keep the account current or pay it off completely, it will not become an issue during your PRSI. If you are already delinquent 180 days or more, contact the creditor, quickly set up a debt repayment plan, and start making payments as soon as possible.

Serious financial issues almost always delay the completion of an investigation, because the issues usually can not be resolved until after a PRSI and/or SPIN has been conducted, credit releases obtained, and credit records reviewed. These investigative actions occur sequentially and almost always involve multiple investigative offices. As each office, in turn, is tasked to accomplish a specific action, a new (later) suspense date is assigned to the case, and the case drags on, and on. To qualify as serious, a financial issue must generally exceed a certain dollar amount and be delinquent more than a certain number of days as reported on your SF86 or in your credit bureau report. The dollar amount of a delinquent debt is based on the past due amount, not the total debt. Some types of financial issues can be serious regardless the duration of time involved.

It is critically important that you know precise details concerning any unfavorable credit information contained in any of the reports available from the three national credit reporting agencies and that you disclose the appropriate information on your SF86 and during your PRSI or SPIN. If you do not provide this information when required, your investigation will be delayed. For each such debt you need to know the name and address of the creditor, account number, current balance, high balance, the amount delinquent, the date of your last payment, how may months you are behind in payments, date the account was open, and payment history. To that end you should contact any creditor with unfavorable information listed on your credit reports and obtain all relevant information directly from the creditor. Remember, OPM will obtain a credit report on you. However there may be a delay of up to three months between the time you submit your SF86 and the time OPM obtains the report. Therefore, if your financial situation changes between the time you submit your SF86 and the time of your PRSI or SPIN, be prepared to provide all relevant information about those accounts (or legal actions) at your security interview.

If any significant information appears on the credit report that you failed to disclose on your SF86 (and if applicable, during your PRSI), it will result in a SPIN. When a SPIN is required for an SSBI or SSBI-PR, it always occurs after all initial investigative actions have been accomplished and the case is being reviewed for completeness. Sometimes SPINs are not tasked until after the case has been sent to the appropriate Adjudicative Facility, and the Adjudicative Facility returns the case to OPM with a request for a SPIN. Most SPINs add one to three months to the final completion time of an investigation.

APPLICABLE ADJUDICATIVE GUIDELINES

GUIDELINE F: FINANCIAL CONSIDERATIONS

Paragraph 18. *The Concern.* Failure or inability to live within one's means, satisfy debts, and meet financial obligations may indicate poor self-control, lack of judgment, or unwillingness to abide by rules and regulations, all of which can raise questions about an individual's reliability, trustworthiness and ability to protect classified information. An individual who is financially overextended is at risk of having to engage in illegal acts to generate funds. Compulsive gambling is a concern as it may lead to financial crimes including espionage. Affluence that cannot be explained by known sources of income is also a security concern. It may indicate proceeds from financially profitable criminal acts.

Paragraph 19. *Conditions that could raise a security concern and may be disqualifying include:*

(a) inability or unwillingness to satisfy debts;

(b) indebtedness caused by frivolous or irresponsible spending and the absence of any evidence of willingness or intent to pay the debt or establish a realistic plan to pay the debt.

(c) a history of not meeting financial obligations;

(d) deceptive or illegal financial practices such as embezzlement, employee theft, check fraud, income tax evasion, expense account fraud, filing deceptive loan statements, and other intentional financial breaches of trust;

(e) consistent spending beyond one's means, which may be indicated by excessive indebtedness, significant negative cash flow, high debt-to-income ratio, and/or other financial analysis;

(f) financial problems that are linked to drug abuse, alcoholism, gambling problems, or other issues of security concern.

(g) failure to file annual Federal, state, or local income tax returns as required or the fraudulent filing of the same;

(h) unexplained affluence, as shown by a lifestyle or standard of living, increase in net worth, or money transfers that cannot be explained by subject's known legal sources of income;

(i) compulsive or addictive gambling as indicated by an unsuccessful attempt to stop gambling, "chasing losses" (i.e., increasing the bets or returning another day in an effort to get even), concealment of gambling losses, borrowing money to fund gambling or pay gambling debts, family conflict or other problems caused by gambling.

Paragraph 20. *Conditions that could mitigate security concerns include:*

(a) the behavior happened so long ago, was so infrequent, or occurred under such circumstances that it is unlikely to recur and does not cast doubt on the individual's current reliability, trustworthiness, or good judgment;

(b) the conditions that resulted in the financial problem were largely beyond the person's control (e.g. loss of employment, a business downturn, unexpected medical emergency, or a death, divorce or separation), and the individual acted responsibly under the circumstances;

(c) the person has received or is receiving counseling for the problem and/or there are clear indications that the problem is being resolved or is under control;

(d) the individual initiated a good-faith effort to repay overdue creditors or otherwise resolve debts;

(e) the individual has a reasonable basis to dispute the legitimacy of the past-due debt which is the cause of the problem and provides documented proof to substantiate the basis of the dispute or provides evidence of actions to resolve the issue;

(f) the affluence resulted from a legal source of income.

NACLC: Obtaining a credit bureau report is a standard part of the NACLC. Any significant delinquent debts (past or present), as well as any "yes" response to question 27a through 27d or to question 28b may result in a SPIN, if the amounts listed under questions 27 and 28 exceed a certain dollar amount.

SSBI/SSBI-PR

Personal Subject Interview: You will be asked to verify the information you provided in this section. Be prepared to provide details of regarding any information you listed on your SF86 and any information you disclose during the interview, as well as the reasons for the indebtedness. You will be asked about any consumer credit counseling you received. If the amounts of your current or past delinquent debts exceed a certain dollar amount, you will be asked to sign releases authorizing OPM to review specific records concerning your debts. You will be asked about gambling. *(See Chapter 2, page 23 for PRSI guidance.)*

Field Investigation: Interviews of all references will include questions regarding financial responsibility, gambling, and evidence of any unexplained affluence. Any indication of financial irresponsibility or unexplained affluence contained in any record that is reviewed will be reported. Effort will be made to corroborate and obtain details of any listed or developed financial problems. If a specific financial release was obtained from the applicant, a review of the financial record will be conducted. Records of any bankruptcies, tax liens, wage garnishments, and civil court judgments will be reviewed.

Additional Investigation For SSBI-PR: Check of the Department of the Treasury's Financial Data Base, under terms and conditions prescribed by the Secretary of the Treasury, to search automated data bases consisting of reports of currency transactions by financial institutions, international transportation of currency or monetary instruments, foreign bank and financial accounts, and transactions under $10,000 that are reported as possible money laundering violations.

EXAMPLES OF CLEARANCE ADJUDICATION

CASE NUMBER: 02-11177.h1
Financial; Personal Conduct
02/14/2005

Applicant's financial difficulties began in 1993, and continued until 2004. Such financial difficulties stemmed primarily from excessive gambling which began in 1993 and tapered off in 2002. In November 2003, he sought the services of a consumer credit counseling service. He embarked on a path of financial rehabilitation, and has successfully resolved all six debts alleged. Two separate minor administrative actions taken against him in 1993 and 1999 do not constitute a pattern of rule violations. Applicant has successfully mitigated security concerns stemming from his past financial and personal conduct. Clearance is granted.

CASE NUMBER: 02-23604.h1
Financial
04/15/2004

Applicant received a discharge of more than $17,000.00 in debts under chapter 7 of the bankruptcy code in July 1993. As of June 2003, he had accumulated more than $21,000.00 in delinquent accounts, and had deferred repayment of approximately $64,000.00 in student loans. He has now either satisfied or made arrangements to expeditiously satisfy his delinquent accounts, and entered into an agreement that will allow him to repay his student loans over the course of the next thirty years. Applicant's belated effort to repay long-standing past-due creditors is insufficient to mitigate the security concern caused by his many years of financial irresponsibility. Clearance is denied.

CASE NUMBER: 02-30017.h1
Financial
06/03/2004

Applicant was granted three Chapter 7 bankruptcy discharges between 1988 and 2002. On each occasion, the circumstances that forced him to seek protection under the bankruptcy code were largely beyond his control. He took advantage of his last financial downturn by obtaining an education and now has well-paying employment with a defense contractor. Applicant has mitigated the security concern that arose from his financial instability. Clearance is granted.

CASE NUMBER: 04-02367.h1
Financial
09/29/2005

Applicant is a 33-year-old veteran who has worked for a federal contractor since 2001. Applicant accumulated delinquent debt while on active duty and continued to add to his debt after he was discharged from the service in 1999. Applicant was unemployed for a short period of time in 1999, but has been fully employed since then and his salary has steadily increased in the past six years. Applicant has made minimal effort to resolve his delinquent debts. Applicant has failed to mitigate the security concerns regarding his financial situation. Clearance is denied.

CASE NUMBER: 03-00929.h1
Financial
07/16/2004

Applicant incurred $80,000 in debt over 10 years. She filed a Chapter 13 bankruptcy in 2001, on which she has paid faithfully for three years. She has one year remaining until discharge. Applicant is an office administrator for a defense contractor. Applicant mitigated the financial consideration security concern. Clearance is granted.

CHAPTER 11

COURT ACTIONS, ORGANIZATIONS, TECHNOLOGY, & SEXUAL BEHAVIOR

CIVIL COURT ACTIONS

SECURITY FORM: Section 29—Public Record Civil Court Actions.
For SSBIs this is a ten-year question, regardless of the instructions on the SF86. In this section you should list any civil law suits in which you were the plaintiff or defendant (not already listed at Section 27). Include any class action lawsuits you joined.

APPLICABLE ADJUDICATIVE GUIDELINES
There are no Adjudicative Guidelines that apply specifically to this section; however, Guidelines such as E: Personal Conduct and F: Financial Considerations could apply to the underlying conducting that resulted in the civil court action. The nature of the civil court action would determine the applicable guideline.

NACLC: There is no standard NACLC coverage for this section. Depending on the nature of a listed civil court action, a SPIN may be required.

SSBI/SSBI-PR
Personal Subject Interview: You will be asked to verify all information you listed in the section and provide details of each matter you listed on the SF86 or disclosed during the interview. *(See Chapter 2, page 23 for PRSI guidance.)*

Field Investigation: Appropriate court records will be reviewed for all listed or developed items.

EXAMPLES OF CLEARANCE ADJUDICATION

There are no DOHA cases specifically related to Civil Court Actions for the same reason that there are no Adjudicative Guidelines that apply specifically to this section.

ORGANIZATIONAL AFFILIATIONS

SECURITY FORM: Section 30—Your Association Record.

Question 30a asks if you were **ever** affiliated with or have **ever** supported (endorsed or provided services or money) any ". . . organization dedicated to the violent overthrow of the United States Government and which engages in illegal activities to that end, knowing that the organization engages in such activities with the specific intent to further such activities?" Basically to answer "yes" to this question you had to understand the goals of the organization and either specifically support the unlawful activities or became affiliated with the organization with the intent to further the unlawful activities.

Question 30b asks if you have **ever** ". . . knowingly engaged in any acts or activities designed to overthrow the United States Government by force?"

If you answer "yes" to either of these questions, you should list name and contact information in the *comment section* for two people who knows about these matters, preferably people who can corroborate your involvement.

APPLICABLE ADJUDICATIVE GUIDELINES

GUIDELINE A: ALLEGIANCE TO THE UNITED STATES

Paragraph 3. *The Concern.* An individual must be of unquestioned allegiance to the United States. The willingness to safeguard classified information is in doubt if there is any reason to suspect an individual's allegiance to the United States.

Paragraph 4. *Conditions that could raise a security concern and may be disqualifying include:*

(a) involvement in, support of, training to commit, or advocacy of any act of sabotage, espionage, treason, terrorism, or sedition against the United States of America;

(b) association or sympathy with persons who are attempting to commit, or who are committing, any of the above acts;

(c) association or sympathy with persons or organizations that advocate, threaten, or use force or violence, or use any other illegal or unconstitutional means, in an effort to:

(1) overthrow or influence the government of the United States or any state or local government;

(2) prevent Federal, state, or local government personnel from performing their official duties;

(3) gain retribution for perceived wrongs caused by the Federal, state, or local government;

(4) prevent others from exercising their rights under the Constitution or laws of the United States or of any state.

Paragraph 5. *Conditions that could mitigate security concerns include:*

(a) the individual was unaware of the unlawful aims of the individual or organization and severed ties upon learning of these;

(b) the individual's involvement was only with the lawful or humanitarian aspects of such an organization;

(c) involvement in the above activities occurred for only a short period of time and was attributable to curiosity or academic interest;

(d) the involvement or association with such activities occurred under such unusual circumstances, or so much times has elapsed, that it is unlikely to recur and does not cast doubt on the individual's current reliability, trustworthiness, or loyalty.

NACLC: There is no standard NACLC coverage for this section. If you answered "yes" to either question, a SPIN may be required.

SSBI/SSBI-PR

Personal Subject Interview: You will be asked to verify your responses to questions 30a and 30b and provide details regarding any affirmative response you listed on the SF86 or disclosed during the interview. You will be questioned regarding any involvement in acts of sabotage, espionage, treason, terrorism, or sedition against the U.S. Government, as well as any association with persons who have committed or are attempting to commit such acts. You will also be questioned regarding any advocacy of or involvement in any unlawful acts designed to prevent others from exercising their rights under the Constitution or laws of the United States or of any state. *(See Chapter 2, page 23 for PRSI guidance.)*

Field Investigation: Interviews of all references will include questions regarding loyalty to the United States and possible involvement with questionable persons or organizations (criminal or subversive).

EXAMPLES OF CLEARANCE ADJUDICATION

There were no DOHA cases in the past ten years involving Guideline A: Allegiance to the United States. When a security clearance investigation develops credible information applicable to Guideline A, the case is almost always closed and referred to other federal investigative agencies, such as the FBI, ICE (Immigration and Customs Enforcement) or ATF (Bureau of Alcohol, Tobacco, Firearms, and Explosives). Consequently these cases are rarely adjudicated for security clearance purposes.

MISUSE OF INFORMATION TECHNOLOGY SYSTEMS

SECURITY FORM: There is no section of the SF86 that specifically addresses misuse of information technology (IT) systems. *Section 23—Your Police Record* covers those criminal offenses for which you were arrested, charged or convicted and *Section 22—Your Employment Record* covers offenses for which employment was terminated. This area of inquiry includes violations of rules, failure to comply with IT security procedures, and misconduct pertaining to IT systems and electronic media, as well as any related misconduct that results in damage to the National Security.

APPLICABLE ADJUDICATIVE GUIDELINES

GUIDELINE M: USE OF INFORMATION TECHNOLOGY SYSTEMS

Paragraph 39. *The Concern.* Noncompliance with rules, procedures, guidelines or regulations pertaining to information technology systems may raise security concerns about an individual's reliability and trustworthiness, calling into question the willingness or ability to properly protect sensitive systems, networks, and information. Information Technology Systems include all related computer hardware, software, firmware, and data used for the communication, transmission, processing, manipulation, storage, or protection of information.

Paragraph 40. *Conditions that could raise a security concern and may be disqualifying include:*

(a) illegal or unauthorized entry into any information technology system or component thereof;

(b) illegal or unauthorized modification, destruction, manipulation or denial of access to information, software, firmware, or hardware in an information technology system;

(c) use of any information technology system to gain unauthorized access to another system or to a compartmented area within the same system;

(d) downloading, storing, or transmitting classified information on or to any unauthorized software, hardware, or information technology system;

(e) unauthorized use of a government or other information technology system;

(f) introduction, removal, or duplication of hardware, firmware, software, or media to or from any information technology system without authorization, when prohibited by rules, procedures, guidelines or regulations.

(g) negligence or lax security habits in handling information technology that persist despite counseling by management;

(h) any misuse of information technology, whether deliberate or negligent, that results in damage to the national security.

Paragraph 41. *Conditions that could mitigate security concerns include:*

(a) so much time has elapsed since the behavior happened, or it happened under such unusual circumstances, that it is unlikely to recur or does not cast doubt on the individual's reliability, trustworthiness, or good judgment;

(b) the misuse was minor and done only in the interest of organizational efficiency and effectiveness, such as letting another person use one's password or computer when no other timely alternative was readily available;

(c) the conduct was unintentional or inadvertent and was followed by a prompt, good-faith effort to correct the situation and by notification of supervisor.

NACLC: There is no NACLC coverage for this issue.

SSBI/SSBI-PR

Personal Subject Interview: You could be asked about any or all of the conditions listed at paragraphs 40a through 40h under Adjudicative Guideline M: Use of Information Technology Systems. *(See Chapter 2, page 23 for PRSI guidance.)*

Field Investigation: Questions similar to those asked during the PRSI may be asked of all references interviewed. Information related to misuse of information technology systems present in any record reviewed as part of the investigation will be report.

EXAMPLES OF CLEARANCE ADJUDICATION

CASE NUMBER: 03-09001.h1
Personal Conduct; Criminal Conduct; Information Technology
02/16/2005

During a two-week period in 1997, Applicant improperly used his company's computer system resulting in the compromise of passwords and other security mechanisms. He resigned his position and was eventually charged with and pled guilty in federal court to a single count of felony computer fraud. During the next 12 months, he was terminated from two subsequent jobs when those employers learned of the charges. However, he has since mitigated the security concerns under Guideline E (personal conduct), Guideline J (criminal conduct), and Guideline M (misuse of information technology systems). His conduct was isolated in that it was a single ongoing event that spanned a brief period in July 1997. It has also been over seven years since that event without any further indication Applicant might repeat his conduct despite clearly having the requisite knowledge and skills to do so. Additionally, Applicant has over several years demonstrated an acceptable degree of reliability and judgment through his church-related duties, which demand a level of discretion and trustworthiness analogous to that required of a clearance holder. His past and current employers, recommend him for a position of trust. They have no doubt he understands his mistakes, feel he has matured a great deal since 1997, and will not again err in this way. Applicant made a single, serious mistake out of inexperience and immaturity. There is clear evidence of rehabilitation. Clearance is granted.

CASE NUMBER: 03-21853.h1
Information Technology; Personal Conduct; Sexual Behavior
02/13/06

Applicant is 43 years old, married with two children, a military retiree, and works for a defense contractor. In 2003, he accessed pornographic web sites on his government information system computer for a six-month period during work hours. Applicant mitigated the misuse of information technology systems, personal conduct, and sexual behavior security concerns, based on two years of not repeating the offense and an otherwise good work record. Clearance is granted.

CASE NUMBER: 02-17345.h1
Information Technology; Personal Conduct
04/10/06

Applicant a retire US Army Colonel held a security clearance during 26 years of active duty. As the director of a defense contractor he accessed pornographic websites on his government computer for two years even after being cautioned against it. Applicant's misuse of his government computer on multiple occasions from 1998 to 2000, and his December 2001 false statement about the circumstances of that misuse, demonstrated that he lacks the judgment, reliability, and trustworthiness required of those with access to classified information. Clearance denied.

CASE NUMBER: 04-03412.h1
Information Technology; Personal Conduct
03/16/2006

Applicant mitigated one allegation of misuse of information technology concerning use of his defense contractor employer's computer to access sexually explicit materials on the internet in 2003. The offense resulted in his discharge after 13 years of employment. He is now employed by another defense contractor. He was under pressure caused by raising two children with a mentally ill wife from whom he divorced in 2005. Psychiatric testimony supported his defense and concluded that there was no evidence the conduct would be repeated and that he suffered from no psychiatric disability. Clearance is granted.

SEXUAL BEHAVIOR

SECURITY FORM: There is no section of the SF86 that specifically addresses sexual behavior. *Section 23—Your Police Record* covers those criminal offenses for which you were arrested, charged or convicted. This area of inquiry includes criminal and non-criminal sexual behavior

APPLICABLE ADJUDICATIVE GUIDELINES

GUIDELINE D: SEXUAL BEHAVIOR

12. *The Concern.* Sexual behavior that involves a criminal offense, indicates a personality or emotional disorder, reflects lack of judgment or discretion, or which may subject the individual to undue influence or coercion, exploitation, or duress can raise questions about an individual's reliability, trustworthiness and ability to protect classified information. No adverse inference concerning the standards in the Guideline may be raised solely on the basis of the sexual orientation of the individual.

13. *Conditions that could raise a security concern and may be disqualifying include:*

(a) sexual behavior of a criminal nature, whether or not the individual has been prosecuted;

(b) a pattern of compulsive, self-destructive, or high-risk sexual behavior that the person is unable to stop or that may be symptomatic of a personality disorder;

(c) sexual behavior that causes an individual to be vulnerable to coercion, exploitation, or duress;

(d) sexual behavior of a public nature and/or that which reflects lack of discretion or judgment.

14. *Conditions that could mitigate security concerns include:*

(a) the behavior occurred prior to or during adolescence and there is no evidence of subsequent conduct of a similar nature;

(b) the sexual behavior happened so long ago, so infrequently, or under such unusual circumstances, that it is unlikely to recur and does not cast doubt on the individual's current reliability, trustworthiness, or good judgment;

(c) the behavior no longer serves as a basis for coercion, exploitation, or duress;

(d) the sexual behavior is strictly private, consensual, and discreet.

NACLC: There is no specific NACLC coverage for this issue.

Ssbi/Ssbi-Pr

Personal Subject Interview: There may be no specific questions regarding sexual behavior. This area of inquiry can be covered by general questions about having been accused or suspected of criminal conduct, involvement in undetected criminal activity, and involvement in conduct that could make you susceptible to blackmail. *(See Chapter 2, page 23 for PRSI guidance.)*

Field Investigation: Questions similar to those used in the PRSI may be asked of all references interviewed. Information related to sexual misconduct present in any record reviewed as part of the investigation will be reported.

Examples of Clearance Adjudication

CASE NUMBER: 03-20165.h1
Personal Conduct; Sexual Behavior
05/12/2006

Applicant has a history of choosing inappropriate locations to masturbate. His decision to masturbate in a church pool in 1986/1987, on three occasions in his office after work hours in 1998, and outside his home in January 2002 raise questions about his judgment and reliability. Such conduct is likely to make him vulnerable to coercion. He has not mitigated the security concerns related to this conduct. Clearance is denied.

CASE NUMBER: 03-21958.h1
Sexual Behavior; Personal Conduct
01/26/2006

In 1995, Applicant began experimenting with bisexual behavior, engaging in sexual acts with men he did not know. He engaged in illegal sexual acts in a public place at least seven times between 1995 and 1997, for which he was twice arrested. In 1996, he was arrested for and convicted of a felony and given a two-year suspended jail sentence. These acts consisted of oral sex and usually took place in the bathroom of a local department store where Applicant knew such activity occurred. Applicant, went to the department store bathroom and exposed himself to a man who turned out to be an undercover policeman. In 1997, while Applicant was awaiting trial on his 1996 charges, he was arrested in the same bathroom for the same conduct. Applicant again exposed himself to an undercover policeman in the next stall. When interviewed during his background investigation, Applicant knowingly made a false statement about the details of his conduct leading to his 1997 conviction. He failed to mitigate the security concerns about his sexual conduct and personal conduct. Clearance is denied.

CASE NUMBER: 05-01106.h1
Sexual Behavior; Criminal Conduct
02/13/2006

Applicant is 63-years-old and married for 40 years. He was arrested for lewd and lascivious acts with a woman not his wife in a car in a public park. The charge was reduced to disorderly conduct, and Applicant received deferred prosecution. He has not told his wife of the incident since it may adversely affect his marriage. Accordingly, the offense is still a basis for undue influence or coercion. Applicant's eligibility for assignment to a sensitive position is denied.

CASE NUMBER: 04-11934.h1
Sexual Behavior; Personal Conduct; Criminal Conduct
04/05/2006

Applicant committed acts of indecent exposure at least twice a month from April 2001 to October 2002. He was arrested in October 2002 and charged with Public Indecency. Between October 2002 and March 2004, he continued to commit acts of indecent exposure on eight occasions. His conduct as well as his deliberate omission of mental health counseling on his security clearance application raise security issues about his judgment and candor. Clearance is denied.

CASE NUMBER: 03-22167.h1
Criminal Conduct: Sexual Behavior; Personal Conduct
02/21/2006

Applicant mitigated security concerns over his criminal conduct, sexual behavior, and personal conduct relating to two arrests for dated, misdemeanor arrests for patronizing prostitution in 1995 and 2001. He has had no subsequent incidents for over four years. Applicant was evaluated by an expert psychologist who assures that Applicant has a normal personality profile with no disorders or addictive behaviors. While he denied to the Defense Security Service (DSS) that he had offered money for a sexual act, he fully disclosed that 2001 arrest and established he had no intent to falsify. He has 37 years of service to his company where his performance has been excellent. Clearance is granted.

CONCLUSION

The primary reason security clearance processing takes so long is that the Department of Defense consistently failed to provide adequate resources to the agencies involved in the process. The math is simple. If an investigator can complete one investigation a day, has 22 cases pending, and receives one new case each work day, case turnaround time in the field is 22 working days. If the average pending caseload per investigator is 44 and the opening and closings are the same, case turnaround time in the field is 44 working days. The same is true of security specialists who receive and processing clearance requests, as well as security clearance adjudicators, except that the numbers are larger and the time is shorter. Unfortunately, in the past the number of investigations requested each year exceeded the number of investigations completed. The number of requested and pending cases was allowed to increase without any increase in security personnel. With OPM taking over responsibility for the vast majority of security clearance investigations, the time it takes to complete an investigation will go down. In the past few years OPM has nearly doubled the number of field investigators conducting background investigations and has recently reduced investigative time significantly. This has been possible because requestors must pay OPM for each investigation they request, and OPM decides how much to charge.

The other two phases of clearance processing—pre-investigation processing and adjudication—have not improved significantly. If you believe OPM, these two phases account for much more than half of the total clearance processing time. Recently DSS announced that the Joint Personnel Adjudication System (JPAS), which is used to request investigations, is in critical condition and any further attempts to fix or upgrade the system could ". . . kill the system." A new system to replace JPAS could take years before it will be ready.

Since government has done such a poor job of managing the process, it is up to others to do whatever they can to reduce the overall processing time. Significant amounts of time can be saved when applicants arm themselves with information about the process and apply that knowledge.

There are three ways that applicants can reduce the processing time when filling out an application form and during their personal interview: 1) providing complete and accurate information, 2) listing the "best" people as references and activity verifiers, and 3) couching unfavorable security and suitability information in terms directly applicable to the mitigating factors detailed in the Adjudicative Guidelines. The first requires inclusion of information that many might regard as insignificant, such short-term residences, employment and school attendance. The second and third may require information beyond that requested by the application form, such as additional employment, school, and residential references/verifiers or a written statement explaining the circumstances surrounding an unfavorable event or situation addressing as many mitigating factors as possible.

Regardless of what others may tell you, there is nothing in the SF86, eQIP, or EPSQ instructions that permit you to omit any residence, school, employment, or period of unemployment within the period of investigation. The instructions do not permit you to list a permanent mailing address instead of a temporary dormitory residence. They do not permit you to omit a job that you quit during the first week of a probationary period. They do not permit you to omit enrollment at a school, because you withdrew during the authorized "drop" period and received a tuition refund. The instructions do not permit these omissions, because of the investigative requirements. Obviously you must use some common sense here. Staying as a guest in hotels and in other peoples' homes, as well as periods of unemployment, of less than a month can be safely omitted, unless you spent three months bouncing from one temporary residence to another. For school enrollment and formal employment you must list all of them (even those that lasted only one day) within the period of investigation.

Look closely at the requirements for your type of investigation (NACLC, SSBI, or SSBI-PR) and pay particular attention to the type and number of references that must be interviewed and the time periods that must be covered in each venue (residence, school, employment, social). Have you provided enough names and contact information, so the investigator will not have to spend time trying to identify and locate them? If you have recently been outside the United States for six months or more, have you provided references, who are currently in the United States and can provide direct coverage for most of the time you were in the foreign country? If you have difficulty providing character references that adequately cover the period of investigation, remember that the requirement is that they, to the extent possible, collectively span the past seven years. This means for an SSBI where a total of four social references are needed, if one reference had at least quarterly contact with you over the entire last seven years, it doesn't matter how long the other social references knew or have known you. You should use the "comment section" of questions 9, 10, and 11 to provide names of additional residence, school, and employment references/verifiers. These should be people who had direct knowledge of your activities, such as neighbors, schoolmates, and work associates.

If you list any information on your SF86 that could be viewed as a potential security or suitability issue (generally in response to questions 14 through 30), use the appropriate *comment section* of the application form and provide names and contact information for people who can verify/corroborate the information. If the issue is serious or complicated prepare a detailed written statement to explain the security/suitability issue and the relevant mitigating factors. The earlier the investigators have all the relevant information, the faster the investigation will be completed and adjudicated.

These recommendations affect all phases of the security clearance process: initial processing, investigation, and adjudication. Each phase involves a significant period of time that can be reduced by applicants through their actions in completing their security form and being proactive during their PRSI or SPIN.

If your SF86 contains all the information needed by the investigators working on your case, your case will be worked on concurrently in different locations in the short amount of time possible. If you fail to provide all the necessary information on your SF86 and the investigators working on your case discover unlisted information, your case will be worked on sequentially and will take significantly longer to complete.

The author welcomes all comments and questions regarding this book. He can be reached by snail mail at: Last Post Publishing, Attn: SCM Author, 1120 Forest Avenue PMB 274, Pacific Grove, CA 93950-5145 or by email at *SCMAuthor@LastPostPublishing.com*. The Last Post Publishing website *http://lastpostpublishing.com* also provides a method of contacting the author, as well as changes that affect the content of this book.

APPENDIX A — REFERENCES

1. Executive Order 12968—Access To Classified Information, August 4, 1995.
2. Executive Order 10450—Security requirements for Government employment, April 27, 1953.
3. Office of the Director of National Intelligence, Intelligence Community Policy Memorandum, Number 2006-700-3, Subject: Intelligence Community Modifications to Annex C, "Adjudicative Guidelines for Determining Eligibility for Access to Classified Information," to DCID 6/4, "Personnel Security Standards And Procedures Governing Eligibility for Access to Sensitive Compartmented Information (SCI), Annex A, Standard C – Single-Scope Background Investigation—Periodic Reinvestigation (SSBI-PR)," July 12, 2006.
4. Office of the Director of National Intelligence, Intelligence Community Policy Memorandum, Number 2006-700-4, Subject: Intelligence Community Modifications to DCID 6/4, "Personnel Security Standards And Procedures Governing Eligibility for Access to Sensitive Compartmented Information," July 12, 2006.
5. Office of the Director of National Intelligence, Intelligence Community Policy Memorandum, Number 2006-700-5, Subject: Intelligence Community Modifications to DCID 6/4, "Personnel Security Standards And Procedures Governing Eligibility for Access to Sensitive Compartmented Information (SCI)," Annex F, "Reciprocity of SCI Eligibility Determinations," July 12, 2006.
6. Director of Central Intelligence Directive 6/4, Personnel Security Standards And Procedures Governing Eligibility for Access to Sensitive Compartmented Information. 02 July 1998.
7. Department of Defense Regulation 5200.2-R, "DoD Personnel Security Program," January 1987 (Administrative Reissuance Incorporating Through Change 3, February 23, 1996).
8. Department of Defense Directive 5220.6, "Defense Industrial Personnel Security Clearance Review Program," February 2, 1992, incorporating through change 4, April 20, 1999.
9. DoD Directive 5210.48, Subject: DoD Polygraph Program, December 24, 1984.
10. DoD Regulation 5210.48, Polygraph Program, January 1985.
11. National Security Directive 63, "Single Scope Background Investigations," October 21, 1991.
12. Army Regulation 380-67, Security, Personnel Security Program, Headquarters, 9 September 1988 (Washington, DC).
13. Air Force Instruction 31-501, Security, Personnel Security Program Management, 27 January 2005.
14. Secretary of the Navy Instruction 5510.30A, Subj: Department of the Navy Personnel Security Program, 10 March 1999, with change 1, dated 19 June 2000.
15. Department of Energy Manual 470.4-5, Personnel Security, 8-26-05.

APPENDIX B — ADJUDICATIVE GUIDELINES

THE WHITE HOUSE
WASHINGTON

December 29, 2005

MEMORANDUM FOR WILLIAM LEONARD
Director
Information Security Oversight Office

SUBJECT: ADJUDICATIVE GUIDELINES

The President has approved the attached revision of the Adjudicative Guidelines for Determining Eligibility for Access to Classified Information as recommended unanimously by the NSC's PCC on Records Access and Information Security. Please circulate the revised guidelines to all affected agencies for immediate implementation. It is important to emphasize that all agencies must honor clearances granted under these guidelines, consistent with Executive Order 12968 and the December 12, 2005 memorandum to agencies from OMB Deputy Director for Management Clay Johnson.

Stephen J. Hadley
Assistant to the President for National Security Affairs

Attachment
Revised Adjudicative Guidelines for Determining Eligibility for Access to Classified Information [63]

ADJUDICATIVE GUIDELINES FOR DETERMINING ELIGIBILITY FOR ACCESS TO CLASSIFIED INFORMATION

1. *Introduction.* The following adjudicative guidelines are established for all U.S. government civilian and military personnel, consultants, contractors, employees of contractors, licensees, certificate holders or grantees and their employees and other individuals who require access to classified information. They apply to persons being considered for initial or continued eligibility for access to classified information, to include sensitive compartmented information and special access programs, and are to be used by government departments and agencies in all final clearance determinations. Government departments and agencies may also choose to apply these guidelines to analogous

---

[63] And further revised by Under Secretary of Defense for Intelligence memo dated 30 August 2006 incorporate the provisions of the "Smith Amendment," Section 986 of Title 10 of the United States Code, as amended. The August 2006 revisions are at paragraph 31(f) and at footnotes 64 through 67.

situations regarding persons being considered for access to other types of protected information.

Decisions regarding eligibility for access to classified information take into account factors that could cause a conflict of interest and place a person in the position of having to choose between his or her commitment to the United States, including the commitment to protect classified information, and any other compelling loyalty. Access decisions also take into account a person's reliability, trustworthiness and ability to protect classified information. No coercive policing could replace the self-discipline and integrity of the person entrusted with the nation's secrets as the most effective means of protecting them. When a person's life history shows evidence of unreliability or untrustworthiness, questions arise whether the person can be relied on and trusted to exercise the responsibility necessary for working in a secure environment where protecting classified information is paramount.

2. *The Adjudicative Process.*

(a) The adjudicative process is an examination of a sufficient period of a person's life to make an affirmative determination that the person is an acceptable security risk. Eligibility for access to classified information is predicated upon the individual meeting these personnel security guidelines. The adjudication process is the careful weighing of a number of variables known as the whole-person concept. Available, reliable information about the person, past and present, favorable and unfavorable, should be considered in reaching a determination. In evaluating the relevance of an individual's conduct, the adjudicator should consider the following factors:

(1) The nature, extent, and seriousness of the conduct;

(2) the circumstances surrounding the conduct, to include knowledgeable participation;

(3) the frequency and recency of the conduct;

(4) the individual's age and maturity at the time of the conduct;

(5) the extent to which participation is voluntary;

(6) the presence or absence of rehabilitation and other permanent behavioral changes;

(7) the motivation for the conduct;

(8) the potential for pressure, coercion, exploitation, or duress; and

(9) the likelihood of continuation or recurrence.

(b) Each case must be judged on its own merits, and final determination remains the responsibility of the specific department or agency. Any doubt concerning personnel being considered for access to classified information will be resolved in favor of the national security.

(c) The ability to develop specific thresholds for action under these guidelines is limited by the nature and complexity of human behavior. The ultimate determination of whether the granting or continuing of eligibility for a security clearance is clearly consistent with the interests of national security must be an overall common sense judgment based upon careful consideration of the following guidelines, each of which is to be evaluated in the context of the whole person.

(1) GUIDELINE A: Allegiance to the United States;

- (2) GUIDELINE B: Foreign Influence;

' (3) GUIDELINE C: Foreign Preference;

(4) GUIDELINE D: Sexual Behavior;

(5) GUIDELINE E: Personal Conduct;

- (6) GUIDELINE F: Financial Considerations;

• (7) GUIDELINE G: Alcohol Consumption;

(8) GUIDELINE H: Drug Involvement;

(9) GUIDELINE I: Psychological Conditions;

(10) GUIDELINE J: Criminal Conduct;

(11) GUIDELINE K: Handling Protected Information;

(12) GUIDELINE L: Outside Activities;

(13) GUIDELINE M: Use of Information Technology Systems

(d) Although adverse information concerning a single criterion may not be sufficient for an unfavorable determination, the individual may be disqualified if available information reflects a recent or recurring pattern of questionable judgment, irresponsibility, or emotionally unstable behavior. Notwithstanding the whole-person concept, pursuit of further investigation may be terminated by an appropriate adjudicative agency in the face of reliable, significant, disqualifying, adverse information.

(e) When information of security concern becomes known about an individual who is currently eligible for access to classified information, the adjudicator should consider whether the person:

(1) voluntarily reported the information;

(2) was truthful and complete in responding to questions;

(3) sought assistance and followed professional guidance, where appropriate;

(4) resolved or appears likely to favorably resolve the security concern;

(5) has demonstrated positive changes in behavior and employment;

(6) should have his or her access temporarily suspended pending final adjudication of the information.

(f) If after evaluating information of security concern, the adjudicator decides that the information is not serious enough to warrant a recommendation of disapproval or revocation of the security clearance, it may be appropriate to recommend approval with a warning that future incidents of a similar nature may result in revocation of access.

GUIDELINE A: ALLEGIANCE TO THE UNITED STATES

3. *The Concern.* An individual must be of unquestioned allegiance to the United States. The willingness to safeguard classified information is in doubt if there is any reason to suspect an individual's allegiance to the United States.

4. *Conditions that could raise a security concern and may be disqualifying include:*

(a) involvement in, support of, training to commit, or advocacy of any act of sabotage, espionage, treason, terrorism, or sedition against the United States of America;

(b) association or sympathy with persons who are attempting to commit, or who are committing, any of the above acts;

(c) association or sympathy with persons or organizations that advocate, threaten, or use force or violence, or use any other illegal or unconstitutional means, in an effort to:

(1) overthrow or influence the government of the United States or any state or local government;

(2) prevent Federal, state, or local government personnel from performing their official duties;

(3) gain retribution for perceived wrongs caused by the Federal, state, or local government;

(4) prevent others from exercising their rights under the Constitution or laws of the United States or of any state.

5. *Conditions that could mitigate security concerns include:*

(a) the individual was unaware of the unlawful aims of the individual or organization and severed ties upon learning of these;

(b) the individual's involvement was only with the lawful or humanitarian aspects of such an organization;

(c) involvement in the above activities occurred for only a short period of time and was attributable to curiosity or academic interest;

(d) the involvement or association with such activities occurred under such unusual circumstances, or so much times has elapsed, that it is unlikely to recur and does not cast doubt on the individual's current reliability, trustworthiness, or loyalty.

GUIDELINE B: FOREIGN INFLUENCE

6. *The Concern.* Foreign contacts and interests may be a security concern if the individual has divided loyalties or foreign financial interests, may be manipulated or induced to help a foreign person, group, organization, or government in a way that is not in U.S. interests, or is vulnerable to pressure or coercion by any foreign interest. Adjudication under this Guideline can and should consider the identity of the foreign country in which the foreign contact or financial interest is located, including, but not limited to, such considerations as whether the foreign country is known to target United States citizens to obtain protected information and/or is associated with a risk of terrorism.

7. *Conditions that could raise a security concern and may be disqualifying include:*

(a) contact with a foreign family member, business or professional associate, friend, or other person who is a citizen of or resident in a foreign country if that contact creates a heightened risk of foreign exploitation, inducement, manipulation, pressure, or coercion;

(b) connections to a foreign person, group, government, or country that create a potential conflict of interest between the individual's obligation to protect sensitive information or technology and the individual's desire to help a foreign person, group, or country by providing that information;

(c) counterintelligence information, that may be classified, indicates that the individual's access to protected information may involve unacceptable risk to national security;

(d) sharing living quarters with a person or persons, regardless of citizenship status, if that relationship creates a heightened risk of foreign inducement, manipulation, pressure, or coercion;

(e) a substantial business, financial, or property interest in a foreign country, or in any foreign-owned or foreign-operated business, which could subject the individual to heightened risk of foreign influence or exploitation;

(f) failure to report, when required, association with a foreign national;

(g) unauthorized association with a suspected or known agent, associate, or employee of a foreign intelligence service;

(h) indications that representatives or nationals from a foreign country are acting to increase the vulnerability of the individual to possible future exploitation, inducement, manipulation, pressure, or coercion;

(i) conduct, especially while traveling outside the U.S., which may make the individual vulnerable to exploitation, pressure, or coercion by a foreign person, group, government, or country.

8. *Conditions that could mitigate security concerns include:*

(a) the nature of the relationships with foreign persons, the country in which these persons are located, or the positions or activities of those persons in that country are such that it is unlikely the individual will be placed in a position of having to choose between the interests of a foreign individual, group, organization, or government and the interests of the U.S.;

(b) there is no conflict of interest, either because the individual's sense of loyalty or obligation to the foreign person, group, government, or country is so minimal, or the individual has such deep and longstanding relationships and loyalties in the U.S., that the individual can be expected to resolve any conflict of interest in favor of the U.S. interest;

(c) contact or communication with foreign citizens is so casual and infrequent that there is little likelihood that it could create a risk for foreign influence or exploitation;

(d) the foreign contacts and activities are on U.S. Government business or are approved by the cognizant security authority;

(e) the individual has promptly complied with existing agency requirements regarding the reporting of contacts, requests, or threats from persons, groups, or organizations from a foreign country;

(f) the value or routine nature of the foreign business, financial, or property interests is such that they are unlikely to result in a conflict and could not be used effectively to influence, manipulate, or pressure the individual.

GUIDELINE C: FOREIGN PREFERENCE

9. *The Concern.* When an individual acts in such a way as to indicate a preference for a foreign country over the United States, then he or she may be prone to provide information or make decisions that are harmful to the interests of the United States.

10. *Conditions that could raise a security concern and may be disqualifying include:*

(a) exercise of any right, privilege or obligation of foreign citizenship after becoming a U.S. citizen or through the foreign citizenship of a family member. This includes but is not limited to:

(1) possession of a current foreign passport;

(2) military service or a willingness to bear arms for a foreign country;

(3) accepting educational, medical, retirement, social welfare, or other such benefits from a foreign country;

(4) residence in a foreign country to meet citizenship requirements;

(5) using foreign citizenship to protect financial or business interests in another country;

(6) seeking or holding political office in a foreign country;

(7) voting in a foreign election;

(b) action to acquire or obtain recognition of a foreign citizenship by an American citizen;

(c) performing or attempting to perform duties, or otherwise acting, so as to serve the interests of a foreign person, group, organization, or government in conflict with the national security interest;

(d) any statement or action that shows allegiance to a country other than the United States: for example, declaration of intent to renounce United States citizenship; renunciation of United States citizenship.

11. *Conditions that could mitigate security concerns include:*

(a) dual citizenship is based solely on parents' citizenship or birth in a foreign country;

(b) the individual has expressed a willingness to renounce dual citizenship;

(c) exercise of the rights, privileges, or obligations of foreign citizenship occurred before the individual became a U.S. citizen or when the individual was a minor;

(d) use of a foreign passport is approved by the cognizant security authority;

(e) the passport has been destroyed, surrendered to the cognizant security authority, or otherwise invalidated;

(f) the vote in a foreign election was encouraged by the United States Government.

GUIDELINE D: SEXUAL BEHAVIOR

12. *The Concern.* Sexual behavior that involves a criminal offense, indicates a personality or emotional disorder, reflects lack of judgment or discretion, or which may subject the individual to undue influence or coercion, exploitation, or duress can raise questions about an individual's reliability, trustworthiness and ability to protect classified information. No adverse inference concerning the standards in the Guideline may be raised solely on the basis of the sexual orientation of the individual.

13. *Conditions that could raise a security concern and may be disqualifying include:*

(a) sexual behavior of a criminal nature, whether or not the individual has been prosecuted;

(b) a pattern of compulsive, self-destructive, or high-risk sexual behavior that the person is unable to stop or that may be symptomatic of a personality disorder;

(c) sexual behavior that causes an individual to be vulnerable to coercion, exploitation, or duress;

(d) sexual behavior of a public nature and/or that which reflects lack of discretion or judgment.

14. *Conditions that could mitigate security concerns include:*

(a) the behavior occurred prior to or during adolescence and there is no evidence of subsequent conduct of a similar nature;

(b) the sexual behavior happened so long ago, so infrequently, or under such unusual circumstances, that it is unlikely to recur and does not cast doubt on the individual's current reliability, trustworthiness, or good judgment;

(c) the behavior no longer serves as a basis for coercion, exploitation, or duress;

(d) the sexual behavior is strictly private, consensual, and discreet.

GUIDELINE E: PERSONAL CONDUCT

15. *The Concern.* Conduct involving questionable judgment, lack of candor, dishonesty, or unwillingness to comply with rules and regulations can raise questions about an individual's reliability, trustworthiness and ability to protect classified information. Of special interest is any failure to provide truthful and candid answers during the security clearance process or any other failure to cooperate with the security clearance process.

The following will normally result in an unfavorable clearance action or administrative termination of further processing for clearance eligibility:

(a) refusal, or failure without reasonable cause, to undergo or cooperate with security processing, including but not limited to meeting with a security investigator for subject interview, completing security forms or releases, and cooperation with medical or psychological evaluation;

(b) refusal to provide full, frank and truthful answers to lawful questions of investigators, security officials, or other official representatives in connection with a personnel security or trustworthiness determination.

16. *Conditions that could raise a security concern and may be disqualifying also include:*

(a) deliberate omission, concealment, or falsification of relevant facts from any personnel security questionnaire, personal history statement, or similar form used to conduct investigations, determine employment qualifications, award benefits or status, determine security clearance eligibility or trustworthiness, or award fiduciary responsibilities;

(b) deliberately providing false or misleading information concerning relevant facts to an employer, investigator, security official, competent medical authority, or other official government representative;

(c) credible adverse information in several adjudicative issue areas that is not sufficient for an adverse determination under any other single guideline, but which, when considered as a whole, supports a whole-person assessment of questionable judgment, untrustworthiness, unreliability, lack of candor, unwillingness to comply with rules and regulations, or other characteristics indicating that the person may not properly safeguard protected information;

(d) credible adverse information that is not explicitly covered under any other guideline and may not be sufficient by itself for an adverse determination, but which, when combined with all available information supports a whole-person assessment of questionable judgment, untrustworthiness, unreliability, lack of candor, unwillingness to comply with rules and regulations, or other characteristics indicating that the person may not properly safeguard protected information. This includes but is not limited to consideration of:

(1) untrustworthy or unreliable behavior to include breach of client confidentiality, release of proprietary information, unauthorized release of sensitive corporate or other government protected information;

(2) disruptive, violent, or other inappropriate behavior in the workplace;

(3) a pattern of dishonesty or rule violations;

(4) evidence of significant misuse of Government or other employer's time or resources;

(e) personal conduct or concealment of information about one's conduct, that creates a vulnerability to exploitation, manipulation, or duress, such as (1) engaging in activities which, if known, may affect the person's personal, professional, or community standing, or (2) while in another country, engaging in any activity that is illegal in that country or that is legal in that country but illegal in the United States and may serve as a basis for exploitation or pressure by the foreign security or intelligence service or other group;

(f) violation of a written or recorded commitment made by the individual to the employer as a condition of employment;

(g) association with persons involved in criminal activity.

17. *Conditions that could mitigate security concerns include:*

(a) the individual made prompt, good-faith efforts to correct the omission, concealment, or falsification before being confronted with the facts;

(b) the refusal or failure to cooperate, omission, or concealment was caused or significantly contributed to by improper or inadequate advice of authorized personnel or legal counsel advising or instructing the individual specifically concerning the security clearance process. Upon being made aware of the requirement to cooperate or provide the information, the individual cooperated fully and truthfully;

(c) the offense is so minor, or so much time has passed, or the behavior is so infrequent, or it happened under such unique circumstances that it is unlikely to recur and does not cast doubt on the individual's reliability, trustworthiness, or good judgment;

(d) the individual has acknowledged the behavior and obtained counseling to change the behavior or taken other positive steps to alleviate the stressors, circumstances, or factors that caused untrustworthy, unreliable, or other inappropriate behavior, and such behavior is unlikely to recur;

(e) the individual has taken positive steps to reduce or eliminate vulnerability to exploitation, manipulation, or duress;

(f) association with persons involved in criminal activities has ceased or occurs under circumstances that do not cast doubt upon the individual's reliability, trustworthiness, judgment, or willingness to comply with rules and regulations.

GUIDELINE F: FINANCIAL CONSIDERATIONS

18. *The Concern.* Failure or inability to live within one's means, satisfy debts, and meet financial obligations may indicate poor self-control, lack of judgment, or unwillingness to abide by rules and regulations, all of which can raise questions about an individual's reliability, trustworthiness and ability to protect classified information. An individual who is financially overextended is at risk of having to engage in illegal acts to generate

funds. Compulsive gambling is a concern as it may lead to financial crimes including espionage. Affluence that cannot be explained by known sources of income is also a security concern. It may indicate proceeds from financially profitable criminal acts.

19. *Conditions that could raise a security concern and may be disqualifying include:*

(a) inability or unwillingness to satisfy debts;

(b) indebtedness caused by frivolous or irresponsible spending and the absence of any evidence of willingness or intent to pay the debt or establish a realistic plan to pay the debt.

(c) a history of not meeting financial obligations;

(d) deceptive or illegal financial practices such as embezzlement, employee theft, check fraud, income tax evasion, expense account fraud, filing deceptive loan statements, and other intentional financial breaches of trust;

(e) consistent spending beyond one's means, which may be indicated by excessive indebtedness, significant negative cash flow, high debt-to-income ratio, and/or other financial analysis;

(f) financial problems that are linked to drug abuse, alcoholism, gambling problems, or other issues of security concern.

(g) failure to file annual Federal, state, or local income tax returns as required or the fraudulent filing of the same;

(h) unexplained affluence, as shown by a lifestyle or standard of living, increase in net worth, or money transfers that cannot be explained by subject's known legal sources of income;

(i) compulsive or addictive gambling as indicated by an unsuccessful attempt to stop gambling, "chasing losses" (i.e., increasing the bets or returning another day in an effort to get even), concealment of gambling losses, borrowing money to fund gambling or pay gambling debts, family conflict or other problems caused by gambling.

20. *Conditions that could mitigate security concerns include:*

(a) the behavior happened so long ago, was so infrequent, or occurred under such circumstances that it is unlikely to recur and does not cast doubt on the individual's current reliability, trustworthiness, or good judgment;

(b) the conditions that resulted in the financial problem were largely beyond the person's control (e.g. loss of employment, a business downturn, unexpected medical emergency, or a death, divorce or separation), and the individual acted responsibly under the circumstances;

(c) the person has received or is receiving counseling for the problem and/or there are clear indications that the problem is being resolved or is under control;

(d) the individual initiated a good-faith effort to repay overdue creditors or otherwise resolve debts;

(e) the individual has a reasonable basis to dispute the legitimacy of the past-due debt which is the cause of the problem and provides documented proof to substantiate the basis of the dispute or provides evidence of actions to resolve the issue;

(f) the affluence resulted from a legal source of income.

GUIDELINE G: ALCOHOL CONSUMPTION

21. *The Concern.* Excessive alcohol consumption often leads to the exercise of questionable judgment or the failure to control impulses, and can raise questions about an individual's reliability and trustworthiness.

22. *Conditions that could raise a security concern and may be disqualifying include:*

(a) alcohol-related incidents away from work, such as driving while under the influence, fighting, child or spouse abuse, disturbing the peace, or other incidents of concern, regardless of whether the individual is diagnosed as an alcohol abuser or alcohol dependent;

(b) alcohol-related incidents at work, such as reporting for work or duty in an intoxicated or impaired condition, or drinking on the job, regardless of whether the individual is diagnosed as an alcohol abuser or alcohol dependent;

(c) habitual or binge consumption of alcohol to the point of impaired judgment, regardless of whether the individual is diagnosed as an alcohol abuser or alcohol dependent;

(d) diagnosis by a duly qualified medical professional (e.g., physician, clinical psychologist, or psychiatrist) of alcohol abuse or alcohol dependence;

(e) evaluation of alcohol abuse or alcohol dependence by a licensed clinical social worker who is a staff member of a recognized alcohol treatment program;

(f) relapse after diagnosis of alcohol abuse or dependence and completion of an alcohol rehabilitation program;

(g) failure to follow any court order regarding alcohol education, evaluation, treatment, or abstinence.

23. *Conditions that could mitigate security concerns include*:

(a) so much time has passed, or the behavior was so infrequent, or it happened under such unusual circumstances that it is unlikely to recur or does not cast doubt on the individual's current reliability, trustworthiness, or good judgment;

(b) the individual acknowledges his or her alcoholism or issues of alcohol abuse, provides evidence of actions taken to overcome this problem, and has established a pattern of abstinence (if alcohol dependent) or responsible use (if an alcohol abuser);

(c) the individual is a current employee who is participating in a counseling or treatment program, has no history of previous treatment and relapse, and is making satisfactory progress;

(d) the individual has successfully completed inpatient or outpatient counseling or rehabilitation along with any required aftercare, has demonstrated a clear and established pattern of modified consumption or abstinence in accordance with treatment recommendations, such as participation in meetings of Alcoholics Anonymous or a similar organization and has received a favorable prognosis by a duly qualified medical professional or a licensed clinical social worker who is a staff member of a recognized alcohol treatment program.

GUIDELINE H: DRUG INVOLVEMENT

24. *The Concern.* Use of an illegal drug or misuse of a prescription drug can raise questions about an individual's reliability and trustworthiness, both because it may impair judgment and because it raises questions about a person's ability or willingness to comply with laws, rules, and regulations.

(a) Drugs are defined as mood and behavior altering substances, and include:

(1) Drugs, materials, and other chemical compounds identified and listed in the Controlled Substances Act of 1970, as amended (e.g., marijuana or cannabis, depressants, narcotics, stimulants, and hallucinogens), and (2) inhalants and other similar substances;

(b) drug abuse is the illegal use of a drug or use of a legal drug in a manner that deviates from approved medical direction.

25. *Conditions that could raise a security concern and may be disqualifying include:*

(a) Any drug abuse (see above definition);[64]

(b) testing positive for illegal drug use;

(c) illegal drug possession, including cultivation, processing, manufacture, purchase,

---

[64] Under the provisions of 10 U.S.C. 986 any person who is an unlawful user of or is addicted to a controlled substance as defined in section 102 of the Controlled Substances Act (21 U.S.C. 802) may not be granted or have renewed their access to classified information.

sale, or distribution; or possession of drug paraphernalia;

(d) diagnosis by a duly qualified medical professional (e.g., physician, clinical psychologist, or psychiatrist) of drug abuse or drug dependence;

(e) evaluation of drug abuse or drug dependence by a licensed clinical social worker who is a staff member of a recognized drug treatment program;

(f) failure to successfully complete a drug treatment program prescribed by a duly qualified medical professional;

(g) any illegal drug use after being granted a security clearance;

(h) expressed intent to continue illegal drug use, or failure to clearly and convincingly commit to discontinue drug use.

26. *Conditions that could mitigate security concerns include:*

(a) the behavior happened so long ago, was so infrequent, or happened under such circumstances that it is unlikely to recur or does not cast doubt on the individual's current reliability, trustworthiness, or good judgment;

(b) a demonstrated intent not to abuse any drugs in the future, such as:

  (1) dissociation from drug-using associates and contacts;

  (2) changing or avoiding the environment where drugs were used;

  (3) an appropriate period of abstinence;

  (4) a signed statement of intent with automatic revocation of clearance for any violation;

(c) abuse of prescription drugs was after a severe or prolonged illness during which these drugs were prescribed, and abuse has since ended;

(d) satisfactory completion of a prescribed drug treatment program, including but not limited to rehabilitation and aftercare requirements, without recurrence of abuse, and a favorable prognosis by a duly qualified medical professional.

GUIDELINE I: PSYCHOLOGICAL CONDITIONS

27. *The Concern.* Certain emotional, mental, and personality conditions can impair judgment, reliability, or trustworthiness. A formal diagnosis of a disorder is not required for there to be a concern under this guideline. A duly qualified mental health professional (e.g., clinical psychologist or psychiatrist) employed by, or acceptable to and approved by the U.S. Government, should be consulted when evaluating potentially

disqualifying and mitigating information under this guideline. No negative inference concerning the standards in this Guideline may be raised solely on the basis of seeking mental health counseling.

28. *Conditions that could raise a security concern and may be disqualifying include:*

(a) behavior that casts doubt on an individual's judgment, reliability, or trustworthiness that is not covered under any other guideline, including but not limited to emotionally unstable, irresponsible, dysfunctional, violent, paranoid, or bizarre behavior;

(b) an opinion by a duly qualified mental health professional that the individual has a condition not covered under any other guideline that may impair judgment, reliability, or trustworthiness;[65]

(c) the individual has failed to follow treatment advice related to a diagnosed emotional, mental, or personality condition, e.g. failure to take prescribed medication.

29. *Conditions that could mitigate security concerns include:*

(a) the identified condition is readily controllable with treatment, and the individual has demonstrated ongoing and consistent compliance with the treatment plan;

(b) the individual has voluntarily entered a counseling or treatment program for a condition that is amenable to treatment, and the individual is currently receiving counseling or treatment with a favorable prognosis by a duly qualified mental health professional;

(c) recent opinion by a duly qualified mental health professional employed by, or acceptable to and approved by the U.S. Government that an individual's previous condition is under control or in remission, and has a low probability of recurrence or exacerbation;

(d) the past emotional instability was a temporary condition (e.g., one caused by a death, illness, or marital breakup), the situation has been resolved, and the individual no longer shows indications of emotional instability;

(e) there is no indication of a current problem.

GUIDELINE J: CRIMINAL CONDUCT

30. *The Concern.* Criminal activity creates doubt about a person's judgment, reliability and trustworthiness. By its very nature, it calls into question a person's ability or willingness to comply with laws, rules and regulations.

---

[65] Under the provisions of 10 U.S.C. 986 any person who is mentally incompetent, as determined by a credentialed mental health professional approved by the Department of Defense, may not be granted or have renewed their access to classified information.

31. *Conditions that could raise a security concern and may be disqualifying include:*

(a) a single serious crime or multiple lesser offenses;

(b) discharge or dismissal from the Armed Forces under dishonorable conditions;[66]

(c) allegation or admission of criminal conduct, regardless of whether the person was formally charged, formally prosecuted or convicted;

(d) individual is currently on parole or probation;

(e) violation of parole or probation, or failure to complete a court-mandated rehabilitation program.

32. *Conditions that could mitigate security concerns include:*

(a) so much time has elapsed since the criminal behavior happened, or it happened under such unusual circumstances that it is unlikely to recur or does not cast doubt on the individual's reliability, trustworthiness, or good judgment;

(b) the person was pressured or coerced into committing the act and those pressures are no longer present in the person's life;

(c) evidence that the person did not commit the offense;

(d) there is evidence of successful rehabilitation; including but not limited to the passage of time without recurrence of criminal activity, remorse or restitution, job training or higher education, good employment record, or constructive community involvement.

(f) *conviction in a Federal or State court, including a court-martial of a crime, sentenced to imprisonment for a tern exceeding one year and incarcerated as a result of that sentence for not less than a year.*[67]

GUIDELINE K: HANDLING PROTECTED INFORMATION

33. *The Concern.* Deliberate or negligent failure to comply with rules and regulations for protecting classified or other sensitive information raises doubt about an individual's

---

[66] Under the provisions of 10 U.S.C. 986, a person who has received a dishonorable discharge or has been dismissed from the Armed Forces may not be granted or have renewed access to classified information. In a meritorious case, the Secretaries of the Military Departments or designee, or the Directors of WHS, DIA, NSA. DOHA or designee may authorize a waiver of this prohibition. Waiver authority may not be further delegated to a member of the Component Personnel Security Appeal Board or the DOHA Security Clearance Appeal Board.

[67] Under the above mentioned statute, a person who has been convicted in a Federal or State court, including courts martial, sentenced to imprisonment for a term exceeding one year and incarcerated for not less than one year, may not be granted or have renewed access to classified information. The same waiver provision also applies.

trustworthiness, judgment, reliability, or willingness and ability to safeguard such information, and is a serious security concern.

34. *Conditions that could raise a security concern and may be disqualifying include:*

(a) deliberate or negligent disclosure of classified or other protected information to unauthorized persons, including but not limited to personal or business contacts, to the media, or to persons present at seminars, meetings, or conferences;

(b) collecting or storing classified or other protected information in any unauthorized location;

(c) loading, drafting, editing, modifying, storing, transmitting, or otherwise handling classified reports, data, or other information on any unapproved equipment including but not limited to any typewriter, word processor, or computer hardware, software, drive, system, gameboard, handheld, "palm" or pocket device or other adjunct equipment;

(d) inappropriate efforts to obtain or view classified or other protected information outside one's need to know;

(e) copying classified or other protected information in a manner designed to conceal or remove classification or other document control markings;

(f) viewing or downloading information from a secure system when the information is beyond the individual's need to know;

(g) any failure to comply with rules for the protection of classified or other sensitive information;

(h) negligence or lax security habits that persist despite counseling by management;

(i) failure to comply with rules or regulations that results in damage to the National Security, regardless of whether it was deliberate or negligent.

35. *Conditions that could mitigate security concerns include:*

(a) so much time has elapsed since the behavior, or it happened so infrequently or under such unusual circumstances that it is unlikely to recur or does not cast doubt on the individual's current reliability, trustworthiness, or good judgment;

(b) the individual responded favorably to counseling or remedial security training and now demonstrates a positive attitude toward the discharge of security responsibilities;

(c) the security violations were due to improper or inadequate training.

GUIDELINE L: OUTSIDE ACTIVITIES

36. *The Concern.* Involvement in certain types of outside employment or activities is of security concern if it poses a conflict of interest with an individual's security responsibilities and could create an increased risk of unauthorized disclosure of classified information.

37. *Conditions that could raise a security concern and may be disqualifying include:*

(a) any employment or service, whether compensated or volunteer, with:

(1) the government of a foreign country;

(2) any foreign national, organization, or other entity;

(3) a representative of any foreign interest;

(4) any foreign, domestic, or international organization or person engaged in analysis, discussion, or publication of material on intelligence, defense, foreign affairs, or protected technology;

(b) failure to report or fully disclose an outside activity when this is required.

38. *Conditions that could mitigate security concerns include:*

(a) evaluation of the outside employment or activity by the appropriate security or counterintelligence office indicates that it does not pose a conflict with an individual's security responsibilities or with the national security interests of the United States;

(b) the individual terminates the employment or discontinued the activity upon being notified that it was in conflict with his or her security responsibilities.

GUIDELINE M: USE OF INFORMATION TECHNOLOGY SYSTEMS

39. *The Concern.* Noncompliance with rules, procedures, guidelines or regulations pertaining to information technology systems may raise security concerns about an individual's reliability and trustworthiness, calling into question the willingness or ability to properly protect sensitive systems, networks, and information. Information Technology Systems include all related computer hardware, software, firmware, and data used for the communication, transmission, processing, manipulation, storage, or protection of information.

40. *Conditions that could raise a security concern and may be disqualifying include:*

(a) illegal or unauthorized entry into any information technology system or component thereof;

(b) illegal or unauthorized modification, destruction, manipulation or denial of access to information, software, firmware, or hardware in an information technology system;

(c) use of any information technology system to gain unauthorized access to another system or to a compartmented area within the same system;

(d) downloading, storing, or transmitting classified information on or to any unauthorized software, hardware, or information technology system;

(e) unauthorized use of a government or other information technology system;

(f) introduction, removal, or duplication of hardware, firmware, software, or media to or from any information technology system without authorization, when prohibited by rules, procedures, guidelines or regulations.

(g) negligence or lax security habits in handling information technology that persist despite counseling by management;

(h) any misuse of information technology, whether deliberate or negligent, that results in damage to the national security.

41. *Conditions that could mitigate security concerns include:*

(a) so much time has elapsed since the behavior happened, or it happened under such unusual circumstances, that it is unlikely to recur or does not cast doubt on the individual's reliability, trustworthiness, or good judgment;

(b) the misuse was minor and done only in the interest of organizational efficiency and effectiveness, such as letting another person use one's password or computer when no other timely alternative was readily available;

(c) the conduct was unintentional or inadvertent and was followed by a prompt, good-faith effort to correct the situation and by notification of supervisor.

APPENDIX C – STANDARD FORM 86

SF86 TIME REQUIREMENTS BY TYPE OF INVESTIGATION

ITEM No.	ITEM TITLE	SSBI	NACLC & SSBI-PR
Item 9	WHERE YOU HAVE LIVED	10 years or age 18*	7 years or age 18*
Item 10	WHERE YOU WENT TO SCHOOL	10 years or age 18*	7 years or age 18*
Item 11	YOUR EMPLOYMENT ACTVITIES	10 years or age 18*	7 years or age 18*
Item 12	PEOPLE WHO KNOW YOU WELL	7 years	7 years
Item 13b	FORMER SPOUSE(S)	No time limit	No time limit
Item 16	YOUR MILITARY HISTORY	No time limit	No time limit
Item 17	YOUR FOREIGN ACTIVITIES		
Item 17a	Current foreign financial assets	Current only	Current only
Item 17b	Foreign employment	No time limit	No time limit
Item 17c	Contact with foreign government	No time limit	No time limit
Item 17c	Foreign passport	7 years	7 years
Item 18	FOREIGN COUNTRIES YOU HAVE VISITED	7 years	7 years
Item 19	YOUR MILITARY RECORD	No time limit	No time limit
Item 20	YOUR SELECTIVE SERVICE RECORD	No time limit	No time limit
Item 21	YOUR MEDICAL RECORD	7 years	7 years
Item 22	YOUR EMPLOYMENT RECORD	10 years or age 18*	7 years or age 18*
Item 23	YOUR POLICE RECORD		
Item 23a	Felony offenses	No time limit	No time limit
Item 23b	Firearms or explosives offenses	No time limit	No time limit
Item 23c	Current pending charges	Current only	Current only
Item 23d	Alcohol or drug offenses	No time limit	No time limit

* Note: If you are under 20 years of age, go back to your 16th birthday.

SF86 Requirements by Type of Investigation (continued)

Item No.	Item Title	SSBI	NACLC & SSBI-PR
Item 23e	Military UCMJ offenses	10 years	7 years
Item 23f	Other arrests & offenses	10 years	7 years
Item 24	YOUR USE OF ILLEGAL DRUGS AND DRUG ACTIVITY		
Item 24a	Illegal drug use	7 years or age 16	7 years or age 16
Item 24b	Illegal drug use while in a position of trust	No time limit	No time limit
Item 24c	Illegal drug involvement for profit	7 years	7 years
Item 25	YOUR USE OF ALCOHOL (counseling/treatment)	7 years	7 years
Item 26	YOUR INVESTIGATION RECORD	No time limit	No time limit
Item 27	YOUR FINANCIAL RECORD (all questions)	7 years	7 years
Item 28	YOUR FINANCIAL DELINQUENCIES		
Item 28a	Debts previously 6 months past due	7 years	7 years
Item 28b	Debts currently past due 90 days or more	Current only	Current only
Item 29	PUBLIC RECORD CIVIL COURT ACTIONS	10 years	7 years
Item 30	YOUR ASSOCIATION RECORD	No time limit	No time limit

Standard Form 86
Revised September 1995
U.S. Office of Personnel Management
5 CFR Parts 731, 732, and 736

Form approved.
OMB No 3206-0007
NSN 7540-00-634-4036
86-111

Questionnaire for National Security Positions

Follow instructions fully or we cannot process your form. Be sure to sign and date the certification statement on Page 9 and the release on Page 10. *If you have any questions,* call the office that gave you the form.

Purpose of this Form
The U.S. Government conducts background investigations and reinvestigations to establish that military personnel, applicants for or incumbents in national security positions, either employed by the Government or working for Government contractors, licensees, certificate holders, and grantees, are eligible for a required security clearance. Information from this form is used primarily as the basis for investigation for access to classified information or special nuclear information or material. Complete this form only after a conditional offer of employment has been made for a position requiring a security clearance.

Giving us the information we ask for is voluntary. However, we may not be able to complete your investigation, or complete it in a timely manner, if you don't give us each item of information we request. This may affect your placement or security clearance prospects.

Authority to Request this Information
Depending upon the purpose of your investigation, the U.S. Government is authorized to ask for this information under Executive Orders 10450, 10865, 12333, and 12356; sections 3301 and 9101 of title 5, U.S. Code; sections 2165 and 2201 of title 42, U.S. Code; sections 781 to 887 of title 50, U.S. Code; and parts 5, 732, and 736 of Title 5, Code of Federal Regulations.

Your Social Security number is needed to keep records accurate, because other people may have the same name and birth date. Executive Order 9397 also asks Federal agencies to use this number to help identify individuals in agency records.

The Investigative Process
Background investigations for national security positions are conducted to develop information to show whether you are reliable, trustworthy, of good conduct and character, and loyal to the United States. The information that you provide on this form is confirmed during the investigation. Investigation may extend beyond the time covered by this form when necessary to resolve issues. Your current employer must be contacted as part of the investigation, even if you have previously indicated on applications or other forms that you do not want this.

In addition to the questions on this form, inquiry also is made about a person's adherence to security requirements, honesty and integrity, vulnerability to exploitation or coercion, falsification, misrepresentation, and any other behavior, activities, or associations that tend to show the person is not reliable, trustworthy, or loyal.

Your Personal Interview
Some investigations will include an interview with you as a normal part of the investigative process. This provides you the opportunity to update, clarify, and explain information on your form more completely, which often helps to complete your investigation faster. It is important that the interview be conducted as soon as possible after you are contacted. Postponements will delay the processing of your investigation, and declining to be interviewed may result in your investigation being delayed or canceled.

You will be asked to bring identification with your picture on it, such as a valid State driver's license, to the interview. There are other documents you may be asked to bring to verify your identity as well. These include documentation of any legal name change, Social Security card, and/or birth certificate.

You may also be asked to bring documents about information you provided on the form or other matters requiring specific attention. These matters include alien registration, delinquent loans or taxes, bankruptcy, judgments, liens, or other financial obligations, agreements involving child custody or support, alimony or property settlements, arrests, convictions, probation, and/or parole.

Organization of this Form

This form has two parts. Part 1 asks for background information, including where you have lived, gone to school, and worked. Part 2 asks about your activities and such matters as firings from a job, criminal history record, use of illegal drugs, and abuse of alcohol.

In answering all questions on this form, keep in mind that your answers are considered together with the information obtained in the investigation to reach an appropriate adjudication.

Instructions for Completing this Form
1. Follow the instructions given to you by the person who gave you the form and any other clarifying instructions furnished by that person to assist you in completion of the form. Find out how many copies of the form you are to turn in. You must sign and date, in black ink, the original and each copy you submit. You should retain a copy of the completed form for your records.

2. Type or legibly print your answers in black ink (if your form is not legible, it will not be accepted). You may also be asked to submit your form in an approved electronic format.

3. All questions on this form must be answered. If no response is necessary or applicable, indicate this on the form (for example, enter "None" or "N/A"). If you find that you cannot report an exact date, approximate or estimate the date to the best of your ability and indicate this by marking "APPROX." or "EST."

4. Any changes that you make to this form after you sign it must be initialed and dated by you. Under certain limited circumstances, agencies may modify the form consistent with your intent.

5. You must use the State codes (abbreviations) listed on the back of this page when you fill out this form. Do not abbreviate the names of cities or foreign countries.

6. The 5-digit postal ZIP codes are needed to speed the processing of your investigation. The office that provided the form will assist you in completing the ZIP codes.

7. All telephone numbers must include area codes.

8. All dates provided on this form must be in Month/Day/Year or Month/Year format. Use numbers (1-12) to indicate months. For example, June 8, 1978, should be shown as 6/8/78.

9. Whenever "City (Country)" is shown in an address block, also provide in that block the name of the country when the address is outside the United States.

10. If you need additional space to list your residences or employments/self-employments/unemployments or education, you should use a continuation sheet, SF 86A. If additional space is needed to answer other items, use a blank piece of paper. Each blank piece of paper you use must contain **your name and Social Security Number at the top of the page.**

Final Determination on Your Eligibility

Final determination on your eligibility for access to classified information is the responsibility of the Federal agency that requested your investigation. You may be provided the opportunity personally to explain, refute, or clarify any information before a final decision is made.

Penalties for Inaccurate or False Statements

The U.S. Criminal Code (title 18, section 1001) provides that knowingly falsifying or concealing a material fact is a felony which may result in fines of up to $10,000, and/or 5 years imprisonment, or both. In addition, Federal agencies generally fire, do not grant a security clearance, or disqualify individuals who have materially and deliberately falsified these forms, and this remains a part of the permanent record for future placements. Because the position for which you are being considered is a sensitive one, your trustworthiness is a very important consideration in deciding your eligibility for a security clearance.

Your prospects of placement or security clearance are better if you answer all questions truthfully and completely. You will have adequate opportunity to explain any information you give us on the form and to make your comments part of the record.

Disclosure of Information

The information you give us is for the purpose of investigating you for a national security position; we will protect it from unauthorized disclosure. The collection, maintenance, and disclosure of background investigative information is governed by the Privacy Act. The agency which requested the investigation and the agency which conducted the investigation have published notices in the Federal Register describing the systems of records in which your records will be maintained. You may obtain copies of the relevant notices from the person who gave you this form. The information on this form, and information we collect during an investigation may be disclosed without your consent as permitted by the Privacy Act (5 USC 552a(b)) and as follows:

PRIVACY ACT ROUTINE USES

1. To the Department of Justice when: (a) the agency or any component thereof; or (b) any employee of the agency in his or her official capacity; or (c) any employee of the agency in his or her individual capacity where the Department of Justice has agreed to represent the employee; or (d) the United States Government, is a party to litigation or has interest in such litigation, and by careful review, the agency determines that the records are both relevant and necessary to the litigation and the use of such records by the Department of Justice is therefore deemed by the agency to be for a purpose that is compatible with the purpose for which the records collected the records.

2. To a court or adjudicative body in a proceeding when: (a) the agency or any component thereof; or (b) any employee of the agency in his or her official capacity, or (c) any employee of the agency in his or her individual capacity where the Department of Justice has agreed to represent the employee; or (d) the United States Government, is a party to litigation or has interest in such litigation, and by careful review, the agency determines that the records are both relevant and necessary to the litigation and the use of such records is therefore deemed by the agency to be for a purpose that is compatible with the purpose for which the agency collected the records.

3. Except as noted in Question 24, when a record on its face, or in conjunction with other records, indicates a violation or potential violation of law, whether civil, criminal, or regulatory in nature, and whether arising by general statute, particular program statute, regulation, rule, or order issued pursuant thereto, the relevant records may be disclosed to the appropriate Federal, foreign, State, local, tribal, or other public authority responsible for enforcing, investigating or prosecuting such violation or charged with enforcing or implementing the statute, rule, regulation, or order.

4. To any source or potential source from which information is requested in the course of an investigation concerning the hiring or retention of an employee or other personnel action, or the issuing or retention of a security clearance, contract, grant, license, or other benefit, to the extent necessary to identify the individual, inform the source of the nature and purpose of the investigation, and to identify the type of information requested.

5. To a Federal, State, local, foreign, tribal, or other public authority the fact that this system of records contains information relevant to the retention of an employee, or the retention of a security clearance, contract, license, grant, or other benefit. The other agency or licensing organization may then make a request supported by written consent of the individual for the entire record if it so chooses. No disclosure will be made unless the information has been determined to be sufficiently reliable to support a referral to another office within the agency or to another Federal agency for criminal, civil, administrative, personnel, or regulatory action.

6. To contractors, grantees, experts, consultants, or volunteers when necessary to perform a function or service related to this record for which they have been engaged. Such recipients shall be required to comply with the Privacy Act of 1974.

7. To the news media or the general public, factual information the disclosure of which would be in the public interest and which would not constitute an unwarranted invasion of personal privacy.

8. To a Federal, State, or local agency, or other appropriate entities or individuals, or through established liaison channels to selected foreign governments, in order to enable an intelligence agency to carry out its responsibilities under the National Security Act of 1947 as amended, the CIA Act of 1949 as amended, Executive Order 12333 or any successor order, applicable national security directives, or classified implementing procedures approved by the Attorney General and promulgated pursuant to such statutes, orders or directives.

9. To a Member of Congress or to a Congressional staff member in response to an inquiry of the Congressional office made at the written request of the constituent about whom the record is maintained.

10. To the National Archives and Records Administration for records management inspections conducted under 44 USC 2904 and 2906.

11. To the Office of Management and Budget when necessary to the review of private relief legislation.

STATE CODES (ABBREVIATIONS)

Alabama	AL	Hawaii	HI	Massachusetts	MA	New Mexico	NM	South Dakota	SD
Alaska	AK	Idaho	ID	Michigan	MI	New York	NY	Tennessee	TN
Arizona	AZ	Illinois	IL	Minnesota	MN	North Carolina	NC	Texas	TX
Arkansas	AR	Indiana	IN	Mississippi	MS	North Dakota	ND	Utah	UT
California	CA	Iowa	IA	Missouri	MO	Ohio	OH	Vermont	VT
Colorado	CO	Kansas	KS	Montana	MT	Oklahoma	OK	Virginia	VA
Connecticut	CT	Kentucky	KY	Nebraska	NE	Oregon	OR	Washington	WA
Delaware	DE	Louisiana	LA	Nevada	NV	Pennsylvania	PA	West Virginia	WV
Florida	FL	Maine	ME	New Hampshire	NH	Rhode Island	RI	Wisconsin	WI
Georgia	GA	Maryland	MD	New Jersey	NJ	South Carolina	SC	Wyoming	WY
American Samoa	AS	Dist. of Columbia	DC	Guam	GU	Northern Marianas	CM	Puerto Rico	PR
Trust Territory	TT	Virgin Islands	VI						

PUBLIC BURDEN INFORMATION

Public burden reporting for this collection of information is estimated to average 90 minutes per response, including time for reviewing instructions, searching existing data sources, gathering and maintaining the data needed, and completing and reviewing the collection of information. Send comments regarding the burden estimate or any other aspect of this collection of information, including suggestions for reducing this burden to Reports and Forms Management Officer, U.S. Office of Personnel Management, 1900 E Street, N.W., Room CHP-500, Washington, D.C. 20415. Do not send your completed form to this address.

Standard Form 86 (EG)
Revised September 1995
U.S. Office of Personnel Management
5 CFR Parts 731, 732, and 736

QUESTIONNAIRE FOR
NATIONAL SECURITY POSITIONS

Form approved:
OMB No. 3206-0007
NSN 7540-00-634-4036
86-111

Part 1 Investigating Agency Use Only | Codes | Case Number

Agency Use Only (Complete items A through P using instructions provided by the Investigating agency).

A Type of Investigation	B Extra Coverage		C Sensitivity Level	D Access	E Nature of Action Code	F Date of Action	Month	Day	Year

G Geographic Location		H Position Code	I Position Title

J SON	K Location of Official Personnel Folder	None / NPRC / At SON	Other Address				ZIP Code

L SOI	M Location of Security Folder	None / At SOI / NPI	Other Address				ZIP Code

N OPAC-ALC Number	O Accounting Data and/or Agency Case Number

P Requesting Official	Name and Title	Signature	Telephone Number ( )	Date

Persons completing this form should begin with the questions below.

1 FULL NAME   • If you have only initials in your name, use them and state (IO).
• If you have no middle name, enter "NMN".   • If you are a "Jr.," "Sr.," "II," etc., enter this in the box after your middle name.

2 DATE OF BIRTH

Last Name	First Name	Middle Name	Jr., II. etc.	Month	Day	Year

3 PLACE OF BIRTH - Use the two letter code for the State.

4 SOCIAL SECURITY

City	County	State	Country (if not in the United States)

5 OTHER NAMES USED
Give other names you used and the period of time you used them (for example: your maiden name, name(s) by a former marriage, former name(s), alias(es), or nickname(s)) If the other name is your **maiden name**, put "nee" in front of it.

Name #1	Month/Year To Month/Year	Name #3	Month/Year To Month/Year
Name #2	Month/Year To Month/Year	Name #4	Month/Year To Month/Year

6 OTHER IDENTIFYING INFORMATION

Height (feet and inches)	Weight (pounds)	Hair Color	Eye Color	Sex (Mark one box) Female Male

7 TELEPHONE NUMBERS

Work (Include Area Code and extension) Day / Night ( )	Home (Include Area Code) Day / Night ( )

8 CITIZENSHIP

a Mark the box at the right that reflects your current citizenship status, and follow its instructions.

- I am a U.S. citizen or national by birth in the U.S. or U.S. territory/possession. (Answer items b and d)
- I am a U.S. citizen, but I was NOT born in the U.S. (Answer items b, c and d)
- I am not a U.S. citizen. (Answer items b and e)

b Your Mother's Maiden Name

c UNITED STATES CITIZENSHIP If you are a U.S. citizen, but were not born in the U.S., provide information about one or more of the following proofs of your citizenship.

Naturalization Certificate (Where were you naturalized?)

Court	City	State	Certificate Number	Month/Day/Year Issued

Citizenship Certificate (Where was the certificate issued?)

City	State	Certificate Number	Month/Day/Year Issued

State Department Form 240 - Report of Birth Abroad of a Citizen of the United States

Give the date the form was prepared and give an explanation if needed.	Month/Day/Year	Explanation

U.S. Passport

This may be either a current or previous U.S. Passport.

Passport Number	Month/Day/Year Issued

d DUAL CITIZENSHIP If you are (or were) a dual citizen of the United States and another country, provide the name of that country in the space to the right.

Country

e ALIEN If you are an alien, provide the following information.

Place You Entered the United States.	City	State	Date You Entered U.S. Month / Day / Year	Alien Registration Number	Country(ies) of Citizenship

Exception to SF85, SF85P, SF85P-S, SF86, and SF86A approved by GSA September, 1995.
Designed using Perform Pro. WHS/DIOR, Sep 95

Page 1

9 WHERE YOU HAVE LIVED

List the places where you have lived, beginning with the most recent (#1) and working back 7 years. All periods must be accounted for in your list. Be sure to indicate the actual physical location of your residence: do not use a post office box as an address, do not list a permanent address when you were actually living at a school address, etc. Be sure to specify your location as closely as possible: for example, do not list only your base or ship, list your barracks number or home port. You may omit temporary military duty locations under 90 days (list your permanent address instead), and you should use your APO/FPO address if you lived overseas.

For any address in the last 5 years, list a person who knew you at that address, and who preferably still lives in that area (do not list people for residences completely outside this 5-year period, and do not list your spouse, former spouses, or other relatives). Also for addresses in the last five years, if the address is "General Delivery," a Rural or Star Route, or may be difficult to locate, provide directions for locating the residence on an attached continuation sheet.

	Month/Year Month/Year	Street Address		Apt. #	City (Country)			State	ZIP Code
#1	To Present								
	Name of Person Who Knows You	Street Address	Apt. #	City (Country)		State	ZIP Code	Telephone Number ( )	
#2	Month/Year Month/Year	Street Address		Apt. #	City (Country)			State	ZIP Code
	To								
	Name of Person Who Knew You	Street Address	Apt. #	City (Country)		State	ZIP Code	Telephone Number ( )	
#3	Month/Year Month/Year	Street Address		Apt. #	City (Country)			State	ZIP Code
	To								
	Name of Person Who Knew You	Street Address	Apt. #	City (Country)		State	ZIP Code	Telephone Number ( )	
#4	Month/Year Month/Year	Street Address		Apt. #	City (Country)			State	ZIP Code
	To								
	Name of Person Who Knew You	Street Address	Apt. #	City (Country)		State	ZIP Code	Telephone Number ( )	
#5	Month/Year Month/Year	Street Address		Apt. #	City (Country)			State	ZIP Code
	To								
	Name of Person Who Knew You	Street Address	Apt. #	City (Country)		State	ZIP Code	Telephone Number ( )	

10 WHERE YOU WENT TO SCHOOL

List the schools you have attended, beyond Junior High School, **beginning with the most recent (#1) and working back 7 years**. List College or University degrees and the dates they were received. If all of your education occurred more than 7 years ago, list your most recent education beyond high school, no matter when that education occurred.

▪Use one of the following codes in the "Code" block:

    1 - High School   2 - College/University/Military College   3 - Vocational/Technical/Trade School

▾For schools you attended in the past 3 years, list a person who knew you at school (an instructor, student, etc.). Do not list people for education completely outside this 3-year period.

▾For correspondence schools and extension classes, provide the address where the records are maintained.

	Month/Year Month/Year	Code	Name of School		Degree/Diploma/Other			Month/Year Awarded
#1	To							
	Street Address and City (Country) of School						State	ZiP Code
	Name of Person Who Knew You	Street Address	Apt. #	City (Country)		State	ZIP Code	Telephone Number ( )
#2	Month/Year Month/Year	Code	Name of School		Degree/Diploma/Other			Month/Year Awarded
	To							
	Street Address and City (Country) of School						State	ZIP Code
	Name of Person Who Knew You	Street Address	Apt. #	City (Country)		State	ZIP Code	Telephone Number ( )
#3	Month/Year Month/Year	Code	Name of School		Degree/Diploma/Other			Month/Year Awarded
	To							
	Street Address and City (Country) of School						State	ZiP Code
	Name of Person Who Knew You	Street Address	Apt. #	City (Country)		State	ZIP Code	Telephone Number ( )

Enter your Social Security Number before going to the next page————————————————▶

11 YOUR EMPLOYMENT ACTIVITIES

List your employment activities, beginning with the present (#1) and working back 7 years. You should list all full-time work, part-time work, military service, temporary military duty locations over 90 days, self-employment, other paid work, and all periods of unemployment. The entire 7-year period must be accounted for without breaks, but you need not list employments before your 16th birthday. EXCEPTION: Show all Federal civilian service, whether it occurred within the last 7 years or not.

● **Code.** Use one of the codes listed below to identify the type of employment:

1 - Active military duty stations	5 - State Government (Non-Federal	7 - Unemployment (Include name of 9 - Other
2 - National Guard/Reserve	employment)	person who can verify)
3 - U.S.P.H.S. Commissioned Corps	6 - Self-employment (Include business name	8 - Federal Contractor (List Contractor,
4 - Other Federal employment	and/or name of person who can verify)	not Federal agency)

● **Employer/Verifier Name.** List the business name of your employer or the name of the person who can verify your self-employment or unemployment in this block. If military service is being listed, include your duty location or home port here as well as your branch of service. You should provide separate listings to reflect changes in your military duty locations or home ports.

● **Previous Periods of Activity.** Complete these lines if you worked for an employer on more than one occasion at the same location. After entering the most recent period of employment in the initial numbered block, provide previous periods of employment at the same location on the additional lines provided. For example, if you worked at XY Plumbing in Denver, CO, during 3 separate periods of time, you would enter dates and information concerning the most recent period of employment first, and provide dates, position titles, and supervisors for the two previous periods of employment on the lines below that information.

Month/Year Month/Year Code	Employer/Verifier Name/Military Duty Location		Your Position Title/Military Rank		
#1 To Present					
Employer's/Verifier's Street Address		City (Country)	State	ZIP Code	Telephone Number ( )
Street Address of Job Location (if different than Employer's Address)		City (Country)	State	ZIP Code	Telephone Number ( )
Supervisor's Name & Street Address (if different than Job Location)		City (Country)	State	ZIP Code	Telephone Number ( )

	Month/Year Month/Year	Position Title	Supervisor
PREVIOUS	To		
PERIODS	Month/Year Month/Year	Position Title	Supervisor
OF	To		
ACTIVITY	Month/Year Month/Year	Position Title	Supervisor
(Block #1)	To		

Month/Year Month/Year Code	Employer/Verifier Name/Military Duty Location		Your Position Title/Military Rank		
#2 To					
Employer's/Verifier's Street Address		City (Country)	State	ZIP Code	Telephone Number ( )
Street Address of Job Location (if different than Employer's Address)		City (Country)	State	ZIP Code	Telephone Number ( )
Supervisor's Name & Street Address (if different than Job Location)		City (Country)	State	ZIP Code	Telephone Number ( )

	Month/Year Month/Year	Position Title	Supervisor
PREVIOUS	To		
PERIODS	Month/Year Month/Year	Position Title	Supervisor
OF	To		
ACTIVITY	Month/Year Month/Year	Position Title	Supervisor
(Block #2)	To		

Month/Year Month/Year Code	Employer/Verifier Name/Military Duty Location		Your Position Title/Military Rank		
#3 To					
Employer's/Verifier's Street Address		City (Country)	State	ZIP Code	Telephone Number ( )
Street Address of Job Location (if different than Employer's Address)		City (Country)	State	ZIP Code	Telephone Number ( )
Supervisor's Name & Street Address (if different than Job Location)		City (Country)	State	ZIP Code	Telephone Number ( )

	Month/Year Month/Year	Position Title	Supervisor
PREVIOUS	To		
PERIODS	Month/Year Month/Year	Position Title	Supervisor
OF	To		
ACTIVITY	Month/Year Month/Year	Position Title	Supervisor
(Block #3)	To		

Enter your Social Security Number before going to the next page ─────────────────►

YOUR EMPLOYMENT ACTIVITIES *(CONTINUED)*

Month/Year Month/Year	Code	Employer/Verifier Name/Military Duty Location			Your Position Title/Military Rank		
#4 To							

Employer's/Verifier's Street Address	City (Country)	State	ZIP Code	Telephone Number ( )
Street Address of Job Location (if different than Employer's Address)	City (Country)	State	ZIP Code	Telephone Number ( )
Supervisor's Name & Street Address (if different than Job Location)	City (Country)	State	ZIP Code	Telephone Number ( )

	Month/Year Month/Year	Position Title	Supervisor
PREVIOUS PERIODS OF ACTIVITY *(Block #4)*	To	Position Title	Supervisor
	Month/Year Month/Year To	Position Title	Supervisor
	Month/Year Month/Year To	Position Title	Supervisor

Month/Year Month/Year	Code	Employer/Verifier Name/Military Duty Location			Your Position Title/Military Rank		
#5 To							

Employer's/Verifier's Street Address	City (Country)	State	ZIP Code	Telephone Number ( )
Street Address of Job Location (if different than Employer's Address)	City (Country)	State	ZIP Code	Telephone Number ( )
Supervisor's Name & Street Address (if different than Job Location)	City (Country)	State	ZIP Code	Telephone Number ( )

	Month/Year Month/Year	Position Title	Supervisor
PREVIOUS PERIODS OF ACTIVITY *(Block #5)*	To	Position Title	Supervisor
	Month/Year Month/Year To	Position Title	Supervisor
	Month/Year Month/Year To	Position Title	Supervisor

Month/Year Month/Year	Code	Employer/Verifier Name/Military Duty Location			Your Position Title/Military Rank		
#6 To							

Employer's/Verifier's Street Address	City (Country)	State	ZIP Code	Telephone Number ( )
Street Address of Job Location (if different than Employer's Address)	City (Country)	State	ZIP Code	Telephone Number ( )
Supervisor's Name & Street Address (if different than Job Location)	City (Country)	State	ZIP Code	Telephone Number ( )

	Month/Year Month/Year	Position Title	Supervisor
PREVIOUS PERIODS OF ACTIVITY *(Block #6)*	To	Position Title	Supervisor
	Month/Year Month/Year To	Position Title	Supervisor
	Month/Year Month/Year To	Position Title	Supervisor

12 PEOPLE WHO KNOW YOU WELL

List three people who know you well and live in the United States. They should be good friends, peers, colleagues, college roommates, etc., whose combined association with you covers as well as possible the last 7 years. Do not list your spouse, former spouses, or other relatives, and try not to list anyone who is listed elsewhere on this form.

Name **#1**	Dates Known Month/Year Month/Year To	Telephone Number Day ( ) Night ( )		
Home or Work Address		City (Country)	State	ZIP Code

Name **#2**	Dates Known Month/Year Month/Year To	Telephone Number Day ( ) Night ( )		
Home or Work Address		City (Country)	State	ZIP Code

Name **#3**	Dates Known Month/Year Month/Year To	Telephone Number Day ( ) Night ( )		
Home or Work Address		City (Country)	State	ZIP Code

Enter your Social Security Number before going to the next page ————————————➤

⓭ YOUR SPOUSE

Mark one box to show your current marital status and provide information about your spouse(s) in items a. and/or b.

☐ 1 - Never married	☐ 3 - Separated	☐ 5 - Divorced
☐ 2 - Married	☐ 4 - Legally Separated	☐ 6 - Widowed

ⓐ Current Spouse   Complete the following about your current spouse only.

Full Name	Date of Birth	Place of Birth (Include country if outside the U.S.)	Social Security Number
Other Names Used (Specify maiden name, names by other marriages, etc., and show dates used for each name)		Country(ies) of Citizenship	

Date Married	Place Married (Include country if outside the U.S.)	State
If Separated. Date of Separation	If Legally Separated, Where is the Record Located? City (Country)	State

Address of Current Spouse, if different than your current address (Street, city, and country if outside the U.S.)	State	ZIP Code

ⓑ Former Spouse(s).   Complete the following about your former spouse(s), use blank sheets if needed.

Full Name	Date of Birth	Place of Birth (Include country if outside the U.S.)	State
Country(ies) of Citizenship	Date Married	Place Married (Include country if outside the U.S.)	State

Check one, Then Give Date ☐ Divorced ☐ Widowed	Month/Day/Year	If Divorced, Where is the Record Located? City (Country)	State

Address of Former Spouse (Street, city, and country if outside the U.S.)	State	ZIP Code	Telephone Number ( )

⓮ YOUR RELATIVES AND ASSOCIATES

Give the full name, correct code, and other requested information for each of your relatives and associates, living or dead, specified below.

1 - Mother (first)	5 - Foster parent	9 - Sister	13 - Half-sister	17 - Other Relative'
2 - Father (second)	6 - Child (adopted also)	10 - Stepbrother	14 - Father-in-law	18 - Associate*
3 - Stepmother	7 - Stepchild	11 - Stepsister	15 - Mother-in-law	19 - Adult Currently Living With You
4 - Stepfather	8 - Brother	12 - Half-brother	16 - Guardian	

*Code 17 (Other Relative) - include only foreign national relatives not listed in 1 - 16 with whom you or your spouse are bound by affection, obligation, or close and continuing contact. Code 18 (Associates) - include only foreign national associates with whom you or your spouse are bound by affection. obligation, or close and continuing contact.

Full Name (If deceased, check box on the left before entering name)	Code	Date of Birth Month/Day/Year	Country of Birth	Country(ies) of Citizenship	Current Street Address and City (country) of Living Relatives	State
	1					
	2					

Enter your Social Security Number before going to the next page ⟶

⑮ CITIZENSHIP OF YOUR RELATIVES AND ASSOCIATES

If your mother, father, sister, brother, child, or current spouse or person with whom you have a spouse-like relationship is a U.S. citizen by other than birth, or an alien residing in the U.S., provide the nature of the individual's relationship to you (Spouse, Spouse-like, Mother, etc.), and the individual's name and date of birth on the first line *(this information is needed to pair it accurately with information in items 13 and 14).*

On the second line, provide the individual's naturalization certificate or alien registration number and use one of the document codes below to identify proof of citizenship status. Provide additional information on that line as requested.

　　1 - Naturalization Certificate: Provide the date issued and the location where the person was naturalized (Court, City and State).
　　2 - Citizenship Certificate: Provide the date and location issued (City and State).
　　3 - Alien Registration: Provide the date and place where the person entered the U.S. (City and State).
　　4 - Other: Provide an explanation in the "Additional Information" block.

	Association	Name		Date of Birth *(Month/Day/Year)*
#1				
	Certificate/Registration #	Document Code	Additional Information	
	Association	Name		Date of Birth *(Month/Day/Year)*
#2				
	Certificate/Registration #	Document Code	Additional Information	

⑯ YOUR MILITARY HISTORY

	Yes	No
ⓐ Have you served in the United States military?		
ⓑ Have you served in the United States Merchant Marine?		

List all of your military service below, including service in Reserve, National Guard, and U.S. Merchant Marine. Start with the most recent period of service (#1) and work backward. If you had a break in service, each separate period should be listed.

•Code. Use one of the codes listed below to identify your branch of service.
1 - Air Force　　2 - Army　　3 - Navy　　4 - Marine Corps　　5 - Coast Guard　　6 - Merchant Marine　　7 - National Guard

•O/E. Mark "O" block for Officer or "E" block for Enlisted.
•Status. "X" the appropriate block for the status of your service during the time that you served. If your service was in the National Guard, do not use an "X": use the two-letter code for the state to mark the block.
•Country. If your service was with other than the U.S. Armed Forces, identify the country for which you served.

Month/Year　Month/Year	Code	Service/Certificate #	O	E	Status				Country
					Active	Active Reserve	Inactive Reserve	National Guard (State)	
To									
To									

⑰ YOUR FOREIGN ACTIVITIES

	Yes	No
ⓐ Do you have any foreign property, business connections, or financial interests?		
ⓑ Are you now or have you ever been employed by or acted as a consultant for a foreign government, firm, or agency?		
ⓒ Have you ever had any contact with a foreign government, its establishments (embassies or consulates), or its representatives, whether inside or outside the U.S., other than on official U.S. Government business? *(Does not include routine visa applications and border crossing contacts.)*		
ⓓ In the last 7 years, have you had an active passport that was issued by a foreign government?		

If you answered "Yes" to a, b, c, or d above, explain in the space below; provide inclusive dates, names of firms and/or governments involved, and an explanation of your involvement.

Month/Year　Month/Year	Firm and/or Government	Explanation
To		
To		

⑱ FOREIGN COUNTRIES YOU HAVE VISITED

List foreign countries you have visited, except on travel under official Government orders, beginning with the most current (#1) and working back 7 years. (Travel as a dependent or contractor must be listed.)
•Use one of these codes to indicate the purpose of your visit. 1 - Business　　2 - Pleasure　　3 - Education　　4 - Other
•Include short trips to Canada or Mexico. If you have lived near a border and have made short (one day or less) trips to the neighboring country, you do not need to list each trip. Instead, provide the time period, the code, the country, and a note ("Many Short Trips").
•Do not repeat travel covered in items 9, 10, or 11.

	Month/Year　Month/Year	Code	Country		Month/Year　Month/Year	Code	Country
#1	To			**#3**	To		
#2	To			**#4**	To		

This concludes Part 1 of this form. If you have used Page 9, continuation sheets, or blank sheets to complete any of the questions in Part 1, give the number for those questions in the space to the right:

Enter your Social Security Number before going to the next page ──────────►

Standard Form 86
Revised September 1995
U.S. Office of Personnel Management
5 CFR Parts 731, 732, and 736

QUESTIONNAIRE FOR
NATIONAL SECURITY POSITIONS

Form approved:
OMB No. 3206-0007
NSN 7540-00-634-4036
86-111

Part 2 OFFICIAL USE ONLY

		Yes	No
19 YOUR MILITARY RECORD			

Have you ever received other than an honorable discharge from the military? If "Yes," provide the date of discharge and type of discharge below.

Month/Year	Type of Discharge

		Yes	No
20 YOUR SELECTIVE SERVICE RECORD			
a Are you a male born after December 31, 1959? If "No," go to 21 If "Yes," go to b			
b Have you registered with the Selective Service System? If "Yes," provide your registration number. If "No," show the reason for your legal exemption below.			

Registration Number	Legal Exemption Explanation

		Yes	No
21 YOUR MEDICAL RECORD			

In the last 7 years, have you consulted with a mental health professional (psychiatrist, psychologist, counselor, etc.) or have you consulted with another health care provider about a mental health related condition?

If you answered "Yes," provide the dates of treatment and the name and address of the therapist or doctor below, unless the consultation(s) involved only marital, family, or grief counseling, not related to violence by you.

Month/Year	Month/Year	Name/Address of Therapist or Doctor	State	ZIP Code
	To			
	To			

		Yes	No
22 YOUR EMPLOYMENT RECORD			

Has any of the following happened to you **in the last 7 years?** If "Yes," begin with the most recent occurrence and go backward, providing date fired, quit, or left, and other information requested.

Use the following codes and explain the reason your employment was ended:

1 - Fired from a job
2 - Quit a job after being told you'd be fired

3 - Left a job by mutual agreement following allegations of misconduct
4 - Left a job by mutual agreement following allegations of unsatisfactory performance

5 - Left a job for other reasons under unfavorable circumstances

Month/Year	Code	Specify Reason	Employer's Name and Address (Include city/Country if outside U.S.)	State	ZIP Code

		Yes	No
23 YOUR POLICE RECORD			

For this item, report information regardless of whether the record in your case has been "sealed" or otherwise stricken from the court record. The single exception to this requirement is for certain convictions under the Federal Controlled Substances Act for which the court issued an expungement order under the authority of 21 U.S.C. 844 or 18 U.S.C 3607

a Have you ever been charged with or convicted of any felony offense? (Include those under Uniform Code of Military Justice)

b Have you ever been charged with or convicted of a firearms or explosives offense?

c Are there currently any charges pending against you for any criminal offense?

d Have you ever been charged with or convicted of any offense(s) related to alcohol or drugs?

e In the last 7 years, have you been subject to court martial or other disciplinary proceedings under the Uniform Code of Military Justice? (Include non-judicial, Captain's mast, etc.)

f In the last 7 years, have you been arrested for, charged with, or convicted of any offense(s) not listed in response to a, b, c, d, or e above? (Leave out traffic fines of less than $150 unless the violation was alcohol or drug related.)

If you answered "Yes" to a, b, c, d, e, or f above, explain below. Under "Offense," do not list specific penalty codes, list the actual offense or violation (for example, arson, theft, etc.).

Month/Year	Offense	Action Taken	Law Enforcement Authority/Court (Include City and county/country if outside U.S.)	State	ZIP Code

Enter your Social Security Number before going to the next page ⟶

24 YOUR USE OF ILLEGAL DRUGS AND DRUG ACTIVITY

	Yes	No

The following questions pertain to the illegal use of drugs or drug activity. You are required to answer the questions fully and truthfully, and your failure to do so could be grounds for an adverse employment decision or action against you, but neither your truthful responses nor information derived from your responses will be used as evidence against you in any subsequent criminal proceeding.

a Since the age of 16 or in the last 7 years, whichever is shorter, have you <u>illegally</u> used any controlled substance, for example, marijuana, cocaine, crack cocaine, hashish, narcotics (opium, morphine, codeine, heroin, etc.), amphetamines, depressants (barbiturates, methaqualone, tranquilizers, etc.), hallucinogenics (LSD, PCP, etc.), or prescription drugs?

b Have you <u>ever</u> illegally used a controlled substance while employed as a law enforcement officer, prosecutor, or courtroom official; while possessing a security clearance; or while in a position directly and immediately affecting the public safety?

c In the last 7 years, have you been involved in the illegal purchase, manufacture, trafficking, production, transfer, shipping, receiving, or sale of any narcotic, depressant, stimulant, hallucinogen, or cannabis for your own intended profit or that of another?

If you answered "Yes" to a or b above, provide the date(s), identify the controlled substance(s) and/or prescription drugs used, and the number of times each was used.

Month/Year	Month/Year	Controlled Substance/Prescription Drug Used	Number of Times Used
To			
To			

25 YOUR USE OF ALCOHOL

	Yes	No

In the last 7 years, has your use of alcoholic beverages (such as liquor, beer, wine) resulted in any alcohol-related treatment or counseling (such as for alcohol abuse or alcoholism)?

If you answered "Yes," provide the dates of treatment and the name and address of the counselor or doctor below. Do not repeat information reported in response to item 21 above.

Month/Year	Month/Year	Name/Address of Counselor or Doctor	State	ZIP Code
To				
To				

26 YOUR INVESTIGATIONS RECORD

	Yes	No

a Has the United States Government ever investigated your background and/or granted you a security clearance? If "Yes," use the codes that follow to provide the requested information below. If "Yes," but you can't recall the investigating agency and/or the security clearance received, enter "Other" agency code or clearance code, as appropriate, and "Don't know" or "Don't recall" under the "Other Agency" heading, below. If your response is "No," or you don't know or can't recall if you were investigated and cleared, check the "No" box.

Codes for Investigating Agency
1 - Defense Department   4 - FBI
2 - State Department   5 - Treasury Department
3 - Office of Personnel Management   6 - Other (Specify)

Codes for Security Clearance Received
0 - Not Required   3 - Top Secret   6 - L
1 - Confidential   4 - Sensitive Compartmented Information 7 - Other
2 - Secret   5 - Q

Month/Year	Agency Code	Other Agency	Clearance Code	Month/Year	Agency Code	Other Agency	Clearance Code

b To your knowledge, have you ever had a clearance or access authorization denied, suspended, or revoked, or have you ever been debarred from government employment? If "Yes," give date of action and agency. Note: An administrative downgrade or termination of a security clearance is not a revocation.

	Yes	No

Month/Year	Department or Agency Taking Action	Month/Year	Department or Agency Taking Action

27 YOUR FINANCIAL RECORD

	Yes	No
a In the last 7 years, have you filed a petition under any chapter of the bankruptcy code (to include Chapter 13)?		
b In the last 7 years, have you had your wages garnished or had any property repossessed for any reason?		
c In the last 7 years, have you had a lien placed against your property for failing to pay taxes or other debts?		
d In the last 7 years, have you had any judgments against you that have not been paid?		

If you answered "Yes" to a, b, c, or d, provide the information requested below:

Month/Year	Type of Action	Amount	Name Action Occurred Under	Name/Address of Court or Agency Handling Case	State	ZIP Code

Enter your Social Security Number before going to the next page ⟶

28 YOUR FINANCIAL DELINQUENCIES

	Yes	No

a In the last 7 years, have you been over 180 days delinquent on any debt(s)?

b Are you currently over 90 days delinquent on any debt(s)?

If you answered "Yes" to a or b, provide the information requested below:

Incurred Month/Year	Satisfied Month/Year	Amount	Type of Loan or Obligation and Account Number	Name/Address of Creditor or Obligee	State	ZIP Code

29 PUBLIC RECORD CIVIL COURT ACTIONS

	Yes	No

In the last 7 years, have you been a party to any public record civil court actions not listed elsewhere on this form?

If you answered "Yes," provide the information about the public record civil court action requested below.

Month/Year	Nature of Action	Result of Action	Name of Parties Involved	Court (Include City and county/country if outside U.S.)	State	ZIP Code

30 YOUR ASSOCIATION RECORD

	Yes	No

a Have you ever been an officer or a member or made a contribution to an organization dedicated to the violent overthrow of the United States Government and which engages in illegal activities to that end, knowing that the organization engages in such activities with the specific intent to further such activities?

b Have you ever knowingly engaged in any acts or activities designed to overthrow the United States Government by force?

If you answered "Yes" to a or b, explain in the space below.

Continuation Space

Use the continuation sheet(s) (SF86A) for additional answers to items 9, 10, and 11. Use the space below to continue answers to all other items and any information you would like to add. If more space is needed than is provided below, use a blank sheet(s) of paper. Start each sheet with your name and Social Security Number. Before each answer, identify the number of the item.

After completing Parts 1 and 2 of this form and any attachments, you should review your answers to all questions to make sure the form is complete and accurate, and then sign and date the following certification and sign and date the release on Page 10.

Certification That My Answers Are True

My statements on this form, and any attachments to it, are true, complete, and correct to the best of my knowledge and belief and are made in good faith. I understand that a knowing and willful false statement on this form can be punished by fine or imprisonment or both. (See section 1001 of title 18, United States Code).

Signature (Sign in ink) | Date

Enter your Social Security Number before going to the next page ⟶

Standard Form 86
Revised September 1995
U.S. Office of Personnel Management
5 CFR Parts 731, 732, and 736

Form approved.
OMB No. 3206-0007
NSN 7540-00-634-4036
86-111

UNITED STATES OF AMERICA

AUTHORIZATION FOR RELEASE OF INFORMATION

Carefully read this authorization to release information about you, then sign and date it in ink.

I Authorize any investigator, special agent, or other duly accredited representative of the authorized Federal agency conducting my background investigation, to obtain any information relating to my activities from individuals, schools, residential management agents, employers, criminal justice agencies, credit bureaus, consumer reporting agencies, collection agencies, retail business establishments, or other sources of information. This information may include, but is not limited to, my academic, residential, achievement, performance, attendance, disciplinary, employment history, criminal history record information, and financial and credit information. I authorize the Federal agency conducting my investigation to disclose the record of my background investigation to the requesting agency for the purpose of making a determination of suitability or eligibility for a security clearance.

I Understand that, for financial or lending institutions, medical institutions, hospitals, health care professionals, and other sources of information, a separate specific release will be needed, and I may be contacted for such a release at a later date. Where a separate release is requested for information relating to mental health treatment or counseling, the release will contain a list of the specific questions, relevant to the job description, which the doctor or therapist will be asked.

I Further Authorize any investigator, special agent, or other duly accredited representative of the U.S. Office of Personnel Management, the Federal Bureau of Investigation, the Department of Defense, the Defense Investigative Service, and any other authorized Federal agency, to request criminal record information about me from criminal justice agencies for the purpose of determining my eligibility for access to classified information and/or for assignment to, or retention in a sensitive National Security position, in accordance with 5 U.S.C. 9101. I understand that I may request a copy of such records as may be available to me under the law.

I Authorize custodians of records and sources of information pertaining to me to release such information upon request of the investigator, special agent, or other duly accredited representative of any Federal agency authorized above regardless of any previous agreement to the contrary.

I Understand that the information released by records custodians and sources of information is for official use by the Federal Government only for the purposes provided in this Standard Form 86, and that it may be redisclosed by the Government only as authorized by law.

Copies of this authorization that show my signature are as valid as the original release signed by me. This authorization is valid for five (5) years from the date signed or upon the termination of my affiliation with the Federal Government, whichever is sooner. Read, sign and date the release on the next page if you answered "Yes" to question 21.

Signature (Sign in ink)	Full Name (Type or Print Legibly)		Date Signed
Other Names Used			Social Security Number
Current Address (Street, City)	State	ZIP Code	Home Telephone Number (Include Area Code) ( )

Standard Form 86
Revised September 1995
U.S. Office of Personnel Management
5 CFR Parts 731, 732, and 736

Form approved:
OMB No. 3206-0007
NSN 7540-00-634-4036
86-111

UNITED STATES OF AMERICA

AUTHORIZATION FOR RELEASE OF MEDICAL INFORMATION

Carefully read this authorization to release information about you, then sign and date it in ink.

Instructions for Completing this Release

This is a release for the investigator to ask your health practitioner(s) the three questions below concerning your mental health consultations. Your signature will allow the practitioner(s) to answer only these questions.

I am seeking assignment to or retention in a position with the Federal government which requires access to classified national security information or special nuclear information or material. As part of the clearance process, **I hereby authorize** the investigator, special agent, or duly accredited representative of the authorized Federal agency conducting my background investigation, to obtain the following information relating to my mental health consultations:

Does the person under investigation have a condition or treatment that could impair his/her judgment or reliability, particularly in the context of safeguarding classified national security information or special nuclear information or material?

If so, please describe the nature of the condition and the extent and duration of the impairment or treatment.

What is the prognosis?

I understand the information released pursuant to this release is for use by the Federal Government only for purposes provided in the Standard Form 86 and that it may be redisclosed by the Government only as authorized by law.

Copies of this authorization that show my signature are as valid as the original release signed by me. This authorization is valid for 1 year from the date signed or upon termination of my affiliation with the Federal Government, whichever is sooner.

Signature (Sign in ink)	Full Name (Type or Print Legibly)		Date Signed
Other Names Used			Social Security Number
Current Address (Street, City)	State	ZIP Code	Home Telephone Number (Include Area Code) ( )

INDEX

Access 17

Access Authorization, 14, 17, 18, 51, 129, 130, 132

Access National Agency Check with Inquiries (ANACI), xiii, 3, 7

Adjudication, vii, xiii, 3, 7, 41—51

Adjudicative Guidelines, B-1—B-19

Agency for International Development (AID), x

Alcohol, 13, 14, 35, 36, 86, 113, 114, 123—125, B-12, B-13

Allegiance, 34, 64, 95, 140, B4—B7

Appeals, viii, 20, 44, 49—51

Applicant, xi

Arrest, 7, 24, 31, 113—115, 123, B-15, B-16

Article 15 UCMJ, 115

Associates/association, 13, 14, 26, 29, 83—89, 140—142, B-4—B-10

Atomal, 17

Background Investigation (BI), x, xii, xiii, 3, 14, 52

Bankruptcy, 15, 21, 26, 134

Birth, 7, 8, 15, 23, 58—64, B-7

Blackmail, 34, 36, B-5, B-6, B-8, B-10

Broadcasting Board of Governors, x

Bureau of Alcohol, Tobacco, Firearms and Explosives (BATF), x, 142

Bureau of Customs and Border Protection, x

Bureau of Engraving and Printing, x

Captain's Mast, 115

Character Reference, ix, 11, 28, 30, 33, 36, 83—85

Charge, 14, 24, 31, 113—115, B-16

Central Adjudication Facility (CAF), viii, 42—51, 128

Central Intelligence Agency (CIA), x, 5, 7, 38, 39

Civil Court Actions, 15, 20, 35, 139—140

Citizenship, 4, 5, 8, 13—15, 23, 35, 57—64, 86—89, B-5—B-7

Citizenship and Immigration Services, 60, 63, 88

Classified Information, 17, 18, 35, 39, 40, 52, 127—131

Clearance (see Security Clearance)

Coercion (see Blackmail)

COMSEC, 17

Confidential (see Security Clearance)

Confidentiality, 35, 45, 52, B-9

Conviction, 24, 113, B-16

Court Record, 24, 114—116, 140

Court Martial, 95

COSMIC Top Secret, 17, 18

Cost of Investigation, xiii, xiv

Criminal Conduct (see Arrest)

Credit Check, x, 7, 9, 11, 15, 21, 22, 26, 31, 33, 132—136

Critical Nuclear Weapons Design Information (CNWDI), 17

CRYPTO, 17

Defense Clearance and Investigative Index (DCII), 4, 130

Defense Intelligence Agency (DIA), x, 38, 39

Defense Investigative Service (DIS), ix, xv

Defense Security Service (DSS), xiv, 19, 20, 51—53, 127

Defense Security Clearance Office (DISCO), viii, xiv, 6, 42—46, 50, 51

Defense Office of Hearings and Appeals (DOHA), viii, xii, 43—51

Department of Energy (DOE), xiv, 4, 17, 128

Department of Homeland Security, x

Department of State, x, 32

Department of the Treasury, x
Detention, 113, 114, 117
Director of Central Intelligence
   Directive (DCID), 17, 51
Directorate for Industrial Security
   Clearance Review (DISCR), 45
Dishonorable Discharge, 95—97, B-15
Dishonesty, 77, 97, B-8—B-10
Divorce, 9, 12, 15, 21, 25, 86, B-11
Drug Involvement, 13, 14, 23—26,
   29, 30, 35, 36, 86, 113, 114,
   118—122, B-11, B-13, B-14
Drug Enforcement Agency (DEA), x,
   38
Drug Waiver, 29
Dual Citizenship, 13, 14, 61—64, B-7
Duress (see Blackmail)
Electronic Personnel Security
   Questionnaire (EPSQ), ix, 19, 150
Electronic Questionnaires for Investi-
   gations Processing (eQIP), ix, 19,
   21, 150
Expanded Background
   Investigation (EBI), 3
Exploitation (see Blackmail)
Education, 8, 9, 14, 15, 21, 35, 30,
   70—72, 100, B-7, B-12, B-16
Employment, x, 3, 6, 7, 9, 11, 14—16,
   20, 30, 35, 42, 72—78, 154, B-9,
   B-16—B18
Expanded National Agency Check
   (ENAC), 3
Entrance National Agency Check
   (ENTNAC), 3, 4
Falsification, xi, 28, 29, 46, B-9, B-10
Federal Bureau of Investigation (FBI),
   x, 4, 11, 38, 84, 114—116, 127
Federal Investigative Services (FIS),
   31, 33
Felony, 114
Files Of Relevant Materials (FORM),
   44
Financial, 8, 9, 11, 12, 20, 25, 26, 35,
   36, 62, 68, 86, 132—136, B-10,
   B-11, B-12

Fingerprint, 22
Foreign
   connections, 8, 13, 14, 23, 25, 35,
      51, 87, 88, 89, 99, 100, 104
   financial, 12—14, 99, 100, 104
   influence, B-5, B-6, B-17
   military, 95, 97, 104
   passport, 13, 14, 63, 65, 99, 100,
      104
   preference, B-6, B-7
   travel, 6, 23, 30, 35, 84, 99, 100,
      104, 105, 150
Former Spouse, 9, 12, 15, 85, 86
Formerly Restricted Data (FRD), 17
Freedom of Information Act, 45,
   51—53
Gambling, 136, B-11
Garnishment, 132, 136
General Accountability Office (GAO),
   vii, x, 13, 14, 41
GENSER, 17
Handling Protected Information, 35,
   130, 131, B-16, B-17
Honesty, 22, 29, 34, 35 (see also dis-
   honesty)
Immigration and Naturalization
   Service, 4, 60, 88 (see also Citizen-
   ship and Immigration Services)
Indebtedness (see Financial)
Interim Security Clearance. (see
   Security Clearance)
Internal Revenue Service (IRS), 5, 21
Interview-Oriented Background
   Investigation (IBI), 3
Investigation (see Personnel Security
   Investigation)
Joint Personnel Adjudications System
   (JPAS), 130
Judgment, 34, 35, 42, 139, B-8—B-17
Juvenile Offense, 115
"L" Access Authorization, viii, 7, 10,
   16, 17, 127, 128
Letter of Intent (LOI), viii, 43
Limited Access Authorization (LAA),
   5, 62

Loyalty, 33—35, 64, 86, 142, B-2, B-5, B-6

Mental Health, 14, 20, 109—112, 122, B-14, B-15

Military Applicants, 27—30

Military Service, 9, 35, 78, 95—97, B-7

Misdemeanor, 26, 114

Misuse of employer's time or resources, B-9

Money Memorandum, 65, 102

National Agency Check (NAC), x, 3—6, 16, 87, 104

National Agency Check with Inquiries (NACI), 7, 127

National Agency Check with Local Agency Checks and Credit Check (NACLC), x, xiii, 3, 6, 7, 10, 14, 16, 21, 27, 31, 34, 67

National Reconnaissance Office (NRO), x, 38, 127

National Security Agency (NSA), x, 38, 39, 127

NATO, 17

Naturalization, 4, 5, 60, 61

Non-Judicial Punishment (NJP), 115

Office of Personnel Management (OPM), ix—xiv, 3, 4, 19, 32, 52, 127, 149

Organizational Affiliations, 35, 140—142, B-4, B-7, B-17

Outside Activities, B-17, B-18

Peace Corps, x, 127

Phased Periodic Reinvestigation (PPR), 10, 12—14, 31

Period of Investigation, 4

Periodic Reinvestigation (PR), xv, 10—15, 17

Personal Conduct, B-8—B-10

Personal Subject Interview (PRSI), ix, xi, 20, 24—27

Police Records, x, 13, 20, 113—117

Polygraph, 10, 37—40

Postal Service, x

Pressure (see Blackmail)

Prior Investigations, 17, 126—131

Privacy Act, 35, 51—53

Psychological Conditions (see Mental Health)

"Q" Access Authorization, x, 4, 10, 16, 17, 127, 128

Reinvestigation. (see Periodic Reinvestigation)

Relatives, 10—12, 87—89
with clearance, viii

Releases, 6, 8, 11, 26, 27, 37, 110—112, 120, 123, 125, 133, 136, B-9

Reliability, 33—35, B-2, B-5—B-19

Repossession, 132

Residence, 9—15, 20, 35, 62, 67—70

Restricted Data (RD), 17

Scope of Investigation, 3—15

Single Scope Background Investigation (SSBI), xiii, 3, 8—10, 15, 16, 20—23, 27, 31, 33—37

Secret (see Security Clearance)

Secret Service, 5

Security and Investigations Index (SII), 4, 130

Security Clearance
Adjudicative Guideline, B-1—B-19
Confidential, x, 10, 15—17, 126, 127
definition, 17
denial, viii, 20, 29, 41—46, 49, 51, 127—131
downgrade, 16
final, 16
interim, 16
number of, xii
processing time, vii, viii
reinstatment, 16
Secret, viii, x, xiv, 7, 10, 15—17, 127
suspension, 1271—131
Top Secret, vii—ix, 10, 12, 15—18, 127
termination, 16

Security Violation, 35, 130, B16, B-17

Selective Service, 106—108
Sensitive Compartmented Information
    (SCI), 16, 17, 51, 127, 128
Sexual Conduct, 26, 86, 145, 146, B-8
Single Integrated Operations Plan, 17
Small Business Administration, x
Smith Act, 122
SPECAT, 17
Special Access Authorization, (see
    Access Authorization)
Special Access Program (SAP), 16,
    17, 38, 39, 127
Special Background Investigation
    (SBI), 3
Special Interview (SPIN), 9, 20, 27,
    33, 134
Standard Form 86 (SF86), viii, ix, xi,
    19—22, C-3
Subject, xi
Subject Interview, 10, 12, 15 (see also
    Personal Subject Interview)
Tax evasion/fraud, B-11
Technology, 142—144, B-5,
    B-17—B19
Tennessee Valley Authority, x
Top Secret (see Security Clearance)
Trustworthiness, 33—35, 57, B-2,
    B-5, B-8—B19
Uniform Code of Military Justice
    (UCMJ), (see Article 15)
Whole Person, 34, 41, 46—49, B-3

Printed in the United States
88556LV00002B/1-99/A